MILITARISM HAS FAILED

WE DISARM THE WORLD

Jesus Christ: "Those who take weapons, perish by them."

© Alan Storkey.
ISBN 9798389082632
Christian Studies Press.
The Old School, High Street, Coton Cambridge CB23 7PL
alan@storkey.com. Response, publishing, contact, translation…

Letter to the reader.

Dear Friend,
Welcome to this book. Apologies for its failings. You will already have faced the issues here in your own terms. We all need little convincing that war and militarism (along with global warming) is the world's biggest problem. Others woke me up to how it might be addressed. It is a big communal task. Your thinking, nationhood, experience will be different and the many ways of addressing this evil matter. Perhaps your contribution will emerge more. My hope is that fairly simple composite conclusions, like war does not work, big problem - big solution, turkeys don't vote for Christmas, and finding a way round the Big Boys will help us, not march, but walk together, a big army for peace, without enemies, to the healing of the nations. No leaders… all with tasks… Warm greetings.

Petition: https://www.change.org/DisarmTheWorld

CONTENTS

Introduction.

Unlearning things is hard. They are in your head, settled down, and you are supposed to take them out. This one, Militarism, has been head resident beyond a human life span – World War One, World War Two, the Cold War and the War in Ukraine yesterday. It is as normal as driving on the left, or the right, but it might be wrong. Around a hundred years ago most of the world and its statesmen were convinced that the Great War should be the War to End All Wars and World Disarmament should happen, but we have forgotten this world majority conclusion. Now we remember it again. Could all this militarism be a failure? Be washed up? Be a dumb way to run the world? Can it be removed in six years? Perhaps it can, and this we think through here.

What is world militarism? In almost all states it is armies, navies and air forces, secret services, arms companies, command centres, government departments, research units and bases which gathers around government like a glove on a hand. It is so big that it is very difficult to see round it or through it, and few people believe it could be demolished. But we, or some of us, have built it. Since about 1840 industrial arms companies have sold weapons and helped states militarise. They have been very successful and most states in the world have substantial armed forces. Militarism rules the world, but perhaps it can un-rule the world. Perhaps arming is a direction mistake, a failure, the tragedy of modern history and it can even *easily* be stopped. So, we take it out of our heads and examine it.

The basic story is not good. Since 1914 something like 150 million have died in war and far more than 200 million people have died through war. A similar number, mainly young, have been seriously injured and suffered damaged living. Then, perhaps two billion people have been traumatised by bombing, attacks, occupation, fleeing as refugees, fighting, losing family and the Holocaust. They suffer depression, suicide, rage or quietly mourn and dwell with the dominance of evil over their loved ones. Apologies if you know, love or miss one of these big numbers; they each matter. Evil continues. We need only think that

Hitler was one of those traumatised by gas in WW1 to see the toxic continuation of aggression. Even now in civilised 2023 there are 100 million refugees who have had to leave their homes, families, cities and countries. Militarism has an obvious damning prospectus.

The economics are even worse. There is immediate government military accounting. Running the military system cost say 10% of world national income in WW1, 30% in WW2 and 10% during the Cold War among the main protagonists (20% in the USSR) and about 3.5% now. A rough calculation using % of world GDP used in Defence and current world GDP says military expenditure since 1900 amounts to $600tn, say $70,000 per person on the planet now, but that is only military running costs.[i] Weapons and wars kill and destroy. War damage is beyond accurate pricing. It wrecks full economies. Dozens of world cities have been bombed 50%, 80% or more. Bombs "take out" infrastructure, factories, offices, churches, power stations, docks, bridges, city centres, equipment, dams, technology, housing and their contents. Decades of building disappear in a puff. It costs a decade or more to rebuild, often at lower standards. When I was a student visiting Eastern Europe, I remember thinking critically about the poor quality of "Communist" buildings, but then learned of the scale of war-time destruction. It was a crisis response to the destruction cost of war. All these costs push the world loss towards a quadrillion dollars.

We can reflect on other losses, like lost work. Perhaps four hundred million years of work went into WW1 and a billion years in WW2 to no constructive purpose. That is a lot of work to waste. You cannot put a price on human life, but usually, the young are killed in conflict; millions of years of their work was lost after both world wars. Millions injured, or traumatized, limp through later work and life. Children's schooling hardly happens. Refugees have to start again from scratch, inefficiently. Trade, manufacturing, health, research, marketing and transport regress. Life is put on hold to do war; it is actually quite difficult to live properly in many wartime locations. Then again, vast resources are diverted to the science, technology and equipment of militarism and away from the stuff which will help us. Millions live merely to survive, or attack, or cope.

These losses cannot be priced. The US wars in Iraq and Afghanistan are roughly costed at $9tn to the US, but nobody even tries to assess the cost to Iraq and Afghanistan. It is obviously far more in terms of real damage and disruption to the states where war occurred. WW1 and WW2 have not really been fully costed or many of the other wars. Appendix One guesstimates the costs. These sums, roughly done, suggest war and militarism has perhaps cost $250,000 for every household on the planet now at today's prices. That gives us a vague idea of how we have all been impoverished by this vast military system. We have no conception of how rich the world could have been without militarism and warfare. Wasting this much of the world economy is criminal.

It is reflected in national debt. The Bank of England started with war debt. The UK's National Debt increased tenfold after WW1. German State finance collapsed in 1923. Much debt in poor countries is paying for weapons and war. War debt is the cesspit of international banking.

Addressing all of this is urgent. If we do not, wars, big and small, will come again. Military kit is accumulating. Nuclear conflict may happen. New weapons will emerge. The scripts are already written. A few years before a big war is usually too late, because the momentum towards it becomes unstoppable. We should address the war problem yesterday.

Crucially, too, world militarism does global warming. It tries to hide the fact, but Defence is the big energy burner. Intensely engineered equipment, flying, missiles, bombs, navies, exercises, defence systems, satellites, bunkers, bases, aircraft carriers and more devour energy. Military operations explode levels of CO_2 and then require rebuilding to replace what is destroyed. "Defence" is one of the biggest polluters on the earth, producing at least 5-10% of world CO_2. Bombing Ukraine and elsewhere, and then rebuilding, is extinction politics. We are heading for climate change catastrophes around the world unless we address this one. Droughts, tempests, floods, famines, refugees and destruction come partly because we do militarism.

For decades military vested interests have tried to hide these issues to keep the profits flowing, but now the urgency faces us direct. Overall, this level of human and economic misery should disqualify militarism from world politics instantly. The question stares us in the face. Why do we still allow it to run the show? Why does disaster after disaster happen without it being addressed?

One part of the answer is fatalism. How can you *stop* it? Fatalism throws up its hands and does not have the faith to answer the question or even ask the question. For half the world's population the Cold War is still in their head, and history is just one damned war after another. It will go on. We can do nothing… Yet, when the question is asked straight, it can be answered. In fact, you could even argue it is easier to end militarism than what we do now, because disarmament and peace cost nothing and most of the process is undoing and not doing. Peace is the bargain of all history. So, let's just lay fatalism aside for a few hours and question this world-wide system of militarism. We can ask what is wrong with it, right down to this Russia-Ukraine War.

The second part is the failure to think. We are taught not to think, but to blame one side or the other. We blame Russia and Russia blames the West. We will blame China next. Blame is a playground level of thinking. We can think beyond blame. When we think about the whole problem of Militarism, really the arguments insult our intelligence. Of course, it is a dumb way to run the world. It is like putting a bull, some kangaroos and a load of geese in a china shop with some fireworks. Nuclear weapons will mess up cities. Guns make holes in people. It is not a great intellectual challenge to realize it does not work. But we blank it. We stay locked into "enemies" and "defence", baddies and goodies. Perhaps we need to do some basic thought about what kind of future we want for the world. Could we eliminate weapons and war and make the planet safe? Why do we not think about this? Why has militarism become so universally accepted? So, we think it through.

1. REMEMBER HITLER. THERE IS ALWAYS A BAD GUY.

A. We remember Hitler.

For many people the central argument is the need to defend ourselves against the bad guys. For they are always about and will attack you sooner or later. You therefore need to defend against them as a preventative measure; if you are strong, they will not attack. Armed defence has been normal throughout history and since 1945 obviously so. Hitler in his conquest of Europe and in the Holocaust was evil beyond dispute and Japan was similarly so in the Far East. Right up to the present we defend against the USSR and Putin to protect our freedoms. There will always be a bad guy and you stay strong. That, in sum, is modern political history.

It kills the idea of disarmament. If you disarm you encourage the bad guys to emerge, because they see the opportunity to overrun their neighbour, as Hitler did when he walked into the Rhineland and Czechoslovakia. To be disarmed is to be weak, as we were in 1939 through Appeasement, and we have to learn that lesson and be strong – better forces, better weapons and be prepared to fight. Being nice does not work. In Churchill's words, "Each one hopes that if he feeds the crocodile enough, the crocodile will eat him last." But you must not feed crocodiles; they are dangerous.

This argument did not even start with Hitler. The bad guys have been around throughout history. Ghengis Khan, Ivan the Terrible, Hannibal, Napoleon and lots more have been out to attack, and suppress, the peoples surrounding them using force. Given this long world history, surely it is futile to expect that disarmament can suddenly happen. You cannot change human nature; you can only guard against it. So, "Remember Hitler" is merely a shorthand for common sense in relation to the long history of conflict and the use of force by bad people. True we now live in democracies, but the same problem is still with us. Ukraine was recently invaded without any justification by an evil ruler intent on expansion. Clearly, he must be shown that he cannot win by superior power, certainly not by disarmament.

B. The good and the bad.

One correction to this argument we must, in honesty, address is the Good Guy - Bad Guy dichotomy. The British in forming the British Empire thought of themselves as the good guys bringing civilisation to benighted places. Actually, much of the time, we were cruel, not just in the era of slavery, selling humans to hard labour and often death, but also later. British treatment of China and India at different times was full of atrocities, and their economic exploitation was beyond measuring. It continued through to the end of Empire. For example, in Kenya between 1952 and 1960 the "Mau Mau problem" was some 90,000 Kenyans being executed, tortured or maimed and 160,000 imprisoned in a pattern of evil control.[ii] The process whereby tens of millions of Indians were wiped out in the United States, or natives in South America by Spain and Portugal, or Africans were treated in the US or West Indies cannot be described as good. The cruelty of the Belgian State in the Congo cutting off the hands of those who did not meet the rubber quota and killing millions, or the Dutch in its colonies, was often extreme. Western wars across the globe have often been devastating, bombing cities and people into the ground. Britain and the US used concentration camps. By almost every definition, we who think of ourselves as the good guys have also been bad, very bad, for millions of other people on the planet.

So, the argument changes shape quite decisively. It is not the Good Guys defending against the Bad Guys, but all sides, partly Good and partly Bad, attacking and defending against one another. In Vietnam, for example, the Vietnamese failed to defend adequately against the Great USA who wrongly bombed them to smithereens. What lesson is the small Vietnam supposed to learn from that? Stalin and the USSR played a big part in defeating Hitler. Was that the Bad against the very Bad? What was the difference between the Battle of Stalingrad and the Battle of Britain? The sacrifice of the USSR with 9 million Red Army soldiers dead and 18 million wounded, and civilian casualties running to nearly

18 million, against Hitler's attack, had to be very good for the world.[iii] So, the Good Guys strong against the Bad Guys will not quite do. The Good are often not good and the Bad are often not bad, or all bad. We need to think further.

C. The Bad Guys examined.

There is an interesting move in the Bad Guys argument. It focusses on individuals. When we think of Hitler's War we think of *him*, slanting hair, silly moustache, examine my armpit, spitting out venom and destroying much of the world. And that is what he did. Of course, personality centred history and politics are there all the time, especially in the media. Partly it is a shorthand for the events, yet it might ignore a quite central issue in Bad Boy politics. What forms them?

Hitler was a corporal in WW1 and in many ways was formed by fighting and war. He was an inadequate figure without a career, gassed, angry, who got together other inadequates still caught up in the war they had just experienced. He milked some rich people to fund his attacks on socialism, later including Henry Ford and Fritz Thyssen, and found a niche market for street violence. Germany had been traumatized by the War and was a place of horrors. He tried to start a rebellion in 1923 by jumping on a table and was imprisoned. Later he became popular when the Great Slump left many poor, out of work and angry. He was seen as useful by rich industrialists and arms people and was one *of many* shaped by militarism and hatred of socialists and Jews. Hitler was shaped into the evil lout he became. Fascist movements everywhere reflected the same ethos of marching, killing and control.

The same was true of Mussolini, more original in the formation of Fascism. He was employed by Ansaldo, the big Italian arms company, during World War One and switched from socialism to supporting a pro-war, militarist stance probably for the money he received. At this stage he was a paid lackey. He was also given £100 a week by MI5 in the last year of the War, partly to beat up peace protesters and keep Italy in the War.[iv] After the War he mobilised Italian war veterans into the goose-stepping fascist squads who would take over the Italian state. Again,

Stalin, the man of steel, was formed in WW1, the Communist Revolution, the war against Poland and famine. He ordered the execution of soldiers to keep his strategies on track. He had enemies everywhere, carried out appalling purges and sent millions to Siberia.

These are the bad people. We state the obvious - these three were militarily formed. It would be easy to extend the list to include Chiang Kai-Shek, Mao Zedong, Idi Amin, Nasser, Mengistu, Saddam Hussein, General Gowon, Kim Jong Il, Jorge Videla, Mengistu and Putin, who was shaped working for the KGB in the Cold War. All of these and many others were *military* men. Indeed, what we call bad is rulers who want to control and kill either their "own" populations or others by force. Embedded at the centre of what we label "the Bad Guys" is militarism, having arms that will murder people wholesale. *So, really, the problem is not the "bad guys" as individuals, (we are all bad in some way or another) but the militarism that has formed them and they then use.* Bad guys trust in weapons. What the argument ignores, we must address. There are baddish guys all over the planet. Dangerous bad guys mainly have arms and want to use them. Disarmament radically reduces that problem.

D. Are Guys the problem?

It is odd that we are talking about men all the time. Whether you rely on the story of Adam and Eve, or experience, there are reasons for thinking that women can be as bad as men. Yet men have been the bad rulers. Of course, the preponderance of men as national political leaders right down to the present is overwhelming, and perhaps that is reflected in the political evils of male conquest which have dogged the planet. Joan of Arc as a baddie or Imelda Marcos's shoes hardly tip the balance. Whatever may be the contributing factors to the long historical pattern, men have done war and weapons, planned conquests, developed the hardness to kill and the skills of battle. Men do militarism, war cruelty, conquest and have justified it with codes of bravery and the necessity of war. Rape as a weapon of war, torture and other unmentionable acts are part of the male culture of militarism. Indeed, we could ask how much of the world-wide pattern of male abuse of women is forged in the cruelties of armed force and war? Bad guys are war formed.

When World Disarmament was being considered in the 1920s and 1930s, women often took the lead. They saw that the Great War should not have been. They did not want to produce babies for generals to kill. They saw the futility of victory in the face of human loss, and they campaigned with petitions of millions and a desire to reform. It is time for them again, around the world, to address this male problem. Garrison Keillor suggests women may have a better perspective on the way to conduct human relationships.

> Girls had it better from the beginning. Don't kid yourself. They were allowed to play in the house where the books were and the adults, and boys were sent outside like livestock. Boys were noisy and rough and girls were nice so they got to stay and we had to go. Boys ran in the yard with toy guns going kksshh-kksshh, fighting wars for made up reasons and arguing about who was dead while girls stayed inside and played with dolls creating complex family groups and learning to solve problems through negotiation and role playing. Which gender is better equipped to live an adult life, would you guess? Is there any doubt about this? Is it even close?[v]

E. We arm the Bad Guys – the record.

Not only does the Bad Guy argument miss the point about militarism, but it has never really been honest because we arm them. The United States armed Hitler and Stalin in the 1930s with military factories despite knowledge of the atrocities committed by both. Chiang Kai-Shek, Pinochet, Batista, Somosa, Suharto, Mobutu, Marcos, Videla and a whole load of other cruel leaders have been armed by the West. We make bad guys worse. The US and Britain evicted a democratically elected President in Iran, Mossadegh, and re-imposed the oppressive Shah, whom they showered with arms while they extracted the oil they wanted. If guys are not bad enough, we even bribe them to make them worse.[vi] We supported long term oppression in Indonesia, Argentina and Chile when they were oppressive. African military dictators galore got their arms. For a short while in the UK around 2000 Robin Cook tried to pursue an ethical arms policy, excluding states from arms sales which were bad. Within a very short time representations from the arms companies to Tony Blair left the policy an empty shell.[vii] For example, after 2005 Blair, Berlusconi and others decided arms sales of €0.8bn to Gaddafi, that paragon of virtue, were fine. Then in the Arab Spring they bombed their own weapons because Gaddafi was now an oppressor. The real joke was Saddam Hussein. He had bad oil money. He wanted weapons. Arms companies backed by their governments flocked to supply him with weapons in the 1980s. He had chemically attacked the Kurds and Iranians, but don't worry about that. Reagan and Rumsfeld offered him a big arms-aid package in 1983. There was an embargo, but the arms piled in; in the UK the famous Supergun was stopped in the docks, although it had been cleared within Government. Then, finally, Saddam was killed in 2006 because Rumsfeld had found out as one of his "unknown unknowns" that he was a baddie although then he had no WMD and could easily be defeated. More recently, *after* a 2014 embargo against Russia for invading the Crimea, European countries, especially France and Germany exported €346m of military equipment to Putin which is now being used in Ukraine. The bad guys have been a sales opportunity.

So, we have to face the fact that the Bad Guys are shaped by arms. In American shoot-outs all the baddies have guns. To say the least, this leaves the Bad Guy argument in a bit of a hole. The military complex is hypocritical. *Be afraid of Bad Guys, while we arm them.* No weapons and bad guys are just eccentrics. Western and other militarists give bad guys their modus vivendi and then say they are the problem. Yet, even given this, perhaps we still need defence in case something happens which threatens us...

2. WE GET OUTSIDE DEFENCE.
A. Do we need Defence?

Most states have a system of Defence, a big defence budget to make it happen, and seek the latest weapons and efficient fighting forces to keep ready for action. There are Ministries of Defence or Departments of Defense in every state. They have military personnel, guns, rockets, bombers, drones, aircraft carriers (if they are rich), tanks, bases, ports, command centres, hospitals, nuclear weapons, submarines and satellites to defend themselves. The world average spend is about 3.5% of GDP (2023). European countries were around 2-2.5%, but the Russia-Ukraine War has changed that. Some middle east countries are big spenders. North Korea spends a *quarter* of its economy on defence and is unbelievably poor.

Because the US has such a big economy, it is by far the biggest in military expenditure, roughly equal to the next half dozen states and about 40% of the total. All states assess who their enemies might be, where the danger of war is coming from and form a complex defence policy. At the same time their neighbours, or if they are super powers, other states across the globe, will do the same. Defences are carefully planned against the threats. Much of the world is in a state of readiness for war and military exercises regularly take place to show they are ready to fight. Several dozen countries have much lower levels of arms and no obvious threat of war but they are usually ignored. Generally, we think we need Defence across the world.

Even at this stage we must inject a bit of peace. Switzerland said it was not interested in war and became neutral in 1815. It spends about 0.75% of its GDP on a basic defence force and has had no wars for two hundred years and threatens and is threatened by nobody. Most of its soldiers are part-time, doing normal jobs and not expecting much military work. It has had no war for two hundred years, few weapons and is it safe. More widely, defence is not needed between many states. France and Germany, long enemies and at war for an industrialised century, now

14

find war mutually inconceivable, as do many other neighbours. The "defence" thing, the idea of threats, is constructed. We notice there is nothing automatic about the "need" for defence.

Yet, worldwide, some kind of defence is entrenched in most, but not all, states. Clearly, in military dictatorships, of which there are several dozen, big and small, around the world, the military also defends the ruler against *internal* threat or attack. Even in democracies, the militaries are often closely embedded in the political system whatever party happens to be in power. They have privileged access to top politicians. The links between the Pentagon and the White House are very close. In London the MOD is immediately across Whitehall from 10 Downing St. The same is true in Paris, Beijing, Moscow and all the other big political capitals of the world. Whatever the comings and goings of party politics, the military are sacrosanct because the nation must be defended. Defence usually is beyond political debate. Wars will come unless you defend against them. It seems unquestionable, but, as we shall see Defence creates the problem it claims to answer. It is, in fact, the dumbest move ever in international politics.

B. Taking the credit.

Normally, Defence takes the credit for defending us against War. If we do not defend ourselves with missiles, aircraft carriers, tanks and armed forces, we would soon be embroiled in a war involving some state or other attacking us. It is our armed forces who keep us safe and you cannot skimp on equipment. We needed Bletchley Park in World War Two and without strong armed forces we would be in constant danger now. This section does not refute this view outright, (though we remember Switzerland's 200 years of unarmed peace), it merely sedates and cuddles it. The idea that states are gagging to go to war with other states, even when they are poorly armed, is somewhat overstated. Most of the time most states live in peace with other states and do not show any signs of aggressive intent. Some continents are like this. South America has hardly had any nation-on-nation war since the Chaco War in the 1930s. They had Cold War interference from the United States and the USSR, but none of the nations of this Continent started attacking their neighbours. New Zealand has not faced a threat in living memory, yet this is what the latest Defence review says, The New Zealand Defence Force "every hour of every day, 365 days a year, contributes to the defence, security and well-being of New Zealand." Really? Is it that tense? "Ow, it's 7 owclok, jist chick whither Austrayalia has started an invaysion yit." Most of this stuff is constructed PR to validate defence, when, really, we like peace. Western Europe since 1945 has done with European Wars. What is the point? There are open borders, holidays anywhere, national differences are fun and war is a hell no-one should consider. Countries arm but often to the American agenda. Though wars are not rare, the idea that we will not have wars only if we are armed strongly is overstated. People do not like war. Armed forces do not like war. Most people can see that wars are not really a good idea. They tend to make a bit of a mess, and not getting on with people on a large scale tends not to be a good idea. Perhaps, we just do not want to have wars much of the time, but weapons provoke them.

So, when the arms manufacturers tell us we must have weapons to stay safe, and governments tell us they are keeping us safe, it may be self-promotion. They are taking credit for dangers that do not exist, like the bloke who built flood defences half way up a mountain and boasted they kept the seawater out. In the UK there is no imminent danger from Belgium, Denmark, Ireland and France. Instead, we have wars with people a long way away in Egypt, Libya, Iraq, Syria, the Falklands and elsewhere which have very little to do with domestic defence. We talk about 1066 and all that, but really there has been very little "all that" for a long time. Maybe, we have been a lot safer than we think.

C. Is peace ideal or real?

There is another bit of the picture in which we are immersed. We are taught to believe peace is ideal, an ethereal hope which can never happen. Everybody "says" they are in favour of peace. All statesmen and women talk about it, even when they are at war. In the Russia-Ukraine War, Dmitry Medvedev, Russia's former president and deputy head of its security council, said recently: "Russia will achieve all its goals. There will be peace – on our terms." Peace becomes, in the famous words of Jeremiah, "Peace, peace, when there is no peace." It is unreal, a vague hope, an ideal and at best the end or absence of war. The real world is wars and rumours of wars and defence budgets, while peace is for Christmas cards. Never, we think, will peace cut it to the realities of politics. But Jeremiah will not be so dismissed. False prophets say false peace; they are greedy for gain and practice deceit. Pretend peace is unreal but real peace is available. Actually, our cities, nations, neighbourhoods and schools work because there is peace most of the time in most places. It is the practical basis of all communal living. It makes traffic work. It is so real, like sleep, that we are not aware of it. There is no peace for the wicked, but not being wicked and unarmed works well all over the place. Peace is basic to all human life.

D. We can think outside De Fence.

Meanwhile, we have lived most of our thinking inside national defence. Some of us practised at school hiding under desks from nuclear attack. Military threats crop up most days on the news. We pay our taxes for defence. We are comforted by our armed forces. Every year there are Remembrance services for the War Dead. State occasions feature the military dressed up. We go to air shows. Our military "punch above their weight". World leaders jostle over power. Secret services uncover threatening plans. Perhaps one film in ten is about war. History is 1066 and all that. Everyone saw 9/11 and remembers it. The British think of "fighting on the beaches" even though it never happened. It is all permanently in our heads.

But we can think outside it. It is interesting that within most of our nations we have moved on. We do not need to do domestic defence. In Britain we had the Wars of the Roses five hundred years ago, but since then, with the odd failure, Yorkshire and Lancashire folk have learned to live together, and it works. People come and go without fear. Yorkshire invades Blackpool. The neighbours do not live in a castle. We work, buy and sell, go on holidays, chat, travel, learn, play games, grow up, make friends and live together without needing weapons or usually making threats. It is ruled out. Killing one another is the most serious crime, requiring a life sentence, and we engage in the normal business of life without thinking of arming. Why, if we do it *within* out nations, can we not live without weapons internationally?

It is even more pointed that that. Most sane people know that Americans have made a mistake by believing a gun under every pillow can keep them safe. We know the US has got it wrong because there are 40,000 or so gun deaths each year, far more than elsewhere. About a million people have died through gun related deaths in the US since 2000, more than all US deaths in international wars back to the Civil War in the 1860s. If the US has got it wrong domestically, perhaps we have all got it wrong internationally. So, we can question this system of thinking and its inevitability. Defence and weapons are a human construction and they can be demolished. Militarism can be ended.

E. Defence is a questionable response.

Criticising defence may be labelled unpatriotic, but it may not be, because disarmament benefits everybody. It may be seen as questioning the sacrifice of the war dead, but most of them probably questioned it before they died. Here, for a couple of hours, we have the freedom to think and see the internal weaknesses of militarism as it has been constructed into our political system. This is not an abstract argument but the main practical, immediate and strategic world issue.

So let us face it more generally. Defence, whether as armour plating, swords, spears, earthworks, castles, cannon, rifles, machine guns, tanks, mortar shells, missiles or nuclear weapons is a "weak" response to other people. Rather than being with them we are against them. Rather than working together, we oppose. In games we oppose, and then shake hands. Political parties oppose, but to a greater good. Couples fight, but then hold hands. We love our neighbour as ourselves. We respect them. Defensiveness is a problem in personal relationships. Barriers give defence, but they are also barriers. To see defence as normal is perverse. It is wrong at a basic human level and then in national relationships, aside its effects. It causes, and has caused, poverty. We could wipe out the planet with militarism in the next decade. There are not just "innocent" victims; all victims are wrongly victims. Defence is the wrong direction in principle. Wars form ten years before they happen. We could spend the next ten years shaping up a war between the West and China, but how tragic and cursed it would be. We can put the idea of defence, the route into distrust, the mutual suspicion, the threats and the power play on hold. We can doubt it,

We need a better way. We already have a hundred million war refugees to care for. Global warming is here with drought, floods, food shortages and violent weather. War and militarism produce 5-10% of all human CO2. That needs addressing now. It is wars and storms. The world needs to survive together. Perhaps militarism needs winding up fast, for the sake of the planet, and we need another response.

F. I'm all right, Jack, or perhaps not.

I feel it in my own soul, and perhaps most of us do. As long as it does not matter in our patch, to us, it does not matter. We are self-centred and for lots of us, if our state keeps us "safe", we will not get worked up about wars and militarism. They happen elsewhere. Our governments have nuclear bombs, advanced weapons, and they have, by and large protected us. They can more or less do whatever they want as long as we are OK. So, we will not get worked up about militarism. It is like our Great Wall of China. Keep War Out and do not bother us.

This view is short-sighted. Wars come home, whether it is World Wars, 9/11, terrorism, or suicidal soldiers. We use endangered forces for our safety in a corrupt deal. "Well, they died or were injured, but at least it was not us." Meanwhile, we do not face that WW2 was worse than WW1, and WW3 will be worse still, and the effects will never end for everyone. Unaddressed, War will come to all of us. It will be horror. It is being built now. The pleasures of tomorrow, or shopping, or media, or myself dominate one day and the next. Whatever will be, will be. Thinking of others goes by the way. Yet, we must stop to think. Really, all wars are our war. All of us stand, or fail, before the Great Command to love our neighbour as ourselves. We know it is the only way to live, whatever we feel. Ignore it, and we will pay. Already two hundred million of our neighbours are dead and a hundred million now are war refugees. We cannot opt out.

G. We move beyond fear

One move might be crucial. Lots of great people have thought about peace, but listening carefully to Jesus is always worthwhile. In the context of talking about getting truth into the public arena, he said: "Do not fear those who can kill the body." What did he mean? Of course, he did what he said, and was calm and fearless before Pilate who would, reluctantly, crucify him. But he was also speaking a general principle. Behind Defence lies this fear, the fear of being overrun or killed. The defence system feeds on fear. At times it is horrifically real. Jesus warned his disciples to see the war problem coming in Jerusalem and flee, and so he was not speaking bravado. Jesus, the world's greatest teacher, deeper. He was confronting his disciples, and us, with the big ask of not living in fear of those who can kill. He drew out the central principles of living, and suggests that putting aside fear, the fear that fuels defence and ties us into militarism, might be a good thing. We can see beyond the petty gods who rule with armies to the Creator of all humankind. He was insistent on God's care for us. We can put aside the fear that runs the military system. We can think fearlessly and see why defence might fail. We give ourselves permission to think about the end of militarism and bringing about world disarmament. This great system that dominates us with fear can be seen from outside. It might not make sense.

3. SELF-DEFEATING ATTACK-DEFENCE.

A. What are the World's military people for?

What are our armed forces for? It is amazing how some important parts of our world are unquestioned. One of these is the armed forces of all the states around the world. What are they for? There are about 28 million highly trained personnel worldwide, additional millions if you include reserves. That is more than the population of the Netherlands and Belgium combined, a vast economy doing something, and so it is worth asking what they do? If you ask what we could do with 28 million highly equipped, usually young fit men, the answer would be a great deal. In fact, you could transform much of the world and end poverty. What are these 28 million trained to do?

They are armed forces. Fairly universally the answer is that armed forces are *for* Defence against other armed forces. Already the problem of this world system opens up. A is defending against B who is defending against A. Let us think what it would really be like if it was really defence. Imagine two big walls, made of stone, facing one another with a gap to prevent A climbing into B or B climbing into A. The walls succeed and there is an empty gap. You watch it for three months and then you get excited about a worm which comes out, swivels round and disappears. That is successful defence, and we all know militarism is not like that. But stay with successful defence. No war. Successful defence and the armed forces do nothing. *Success is 28 million well-trained, highly-equipped men and women doing nothing.* It is the Grand Old Duke of York updated.

> The Grand Old Duke of York
> He had ten thousand men.
> He marched them up to the top of the hill,
> And he marched them down again.

If there is no war, the system is not used. If that is "successful" defence, what, we may ask, is failure? Of course, the militaries try to cover this by saying they are "keeping the peace" or "defending" us. So, what is defence?

B. Real military "Defence" has usually failed.

Defensive militarism has been thought about for a long time. There were Castles and Hadrian's Wall and the Great Wall of China, and armour which covered the body in iron plates with a little slit for eyes, but usually they failed. There were shields against arrows, but the shielded had to attack sometime and armour was heavy. The archer won. He killed the horse and a clump of iron was left on the ground. Since William the Conqueror a whole load of invaders, or attackers, have been successful all round the world. In the First World War trench warfare was nearly an effective defence against heavy pounding with shells, but towards the end of the war the trenches were over-run by tanks, and there were heavy losses anyway as troops were shelled in the trenches, drowned in mud and slept face to face with rats. The trench system became history. Then in the 1930s France built the Maginot Line, a vast defensive fortification. It used up 55 million tons of steel and cost a lot, but when war came the Nazis simply went round it and it probably hindered the French defence. Since then, with bombers and the understanding that "the bomber will always get through", attack weapons have largely dominated world militarism over defence. You build strongly defended warships, tanks, but mainly so they can attack.

There is one recent exception to the primacy of attack. Ronald Reagan, not the brightest guy on the planet, had watched the Star Wars Film and this generated some idea of zapping incoming missiles with lasers and other things. Really, Edward Teller, who had a background in nuclear weapons, put the idea firmly in his head to make a lot of money for himself. It became US policy and was called the "Strategic Defense Initiative". Initial developments costs were some $30bn, but the idea had to be dropped because it was not going to work. It was described as hitting a bullet with a bullet and the cost of zapping an incoming missile was going to be many times the cost of making them. That was the last really big example of defensive militarism, although many defence systems exist. What Reagan actually did during this period was send nuclear bombers screaming over the North Pole towards the USSR before peeling off at the last moment. He was an attacker too.

Generally, it is cheaper and more effective to attack than defend. Although defensive kit is used, the military is overwhelmingly attack-based. Guns, rifles, fighters, bombers, missiles, nuclear weapons, aircraft carriers, subs and drones attack the other side. The Pre-emptive Strike where the attacker has an advantage makes nuclear weapons' policy jittery, as everybody has to be the first to attack. Attack dominates defence and the main defence against attack is threat or counter attack. Defence is Attack-defence. Really all our Departments of Defence should be called Departments of Mainly-Attack-Defence.

C. The World's militaries are all Attack-Defence.

So, we defend by attacking. The UK has a "Continuous At Sea Nuclear Deterrent". How does it defend us? By threatening to shoot nuclear warheads at any aggressor at any time. (Of course, in reality it is completely ignored and is merely there to make us feel good.) All the time States threaten attack to do defence, but *attack as defence creates the problem it sets out to solve.* A must threaten to attack to defend itself against B and vice versa. It is obvious. Both A and B will arm against the potential other attacker. For 45 years the Cold War perpetuated this pattern with tens of thousands of nuclear weapons aimed mutually at each other in what came to be known as Mutually Assured Destruction.

More than sixty years ago we were driving through the Fens and suddenly there was a great long rocket on another road driving along. It was probably, Dad said, a mobile nuclear ballistic missile trying to avoid being attacked by another nuclear ballistic missile, but it was secret and so we hadn't seen it... Attack-Defence creates and deepens the problem it sets out to solve. It is, as we say, a two-edged sword. Moreover, since the time of Krupp and Armstrong arms companies have insisted on the right to sell to the other side. The Other Side also learns to copy attack weapons. The West had nuclear bombs and drones, and soon its enemies do as well. It is Self-Defeating Defence.

The same pattern is everywhere. "Defence" is threat, aggression, building instruments of annihilation, calculating that you can win wars, showing off weapons so the other side knows you can attack because aggressive weapons are more successful. Attack militarism escalates. It generates arms races. Each side raises the threat level and lives in it fearing the other. North Korea fears US nuclear powers and threatens back with its nuclear weapons and missiles. China and Japan mutually arm in distrust. Russia and NATO do the same. Iran and Saudi Arabia increase their threat levels. Israel-Syria, Turkey-Greece, North and South Sudan and other examples show the same mutual threat pattern. Everywhere armed forces are potentially aggressive. Soldiers sit at drone and missile controls selecting targets. Militaries are organised with war plans, strategies, counter-offensives to attack. Defence is attack and that guarantees a continual escalating problem if the politicians buy into it, which they do. India and Pakistan have several dozen nuclear weapons with the missiles to deliver them pointing at one another – an astronomical cost and not a good way to live. *Thus, the insoluble problem with "Defence" is it is Attack.*

Attack-Defence cannot work. It creates the problem it does not solve. The words of Christ nail it. "Those who take the sword perish by the sword." If you buy into this stuff, it gets you. That is immediately inaccurate. If you have the sword, the other guy is likely to be skewered, but Jesus' words are big, gigantic, beyond the immediate. You take up the sword and you enter the system. You believe you will win, even that you are safe, but the weapon creates the problem for you. Hitler and the Japanese took the sword in WW2 and it got them. The colonial powers took the sword and the Maxim gun around the world, but it got them in 1914-18. Donald Rumsfeld sold swords to Saddam Hussein, but he would be fighting him later. If you are in the system, says Christ, it will get you. Defence is Attack-Defence and the Attack gets your Defence sooner or later.

D. The System has failed.

There is no escape from this. Technology will not do it; in fact, technology makes it worse, because the next "better" weapon will be the game changer which threatens the other side again. We have tried cannon, machine guns, howitzers, tanks, bombers, rockets, missiles, drones, stealth bombers and then the other side gets them or something else. It will be cyber warfare or armed outer space. Weapon escalation is the arms companies' normal business plan. But the weapons do not even have to be high tech. If people are annoyed enough by being invaded, they become terrorists and the terrorist will always get through, as 9/11 showed; you then spend shed-loads of money trying to stop them. Attack-Defence cannot work to bring peace and stability. We have a hundred and fifty years of modern overwhelming evidence. It fails. It kills. It destroys. It costs, and it is always mind-numbingly stupid. Putin thinks he is defending Russia while attacking Ukraine. Now where did that come from? The same old place.

We can go on with this long organisation of Attack-Defence. The militarists want us to stay blind inside - seeing the other side as the problem, but both sides, including us, attack-defend. The military system has already planned the next twenty years of opposition - China against Japan and the West, Russia and NATO in Eastern Europe, Iran and Saudi Arabia and chaos in the Middle East, troubles in DRC and other parts of Africa, rivalries in South America, cyber warfare, space warfare, terrorism, new weapons, new threats to keep us fearful. The budgets will grow, defence companies will get even richer, militaries will flourish, democracy will continue to dive, we will not have the resources to address global warming and militarism will make it worse. Inevitably, small wars, big wars or nuclear war will break out. We can stay in this tunnel of destruction and failure OR we can address it clearly and thoughtfully. Obviously, we must do the latter. We have seen the problem and are outside the tunnel; we cannot opt back into the dark.

4. ARMS CAUSE WARS. WE FORGET WHAT WE KNEW.

A. Arms companies are the engine for War.

So, we coolly see arms are a problem. Wars do not just happen. They emerge through commitments to weapons and using them. Ah, people say, weapons are neutral; it is only when they are used that they become evil. But all manufacturing is purposive. Cars drive on roads, spanners turn nuts, and weapons attack to kill. You cannot go to work on a tank, fly on a missile or cook with a rifle; they are made to rip and destroy. We could say that weapons have amplify human anger and the desire to dominate into killing and war. They are centrally formers of conflict. The main drivers of war are not those who fight; they often die and even hate it. The real impetus has lain with the industrial arms companies who make and promote weapons to kill. Their sales pitch, aggressively pushed for nearly two centuries, is that arms will win through aggression, killing and destruction. They began in earnest with Krupp's cannon, Armstrong-Whitworth's battleships, Vickers Maxim Gun, Mauser rifles, the Schneider 105 canon, Nobel dynamite and so on. They provided colonial control by the British, French, Belgians, Russians, Ottomans; the natives who objected to being Empire were shot. At one stage Birmingham was the gun centre of the world feeding British and other armies. Year by year they developed better, i.e. worse, weapons to kill, maim and expand the military enterprise. We must focus on them.

Arms companies have become one of the world's biggest and most successful industries. They sell different and competing products, and their products are promoted as the *best*, better than their rivals, or other incentives are offered. They have developed the world's most advanced technologies to win wars. They exploited steel. They developed explosives. They did airships and took over aeroplanes, did big cannon, submarines, gas warfare, mass shooting guns, biological warfare, nuclear weapons, missiles and vast supporting technologies in communication, weather, logistics, clothing, information and more to win wars. The model was the same as Krupp; if you produced cannon which shot further and killed more people, you won. Success was killing and destroying the other side. Success was gassed men in the trenches. They advertised and competed, and the best weapons won.

Wars were good business. The arms companies fuelled and were fuelled by wars. Each war expanded their business. After 1850 the Crimean War, the Second Opium War, the Indian "Rebellion", the US Civil War, the French Invasion of Mexico, the Paraguayan War, the Austro-Prussian War, the Cuban fight for independence from Spain, the great Franco-Prussian War, the Anglo-Zulu War, the US Wars against the Indians, the Anglo/Italian/Ethiopian War, the Matabele Wars, the First Sino-Japanese War, the Boxer rebellion, the Russo-Japanese War and the Second Boer War were good for trade. Across the world colonial powers needed weapons to fight, or "keep the peace". All of them involved weapons, rifles, cannon, warships sold wholesale by industrial arms companies. The industry proliferated world-wide before World War One. The arms trade was for war, and its success depended on having wars. It generated the modern industrial militarism within which we have lived ever since. It sold the war model internationally, but did not call it that. Salesmen, like Sir Basil Zaharoff, probably the richest man in Europe at the time, did deals, often with bribes, to pull states into the War Model. As shoe shops depend on walking, so arms companies depend on war.

B. Arms caused World War One.

The First World War was not about territory. Germany had enough lebensraum. It was about a complex of arms issues, whether battleships, the Schneider-Krupp canon rivalry or France and Britain arming Russia. The weapons, and the fear of attack, gave power to scares, especially the Dreadnought Scare, to create pressure for more orders. There were four arms races – Britain-Germany (naval), Germany-France (land arms), Russia-Germany (land arms) and Austro-Hungary-Serbia/Russia (land arms). The last one sparked around Sarajevo and the Archduke's assignation by Gavrilo Princip using a Belgian pistol. Even the issue then was arms. The big Austro-Hungarian arms firm, Skoda, wanted an arms deal with Serbia, which Serbia did not want, mainly because Austro-Hungary was its most likely enemy. It punished Serbia with the "Pig War", and then with the assassination at Sarajevo the whole fireworks box went off as the Austro-Hungarian Empire invaded Serbia. Often Germany is blamed, but because Britain and France were arming Russia, it faced potential attack from both West and East, which made it jittery. In response, the Schlieffen Plan of attack primed the War to start fast. In the decade before the War the arms companies in Britain, France, Germany, Russia continually pushed for bigger contracts and demonized the potential enemies. The war was caused by weapons, and Attack won over Defence. It was not a surprise.

C. The prophets of what was to come.

This is no new insight. The world had been warned about the dangers of munitions and war by a large number of leaders, including Gladstone, Adin Ballou, Frédéric Passy, Charles Booth and Count Komarovsky. Here is Gladstone in 1893, twenty years before the Great War, being pressured to fund more battleships.

> "If a stood alone in the world on this question, I could not so be moved; so strongly am I convinced that this large increase in the Navy will lead to disaster in Europe – Europe is my watchword.."[viii]

He was right, but he was "moved"; the Naval lobby eased him out of being Prime Minister. Big groups also pushed disarmament. The Christian Anabaptist tradition lived peace. Leo Tolstoy had slain the militarists in a vast outpouring of Christian sense… You abhor murder and then back mass murder by the state. You talk of conscience and then train people to kill and to obey without questioning. The Kaiser wants an absolute loyalty which demands you would even kill your family. A wheelbarrow is more use than all the world's weapons. Let those who start wars go to the frontline… People got the point from Tolstoy and many others. The 1890 London Peace Conference laid out how to do peace. Christian organisations organised for peace as international policy. It was followed by the 1899 Hague Peace Conference with 26 delegations from the main world states. Sadly, the hypocritical British

Government went cold on the proposals because they wanted to be off to fight the Second Boer War (with concentration camps) for gold and diamonds - not our finest hour. Marx had explained the links between capitalism and war. Keir Hardie, Ramsey MacDonald, Philip Snowden and Arthur Ponsonby pointed the Labour Party away from militarism. Jean Jaurès did the same in France before he was murdered. Bertrand Russell, Fenner Brockway, Maude Royden, Alfred Friend, Karl Liebknecht, Rosa Luxemburg, Bertha von Suttner, Jane Addams and many other world leaders saw the war catastrophe coming. Pope Benedict criticized it scathingly and tried to stop it with the Christmas truce of 1914. There was a 1915 International Congress of Women against it in the Hague. So, no-one could be surprised when this War turned out to be a catastrophe which all sides lost; they had been warned.

But the military-industrial complex got their War. Krupp was at the Kaiser's elbow when he finally decided for combat. Vickers and Co had the unassailable Navy; the Dreadnought Scare of Mulliner and others would be forgotten. The arming of Russia would now help the Allies. The French could test their new cannon. Jingoism ruled in the Daily Mail and elsewhere. *Thus, an assassination at the other end of Europe, really a small tragedy, exploded into the First World War because everybody was doing arms. Arms caused World War One.*

D. A hundred years ago we understood this.

This chapter says nothing new. It largely recycles what we knew a hundred years ago from Tolstoy, Passy, Keir Hardie and others, but have forgotten. Hear now the considered judgement of Lord Grey, the British Secretary of State for Foreign Affairs in the decade leading up to 1914, perhaps the best placed person *of all* to assess the Great War. He could have blamed Germany, but this is his conclusion about the War.

> "The moral is obvious; it is that great armaments lead inevitably to war. If there are armaments on one side there must be armaments on other sides...

The increase of armaments that is intended in each nation to produce consciousness as strength and a sense of security, does not produce these effects. On the contrary, it produces a consciousness of the strength of other nations and a sense of fear. Fear begets suspicion and distrust and evil imaginings of all sorts....

But, although all this [diplomatic difficulties with Germany] be true, it is not in my opinion the real and final account of the origin of the Great War. The enormous growth of armaments in Europe, the sense of insecurity and fear caused by them - it was these that made war inevitable. This, it seems to me, is the truest reading of history, and the lesson that the present should be learning from the past in the interests of future peace, the warning to be handed on to those who come after us."[ix]

We merely have to hear Edward Grey speaking to us the same sane moral conclusion for today. The lesson has not changed. A whole generation after WW1 understood this and the role of the private arms companies. There was a joke at the time where a young girl asks her father who was an arms dealer, "Daddy what did you do in the war? and he responds, "Well, darling, I did everybody."

E. The War to End All Wars and World Disarmament.

The horrors of the Great War was evident to all. Fifteen to twenty million died and some twenty to twenty five million were injured. Tens of millions more suffered shell-shock, or trauma. A mere two of them were Hitler and Stalin, and look what they did later. Towards the end of the War "Spanish" flu spread by the troops killed a further 50-100 million around the world, mainly the young, because people had been weakened by the War. Graves stretched to the horizon. The whole world was devastated by what we had done to ourselves.

At Versailles and in the League of Nations they understood world disarmament was necessary. The Covenant stated: Members "recognise that the maintenance of peace requires the reduction of national armaments to the lowest point consistent with national safety and the enforcement by common action of international obligations...The Council... shall formulate plans for such reduction for the consideration and action of the several Governments...After these plans shall have been adopted by the several Governments, the limits of armaments therein fixed shall not be exceeded without the concurrence of the Council... The Members of the League agree that the manufacture by private enterprise of munitions and implements of war is open to grave objections. The Council shall advise how the evil effects attendant upon such manufacture can be prevented... (Article 8, Covenant of the League of Nations) A Disarmament Commission was set up to prepare the Conference which would disarm the world. Arms are the problem; they produce evil.

This was no fringe understanding. The world's key figures were behind it, President Wilson before he was ill, Pope Benedict XV, Albert Einstein, Lloyd George, Vera Brittain, Bertrand Russell, Mahatma Gandhi, Lord Robert Cecil, Archbishop Cosmo Lang, Jane Addams, Arthur Henderson, Charles Raven, George Lansbury, H.G. Wells, Sigmund Freud and many others saw it as the obvious way to go. There was overwhelming support for World Disarmament with millions of ordinary people signing petitions, and, as Noel-Baker points out, the organisations finally present at the conference – churches, trade unions, socialists, veterans, women, Co-operatives, League of Nations groups and many more, represented about a thousand million people, more than half the adult population of the world.[x] They were pressing that World Disarmament be done, because they understood that arms caused wars and would continue to do so if they were not abolished. The private manufacture of the weapons to kill had to stop.

This central lesson was accepted around the world. Millions understood this because the Great War had forced them to see the big picture. They suffered and saw beyond hate. The soldiers lived it and were cynical of the whole operation. "Oh, oh, oh what a lovely War!" There were the generals who gave the orders and the soldiers who carried them out.

They were "Up to your waist in water, Up to your eyes in slush… " and finished hanging on the barbed wire.

> When this bloody war is over
> Oh, how happy I will be;
> When I get my civvy clothes on
> No more soldiering for me.

> No more church parades on Sunday
> No more begging for a pass;
> I will tell the Sergeant Major
> To stuff his passes up his ass.

They knew war had to be stopped. It was the same for all sides. Soldiers were "cannon fodder". But they saw it then, why are people so different now? Ordinary Ukrainian and Russian soldiers now are mouth-open dead. Given this awareness *then*, we need an explanation of why World Disarmament has been eradicated from public debate and discourse *now* and Militarism has won. More than that, we need to plonk this obvious conclusion about War back in the centre of world politics.

F. War against War. Who are the enemy?

We need to war against war, now as then. But how do you war against war? Who are the enemy? Whom do you fight? What does it mean to fight against war? Obviously, you can't kill anybody. Jesus tends to put his finger deep on issues like this, and the Sermon on the Mount does it in a sentence. "Beware wolves in sheep's clothing." Well, actually he carries on in case we don't get it. They come in sheep's clothing, but inwardly they are ferocious wolves. Test them by their fruit. You don't pick grapes from thornbushes or figs from thistles. If you get a War, it came from a War Tree, however fluffy the outside, to mix metaphors. We have to get beyond the way leaders present themselves. They can talk peace, when actually they are planning war. If Militarism causes war, and it does, saying, Peace, peace" when there is no Peace, is a false show and we must expose it. The pretence is dangerous.

But who are the enemies? To War On War, (WOW), we need to know the enemy. They are those who believe in, or push, Militarism. They are often influential and in charge. In Britain, Thatcher was a militarist and her son was an arms trader. So were Blair, Cameron, Johnson and others. Reagan, Clinton, Bush and Trump were. Some politicians are mild militarists. There are a lot of them, and they are only slightly troubled by what they back; they have not really learned anything but the defence mantra over a long period of time. They dress up their policies in nationalism and goodness, and probably even deceive themselves. But the full-time ones are the arms manufacturers. Whatever they say, *wars are their business*. They work at it. They masquerade as keeping the peace, while selling death. Killing is washed clean away from their websites. They use words like, "lethality" and they do no wrong. They provide employment. They defend us (by selling weapons around the world). They are there to "avoid" war (although they profit vastly from it). And they are nearly invisible, except they fund research, and often help politicians along. They are rich and use the money they have to bribe and influence, and they are inside politics. Most important of all, since their exposure in the 1920s and 30s as the Merchants of Death, they lie low and pretend that arming the world is normal, when it is a political choice they have engineered since Krupp. Wars are "accidents" which require their remedy. They have changed emphasis as history has changed, but each has contributed to the overall ethos and direction. Once you are inside the system, and earning your living from it, you will assert that the way of weapons is right, necessary and unavoidable. Some militarists are small ones or even great ones like Churchill, Eisenhower, earlier in his life, and De Gaulle. Others operate within the systems they have set up and do what they are told to do professionally. Once you have weapons in your head, you are part of the system. Many like money, because the system spins money, and they go home to affluence. Many of them are likeable, doing what is right in their own terms and operating within the legitimate structures of the state and nation. Yet really, they are the enemy, if we are to fight the system.

But again, we have to listen to Christ. "Love your enemies." Really, the enemy is quite pleasant. A lot of them are decent. They want to be in power and stay in power, but their kind always have. They are locked in the box of their own thinking; they need more weapons. They have quite a bit of money or property and do not ask too many questions about business deals. They think within their brief; they distrust those who oppose armaments. "We do not want troublemakers about," they say. Yet, really, they are quite like us. They might be us. We might be partly wolves through our voting and our investments. We pay our taxes for arms. The key about this fight is that it is *not* ultimately one side against the other. It is against worshipping this systemic force of destruction and destroying *it*.

And so, we are in the business of a new kind of war. Nobody will be killed. In this war we all finish fighting on the same side. We do not use clobbering weapons, but evidence, arguments, presenting what is true, changing people's viewpoints, petitions, peaceful marches, democracy, respect for the UN, speaking to people's good principles and conscience and we do disarmament as practical politics. We look for conversions, like John Newton from the slave trade. We love our enemies, but they also need defeating. Wickedness has to be named and truths need to be stated. Our peace army is democratic, ordinary people voting until there is no against, and the enemy disappears because peace is good for us all and the dogs of war should not be loosed with sharpened teeth. The real enemy is Militarism, a world consuming god of nothingness we have constructed, not other people. Let us investigate how it came to rule.

5. THE 1932 WORLD DISARMAMENT CONFERENCE AND TORY SABOTAGE.

A. The World meets for Disarmament.

Let us look at how disarmament and peace were pushed from being a world-settled conclusion in the 1920s, partly so that we can learn from the mistakes. The Tory Government of 1924-29 delayed the World Disarmament Conference set up after the formation of the League of Nations, because it was quietly against disarmament and for Empire, despite the public pressure for disarmament. It came to power partly through the fake Zinoviev Telegram in the second 1924 election. The Preparatory Commission was set up in 1925, but it was not until the Labour Government returned in 1929, with Lord Robert Cecil, Arthur Henderson and Philip Noel-Baker as key British figures, that it had momentum of government to plan the Conference. Even then, in 1931, the Labour Government was ousted, but these three carried on with little Government support into the actual World Disarmament Conference. Nansen, the Arctic explorer, another key figure died just before it opened. It was a global event with delegates from all over the planet. Surely now World Disarmament would happen.

Key figures everywhere backed disarmament. Albert Einstein was merely one committed to it. Here is part of his good wishes.

> Without disarmament there can be no lasting peace. On the contrary, the continuation of military armaments in their present extent will with certainty lead to new catastrophes.

> Hence the Disarmament Conference in Geneva in February, 1932, will be decisive for the fate of the present generation and the one to come. If one thinks back to the pitiful results achieved by the international conferences thus far held, it must be clear that all thoughtful and responsible human beings must exercise all their powers again and again to inform public opinion of the vital importance of the conference of 1932. Only if the statesmen have,

to urge them forward, the will to peace of a decisive majority in their respective countries, can they arrive at their important goal. For the creation of this public opinion in favour of disarmament every person living shares the responsibility, through ever deed and every word.

The failure of the conference would be assured if the delegates were to arrive in Geneva with fixed instructions and aims, the achievement of which would at once become a matter of national prestige…. We can only hope for a favourable outcome in this most vital conference if the meeting is prepared for exhaustively in this way by advance discussions in order that surprises shall be made impossible, and if, through honest good will, an atmosphere of mutual confidence and trust can be effectively created in advance.

Success in such great affairs is not a matter of cleverness, or even shrewdness, but instead a matter of honourable conduct and mutual confidence. You cannot substitute intellect for moral conduct in this matter–I should like to say, thank God that you cannot!

It is not the task of the individual who lives in this critical time merely to await results and to criticize. He must serve this great cause as well as he can. For the fate of all humanity will be that fate which it honestly earns and deserves.

So, everyone needed to be part of this great convening of humankind for peace, and especially the governments needed to be prepared with moral commitment.[xi]

You would think that is the right spirit for world disarmament. In Britain it was supported by King George V, three Prime Ministers, two Archbishops and was established national understanding and it was similar in many other countries.

B. Britain is crucial.

The Great Disarmament Conference met at Geneva on 2nd February 1932. You, like me most of my life, have probably not heard of it, because it has been buried by the militarists. They do not want us to think about it or to understand what went on there. But we need to, *because the world is going to do this again and get it right.* You need to know how the powerful can strangle disarmament, simply by finding "difficulties" and delaying.

The great petitions of tens of millions were received, and it began. Britain was the lead nation. We were then the seeming world superpower and Lord Cecil and Arthur Henderson, British politicians, were the key figures running the Conference. The plan was for an ordered reduction of arms in all nations, across land, sea and air, but actual action depended on governments agreeing. There was an especial focus on aggressive weapons like the new bombers and big guns. Japan was a problem because it was attacking China and not at the Conference. France wanted special guarantees about collective security against possible German aggression. But the main issue was Britain. If Britain, especially, if it co-operated with the US, did World Disarmament, it would happen. Germany, unarmed, would come in line, France too. The USSR was for it, and dozens of other countries. Britain had "won" in 1918 and the British Government had to take the lead, but the British Government was not what it seemed.

C. The "National Government" and the Tory Story.

Formally, in 1932, Ramsey MacDonald was the Prime Minister in charge of the National Government. He had been persuaded by Conservatives to lead a "National Party" in the 1931 election, separating from his party, the Labour Party. Labour actually had a better policy to address the recession than the Nationalists, but Keynesian economics was not understood then and a patriotic general appeal saw the mainly Tory "National Party" in. It won the election with an inflated 345 majority. Labour (for disarmament) was cut from 287 seats in 1929 to 46 in 1931 while the Tories had a totally dominant 473 MPs, and not a very talented bunch at that. They easily moved from Westminster to the West End dining clubs and had strong aristocratic networks across the country. MacDonald was thus a figurehead in a mainly Conservative Cabinet. Parliament was dominated by a massive Conservative body of MPs who were mainly pro Empire, pro-military and against disarmament. Most of them were worried by Socialism and the threats it posed to their wealth and looked to right wing military groups as a bulwark against the socialist menace. They were Land of Hope and Glory, warry, gory, dilatory, vindicatory, expostulatory, obfuscatory, a priori, militory Tories and they were not going to do World Disarmament. Their hero was the Duke of Wellington. MacDonald was now probably a bit senile into the bargain and was being flattered by Lady Londonderry and her social circle on Park Lane.

Publicly, the Cabinet said it was for disarmament, like MacDonald, because it had such overwhelming public support, but actually it was against it and for empire, the navy, British supremacy and the arms industry. They were wolves in sheep's clothing. The key figures in the Cabinet on international issues were Neville Chamberlain - the Chancellor of the Exchequer, Sir John Simon - Foreign Secretary, Sir Philip Cunliffe-Lister - Colonial Secretary, Lord Hailsham - Secretary of State for War, Sir Samuel Hoare - Secretary of State for India, the Marquis of Londonderry – Secretary of State for Air, Sir Bolton Eyres-Monsell – First Lord of the Admiralty, Walter Runciman, and in 1932 Stanley Baldwin, who was effectively Prime Minister. These, aside Baldwin, would later become the Appeasers because they were right wing, pro-military figures who quite liked Hitler. Sir Maurice Hankey, Secretary to the Cabinet, was also against the League of Nations and Sir Robert Vansittart at the Foreign Office wanted an alliance with Mussolini. The pull away from disarmament was strong.[xii]

It is easy to blame this group for their later support of Hitler, but, really, they were Nationalist and Imperial all through. First, they were for Empire and wanted an international settlement which would allow them to carry on ruling British colonies around the world with armed forces. Second, they wanted naval supremacy to keep the Empire in shape;

Britain had run down its navy in the 20s quite a bit. Third, of course, they were anti-Communist and anti-Socialist. Fourth, they were a bunch of upper-class aristocrats tied to Britain's glory and landed wealth.

Slowly they formed the idea that an alliance with *Germany* against France and the USSR was the best European alignment. Germany was not really interested in a far-flung empire or a big navy and so it "fitted" us. It seemed to want only about 35% of our Navy because it had few overseas territories and was not a challenge to the British Empire; its focus was within Europe. It alone could attack the USSR, while France had Socialist Governments in or near power in the early 30s. It was not an obvious Tory ally. This orientation also appealed to Edward VIII, linked by family ties to Germany. The aristocracy liked them and went hunting with them. We remember Sir Oswald Moseley was Lord Curzon's son-in law; Fascism and the Tory Party were intermarried. This group aimed to make foreign policy on their own terms without disarmament or international law, because Britain was Great Britain. At this stage Germany was largely without arms and a navy. Given all this, the Tories could easily shape a strategy against Socialism, for the Empire and links with Germany and they were not going to back disarmament.

The problem was not seeming to oppose this great world disarmament movement because it was so popular. This they did in the normal establishment way – the best policy is to do nothing. The Cabinet stalled, as did Sir John Simon, the Foreign Secretary, who was half in favour of disarmament. Initially, it was not discussed in the House of Commons, but the Labour forced an adjournment debate on the 13th May, 1932 just before the recess. Sir John Simon gave a long speech going nowhere. The Chiefs were not for disarmament of the Navy, Air Force and Army and demurred in Cabinet. The Government did nothing and said they were trying. Questions from George Lansbury and others in the Commons before the long summer recess were unanswered. Throughout the Spring and early Summer this great Conference stalled, while the Tories sat on their hands. Lord Cecil, Arthur Henderson and Philip Noel-Baker and the delegates from other countries could do nothing…

D. The Hoover Plan.

Then President Hoover stepped in with a breath-taking proposal to cut by a *third* the armament burden of the world and totally abolish the most aggressive weapons - all bombing planes, all large mobile guns and all instruments of chemical warfare. It would launch full World Disarmament. Hoover put all the US cuts on the table immediately, saying, "We will do them." The United States, the world's biggest economy, was leading for disarmament. A tide of support followed from the USSR, Germany, Italy (the Pope had done his work), Spain, Canada, Belgium, Brazil, Turkey, Cuba, Austria, Norway, Dominican Republic, Finland, Hungary, Denmark, Mexico, China, Sweden, Estonia, Switzerland, New Zealand, Persia, Venezuela, Argentine, the Netherlands, Lithuania, Afghanistan, Colombia, Latvia, Portugal, Bolivia, Bulgaria, Yugoslavia and other smaller states. Of course, colonies did not have a vote, and so this represented easily most of the world's states and population. There was a large majority of support for President Hoover's drastic world disarmament and also backing from the British public. Surely, now it would happen.

The British and French Governments agreed, though with reservations. France wanted security with Germany, which could be addressed within disarmament with the correct guarantees, and Britain, with its Empire including most of the rest of the world population, *dithered*. Britain was key. Sir John Simon was Foreign Secretary and he said that the US proposals were good, but Britain would come up with some other ones. Again, the Government stalled. Lloyd George's verdict on Sir John Simon was that he "sat on the fence so long that the iron entered his soul". Sir Anthony Eden had "contempt" for him. Harold Nicholson described him as "a toad and a worm". But he was dominated by, and later joined, the militarists in the Cabinet and among the Tory Party. Eyres-Monsell (Navy) and Lord Londonderry (Air) insisted on not depleting their forces, although they were not very efficient at doing it, and the Cabinet carefully undermined progress on the Hoover Plan. Partly, it was jealousy that the US was the new Superpower, replacing Britain, making proposals; it was that pathetic. Hankey and Vansittart also skilfully avoided addressing the Hoover proposals and even organised a visit of MacDonald to Mussolini. The British discussions mired in different military complexities and nothing of substance happened through July, August, September and October. The world kept asking, while the British Government quietly scuppered President Hoover's radical world disarmament proposals. It was a tragedy. If the United States, Britain, France, the USSR, Italy and fifty or so other states had backed the Hoover Disarmament Proposals when Germany was largely unarmed except for a few illicit deals, *then Germany would have stayed disarmed and Hitler would not have come to power.*

E. The Oxford Union 'King and Country' debate.

The defeat of disarmament in 1932 was a big event in the public's mind. We now do not understand the disappointment and anger it produced. So, for example, most people have heard of the Oxford Union debate of 9/2/1933 where it voted 64% for the motion: "This House would not in any circumstances fight for king and country." Were they just unpatriotic? Oxford University was mainly peopled by fairly rich, Tory members of the British establishment. Why should it vote so strongly against this patriotic resolution? A later vote was even more extreme. Note the date. They were not being unpatriotic, but were angry that the Government had messed up Disarmament at Geneva and Hitler was in power. They had a point. A lot of them would die in WW2. They knew the way things were going and did not feel like being dead patriots...

F. We now do not know this.

All of us living now are cut off from this stuff. It is edited out of most British, and World History. We do not know World Disarmament existed, was world dominant and nearly won before Hitler came to power. History after 1939 was dominated by Hitler - defeating the bastard - and then the Cold War. The militarists banished it from world discussion. Disarmament talk became "unrealistic"; it was being a traitor. It was *appeasement* and it let people like Hitler in. We ignore the truth that those who scuppered the Hoover Plan then and later, as the

Appeasers, were *militarists who opened the door to world rearmament and saw Germany and Hitler as a potential ally.* In fact, we get Appeasement completely the wrong way round. That mistake is so big we spend the next chapter on exposing the illusion.

G. Two big lessons.

One lesson from Geneva for us now is that militarists in power can kill disarmament through *process* - complexity, minute discussions of weapon systems, fears, negotiations -and will try to do it again if they are in charge. **Turkeys do not vote for Christmas.** Military establishments live inside their thinking, planning, calculations of power and cannot get out; they will kill proposals if they can because it ends their business. Full world disarmament must be clean, direct and cut to action. It must be done on clear terms for all of us, not ones shaped by the military-industrial complex, the Big Boys, and their priorities. They have killed disarmament for a hundred years, still know how to do it, and will do it again. You are warned. The military establishment cannot do disarmament. It is like asking a tiger to do surgery.

There is a second lesson. *Partial* disarmament merely deals in mutual mistrust. It retains the suspicions of attack and competitive arming and allows introducing complications. Militarists have been taught to want more than the other guy and bargain against the process. They will discuss "problems" endlessly as they did in the 1960s. Full disarmament for everybody avoids these stalemates. We go for the full deal. Why should we not get rid of all weapons? Our cities function without any weapons and the world can too; a gun in every fifth house on the High Street is absurd. Then we failed and were sabotaged. Now we succeed and they all go.

6. APPEASEMENT – THE WORLD'S BIGGEST MILITARY LIE.

A. Hitler and Appeasement.

Even now around the world, "appeasement" is seen as the main argument against disarmament and world peace. People vaguely see disarmament as the cause of War. That is inside their heads. "Remember Hitler" is the refrain. The world now understands the necessity of militarism through the supposed lesson of how World War Two started. The general conclusion is as follows:- "You will always get people like Hitler. If you try to *appease* them by not arming, they will take advantage of you and rule the world. So, always be strong and arm against the next Hitler. The lesson of the 1930s is *do not disarm*. Stay strong, or another Hitler will get you. Being soft and disarming is not an option; it is for the fairies. The arms companies stopping us being overrun. They prevent war rather than cause it. They are always on our side. Be strong and arm and then we will all be safe. Disarmament means war and arming means peace." A billion people probably vaguely believe that message, *although it is the direct opposite of history and of the truth.*

First, we take "Hitler" out of the fantasy. WW2 was bigger than Hitler. From 1918 a large group of Fascists in Nazi Germany, Italy, Poland, Japan, France, Britain and the US who were committed to military type, anti-socialist governments. As we see later, Hitler was merely the most successful leader of these vast movements. There was the Holocaust, obviously the greatest evil, but also atrocities in many other places because mass military cruelty was again let loose. Cities were viciously bombed across the globe - killing and mangling millions. People were left to famine, were raped, were enslaved, were left to die, because inhumanity became normal. WW2 was generated across the globe, not just in one place, and we need an adult understanding of all this evil, all this darkness which descended on the earth. In particular, before Hitler came to power, the world had reinvested in the means of killing, the weapons which lead to war. The darkness was long coming and we must face it. World-wide militarism, not one man, caused WW2.

Then, the appeasement lie must be held in the light, because it has become the "truth" and disarmament has been rubbished all our lifetimes. We look again at the history of militarism between the wars and see that, *as weapons caused WW1, so they caused WW2*. The Appeasers were the Militarists. Real historical "appeasement" is the opposite of the supposed lesson of the arming people. The militarists, acting together, appeased Hitler, because they were on his side. They opened up arming world-wide, kitted him out with weapons and brought on WW2. Exactly, it is the false conclusion. There are multiple processes whereby arms and war caused WW2. Let us examine some of them.

B. WW1 Militarism becomes goose-stepping Fascism.

As we have seen, WW1 was caused by the build-up of arms and four arms races. It then involved four years of horrific fighting, *but war does not end with Armistice.* It has consequences for decades. Some 70 million troops fought in the War. 10-12 million were killed, but what of the others. Fifty to sixty million soldiers carried on, an enormous population mainly in Europe, traumatized, still marching, poor, often injured, looking for an income. They were often still fighting war and believing myths like the Nazi Jewish plot. Let us look at the way these people helped form Fascist politics. It was the same in many countries.

In Italy Mussolini, was paid by Ansaldo, the Italian arms company, during WW1. He then formed Fascist Blackshirts, the Squadristi, the first goose-stepping mercenary group who warred against Communists and anyone they did not like in Italy. There were eventually some 200,000 of them. In October 1922 about 30,000 led the coup that made Mussolini the first Fascist dictator and later Hitler's ally.

In Russia the defeat and cruel occupation by Germany led to the Bolshevik Revolution and a long internal Civil War between White and Red forces. Churchill as British Minister for War from January, 1919, contributed to this confrontation. It lasted until 1923 and Poland also continued warring against the new USSR. Thus, Russia faced nine years of raw, devastating war, followed by famine, with fighters facing and making horrific conditions for national life. The USSR remained ravaged by violence through to 1939.

In Germany Hitler's Brownshirts, the Sturmabteilung, were largely ex-soldiers recruited into a thug army, one among other ones. Hitler paid them a pittance from his rich friends. There were other traumatized military units carrying on war against Socialists in Germany, murdering Karl Liebknecht and Rosa Luxemburg, the socialist leaders. Hitler and his thugs tried the Munich Putsch in 1923, which failed and landed Hitler in prison. The militarist model dominated the Nazi movement all through with lots of leaders similar to Hitler in the Nazi and other groups. Hitler became merely the most successful of them.

In France the Croix de Feu and Action Française mobilised ex-military personnel and the same Fascist style into demonstrations of more than 50,000 in the 1930s. There were a million injured soldiers in France, life spoiled by war, looking for redress.

In Britain Oswald Mosley marched his Blackshirts around the East End spouting antisemitism with wide support. The Daily Mail was "Hurrah for the Blackshirts". The British Union of Fascists was strong and supported by many establishment figures until Hitler loomed as a threat. Hitler was even seen as an ally into WW2 by many of them.

In Japan the World War One militarists, linked to the big dominant companies - the Zaibatsu - moved into permanent dominance. Spain and Portugal had Fascist revolutions through to 1939. Other aggressive militaristic units followed on from 1918 in other countries.

So, World War One and its militarism, often linked to war trauma, carried through towards World War Two, providing the foot soldiers and leaders of Fascism. It was a general world pattern. These groups were not incidental. Usually, they influenced politics and government strongly as in Italy, Germany, Japan, and even Britain and the US, for war and militarism. As so often, War helped cause War and only peace can heal it. That is background to the whole period.

C. Reviving the Arms Trade.

The Arms Trade is quite precarious, and the most difficult time is after a war. Weapons have been produced on a vast scale to win, or lose, the War and then the War ends with no further conflict in sight and demand for arms drops to zero. This happened in 1918 on a grand scale. Because everybody had fought in the World War, war ended for everybody. Actually, conflict did carry on in Russia and elsewhere, but that was with the vast surplus of weapons after 1918. The common-sense understanding was that no war or substantial armaments sales were thinkable for a decade. And die back the arms trade did. Of course, they had vast stored profits. In Germany the end of arms production was required of Krupp and the others, but Krupp had money in the Netherlands and wanted to resume arms production deviously if necessary. In France and Britain demand dived and the industry suffered. Armstrong-Whitworth and Vickers merged with Government help. Schneider linked with Skoda in Czechoslovakia in a deal to keep output going. In the States Du Pont, Singer, Remington and others were very rich, but suddenly without demand. Of course, they could buy up other companies (as Du Pont did General Motors), diversify or recreate a demand for arms. Groups of shareholders, politicians and militarists tried the latter, but with difficulty. Throughout the 1920s the arms trade was low and struggling.

Yet, they found their ways through. One was through bribery. Another was through scares. Another was through pressure on governments either from inside, or though agents. One agent, employed to scupper the 1927 Geneva Naval Conference for $25,000, was William Shearer. He was largely successful and then tried to get $250,000 from his Naval Employers and went to court, so everyone then knew what was going on. Another was through exploiting tensions; even in 1919 the French were arming the Turks fighting the Greeks armed by the British; Lloyd George and Sir Basil Zaharoff helped set that one up. Another was through patriotic groups and campaigns from the press, often part owned by military interests.

However, the real bonanza came with China and Japan. There was big business in equipping the Chinese warlords and the now militarised Japan. Both intensified when Japan invading China in the Manchuria Incident. From about 1929 the Far East was taking all the arms it could from British and French yards, *with arms companies ignoring the League of Nations Covenant*. Ships went almost daily from Hamburg, poorly disguised, with weapons and ammunition. Exports from Britain, France, Germany, Czechoslovakia, Switzerland, Holland, Belgium and Norway went to Japan and China. British arms exports were £12m officially between 1929-1931 but really more. We are talking five hundred bombs to China and a million rounds of machine gun ammunition to Japan in one month. One hilarious incident is reported in Hansard on 27/2/1933 by MP Morgan Jones. Apparently, Chinese and Japanese representatives turned up at a factory to inspect their arms purchases and both discovered that they were being overcharged and together delivered an ultimatum to their supplier to cut the price.[xiii] Given these big sales, neither the French or British Governments were really going to sanction Japan for its invasion of Manchuria. Already before the Geneva Disarmament Conference the arms industry was off its leash and the arms trade was booming.[xiv] Note these were arms sales around the world, before the arms race towards WW2 took place in Europe.

D. The arms companies unleashed.

The failure of the Geneva Disarmament Conference was another green light to the arms companies. By 1933 they were back in business; their share prices were up. Sir John Simon tried, not very hard, to stop the weapons supply to Japan and China and it grew. Really, many Tory MPs were complicit within the business with shares and interests. The politicians still talked peace to the public, but really the militarists and arms traders were now in charge and the vast money-making machine from before WW1 was again churning out weapons. The wars were now coming – 1931 Manchuria, 1932 the Chaco War, 1934 the Saudi-Yemeni one, 1934 the Austrian Civil War, 1935 the Italian invasion of Ethiopia, 1935 the Yazidi Revolt, 1936 the Arab revolt in Palestine and 1936 the Spanish Civil War, another big one. They all needed arms. British, Czech, French, Spanish and German arms fuelled them. The factories were back in business, selling around the world, to supply the new wars.

Picasso painted Guernica in 1937, another warning, but half a million died in the Spanish Civil War and it was a practice ground for Fascist and Soviet planes. It was not as though the Fascists could not be understood before Munich. Through 1935 and 1936 Haile Selassie witnessed to the barbarism of Mussolini's invading forces and Japan's invasion of China would move seamlessly into the Second World War. The war machine was up and running across the globe, and everywhere the arms company factories were humming with the demands for war because *governments allowed it to happen*. This was not just Hitler but the whole of the western military system, as we see from the evidence below. World War Two was set in motion by nearly a decade of arms expansion.

E. Pretend Peace.

Had the Geneva Conference failed? Actually, it dragged on well into 1933 and throughout the world people who knew disarmament was right waited with hope. Crucially, the British National (really Tory) Government spent the mid-30s saying they were for peace when they had buried disarmament. Baldwin went to the 1935 election standing for peace. As the Manifesto says, "Peace is not only the first interest of the British people; it is the object to which all their hopes and efforts are diverted." Baldwin talked peace, rearmament and "defending" the Empire at the same time. He actually lost two hundred and fifty MPs in 1935 mainly because of people angry at the failure at Geneva, but it was not catastrophic. He still had 52% of the vote and a massive majority in the Commons. At this stage Hitler was not much of a threat, for three reasons we consider below, but it was a period of pretend peace. MacDonald was a token Prime Minister, largely senile through to June 1935 when he resigned. It was in this unreality of this situation, the idea that the Baldwin Government were for disarmament when they had scuppered the Hoover Plan, that the myth of appeasement was born.

Historians often still moan that there was a failure of the British military to respond adequately to the arrival of Hitler. Why did we not arm properly against this evil man, we ask? Partly, it was poor political leadership among the group who were governing. They were quite lazy aristocrats with servants and used to leisure. They were not good at doing things efficiently. Partly, too, it was the arms companies. Britain had the largest arms business, but they were geared to exports, not national defence. Again, the Government was not against arms but it was not very efficient at arming fast. The task of confronting the Nazis was very different from that of selling arms to various conflicts in other places, and someone needed to shape up that task. Fourth, Britain was developing slowly from existing arms supplies, whereas the German military was starting from scratch and could be more strategic.

F. The arms companies exposed, hiding and invisible.

There was also a change in situation of the arms companies. They were now back in business, but they were also suddenly receiving world attention. The 1932 Geneva Disarmament Conference was about getting rid of them, and many of the public suspected they had undermined it. Now arms were flowing, but they were exposed, no less than by the President of the United States. Here is Roosevelt on the 18th May, 1934 in a message to the Senate. Note the early date; it was a "mad race in armament" five years before WW2.

> The peoples of many countries are being taxed to the point of poverty and starvation in order to enable Governments to engage in a mad race in armament which, if permitted to continue, may well result in war. This grave menace to the peace of the world is due in no small measure to the uncontrolled activities of the manufacturers and merchants of engines of destruction, and it must be met by the concerted action of the peoples of all Nations.[xv]

Roosevelt was right. He truly saw the problem, the enemy, but no concerted action came. His enemies did not actually win politically, although they were planning to oust him. A few months later in November what came to be known as the Business Plot, a Fascist Coup attempt against the US President, planned in 1933-4, was exposed by General Smedley Butler who had been asked to take part. Wall Street business leaders and arms manufacturers had planned a Mussolini style coup, led by US veterans storming the White House, to overthrow Roosevelt, the elected US President. They planned to have half a million veterans march on Washington, take over, declare Roosevelt too ill to govern and put in their stooge. Butler reported it to the Senate and the plot failed. Roosevelt hit back against his attackers. He set up a Senate Committee, chaired by Senator Nye between April 1934 to February 1936, to investigate and expose them. That year, *The Merchants of Death* by H.C. Englebrecht and F.C. Hanighen (NY: Dodd, Mead and Company, 1934) was published. It showed how the military-industrial complex encourages war and profited from it. The phrase, "the Merchants of Death", went round the world, describing this group selling death so well. Suddenly, their policies of pushing weapons and stoking war were exposed to everyone. In Britain Philip Noel-Baker documented them further in his book, *The Private Manufacture of Armaments*, published in 1936. It woke me up sixty years later. The Merchants of Death came blinking in the limelight. What did they do?

The answer, important to the world, is that they went into hiding. The Du Ponts funded the "Liberty League" to attack Roosevelt in the States. It was a front organisation to undermine Roosevelt politically, but he exposed who was behind it and won elections decisively. So, they were not immediately successful. They retreated from the glare of publicity. They could quietly send weapons, and weapon factories anywhere. They disappeared. They sold where the wars were, and by cultivating the people in government, grew their business. As the arms race to World War Two speeded up, they were shaping what was to come, by supplying Hitler, but it was not publicly clear what they were doing.

So, in the mid-late 1930s there was huge public distrust of the arms companies but they continued to sell and grow under the radar, as we say. Especially, the combination of the Wall Street banks, firms and arms companies kitted the Nazis out for war. We now come to the three great reasons why the Militarists did Appeasement.

G. On the same side in the world class war.

First, quite central to modern world history, aside the big wars, is class. Crudely, it is true throughout modern history that the rich live off workers, either in colonies, factories, as servants, farmers, miners or employees to support their luxurious lifestyle. Full on slavery was stopped in 1865, but still the power of the capitalists controlled and extorted from workers. Marx focussed on this exploitation, as did many Christian reformers, but with the Russian Revolution in 1917 it became a world issue. A great country was Communist. The aristocracy was murdered or fled, because they had been rich oppressors and fear went round the world. There was a Red Scare in America in 1918, partly faked to keep the workers down, but a Scare nonetheless. Of course, many Socialists were democrats and reformers, but the Class War was close to Real War, especially with Marxist Socialist parties. Throughout the 20th Century the class war was threatening for the rich, and they looked to the military to protect their wealth and position. Really, kings and emperors, have been doing the same throughout history. You pay the military to keep the serfs, workers, proletariat in their place.

It shaped events from 1918 decisively. Consider how Hitler, a jumped-up corporal, was receiving money in the early 20s from Henry Ford, the mega US businessman. Both were antisemitic then, but Ford went on to supply weapons factories to Hitler in the 1930s because they were on the same side against the workers. Hitler was beating up workers and Jews to keep them "in their place". Indeed, *antisemitism was largely an upper class ideology*, because the rich felt threatened by efficient Jewish bankers and businessmen. The rich looked to armed militias, the forces and the arms providers to support them against the workers in Italy, Spain, Portugal, the US, Greece, Japan, Brazil, Britain, Poland or where-ever and ex-WW1 soldiers were ideal. Lord Curzon's Son in Law was Oswald Mosley. The Rich and the Fascists were hand in glove everywhere.

This was the main reason why Hitler was seen as benign. The rich across the world looked to Fascist and Nazi militarism to protect wealth. Spain, Portugal, France, Poland, Greece and other European states had similar movements. We can see it in Japan, where the rich Zaibatsu companies destroyed democracy and set that great state on the warpath. In China the warlords were similarly rich and buying weapons. Fascism was present in Brazil, Argentina and throughout most of the world supported by the rich against the workers, often with theatrical leaders to take in the masses in elections. Populism, mass rallies and marches were all part of the show to insist that we remain in control.

We focus on the Nazi menace, but ignore the picture in which it is set. Fascist sympathizers were not mainly supporting Fascism, but looking after their money. The Rich calculated Fascists kept their wealth safe if they were paid; it was a deal. The pattern in Britain was the same as elsewhere. It included a lot of the British Establishment – the Dukes of Westminster, Buccleuch, Hamilton, Lord Rothermere, the Mitfords, John Amery, Archibald Ramsey, Lord Londonderry, Viscount Halifax, the Editor of the Times, Neville Chamberlain, Quentin Hogg, King Edward VIII and many more of the rich and landed. Often people focus on this as though it were some kind of wicked conspiracy, which occasionally it became with Sir Oswald Mosley, Lord Haw Haw and even Edward VIII, but usually it was a broader political position. The Conservative Right in Britain and elsewhere were rich with land, estates, town houses in London, servants, businesses, factories, banks and trade and an elegant lifestyle which they considered necessary and normal. But it was threatened. In Britain the vote had been extended in 1918 to all men over 21 without a property qualification and all women over 30 where either they or their husband met a property qualification (two thirds of them). Suddenly the old governing class were outnumbered by the workers. Then in 1928 all men and women over 21 got the vote. The change was enormous. Previously property had ruled. Now it was universal suffrage. Even in 1923 the Labour Party was the strongest party. The fake

Zinoviev Telegram, a wicked electoral fix just before the polls, kept Labour out of power after November 1923 through to the late 20s. The National Government of 1931 also gave the Tories a massive majority of MPs against real party allegiance. They were in government when they should have been in a minority. They were insecure; Socialist reform was threatening much of their wealth and property. They could be facing the remains of the day and a long socialist night.

Thus, worldwide the link between the aristocracies and the industrial rich and Fascism and the Nazis was protection money. Of course, it was dangerous, because Hitler the Servant become Hitler the Master, and the rich were very slow spotting that. In addition, the arms industry had its own momentum, but mainly the rich funded paramilitaries to keep their wealth safe. Always money was there. The Apostle Paul said the love of money is the root of all evil. It is certainly correct in relation to militarism. In the 18th and 19th centuries European militarism had centred around making money through world-wide colonialism. In the 20th century Fascist and Nazi militarism arose to defend money against socialism. *The love of money lurks behind militarism and War. It was the reason why the Tories and American capitalists were drawn to Fascism and to Hitler, and when Munich came, Chamberlain and his coterie backed Hitler. They were on the same side because of money.*

H. The United States arms Nazi Germany.

We have seen how the Du Ponts and the other arms, banking and business elites were defeated by Roosevelt politically, but they were still successful in producing a massive pattern of arms sales both to the USSR and Germany in the 1930s. The US was the industrial powerhouse of the world, especially in mass production factories and they would sell wherever there was money. Notice that this was not strongly ideological, otherwise US companies would not sell to the USSR. Chase Manhattan, the Caterpillar Tractor Company, Ford, Gulf and Western, Honeywell, Martin, Douglas, Pratt and Whitney, Du Pont and other US companies provided the USSR with the most up to date weapons factories on the planet. It was fortunate, because these factories produced vast quantities of munitions which later helped defeat the Nazis. The USSR could pay in gold and the arms factories began production in the mid-late 1930s.

The bigger problem is the even stronger links to the Nazis in selling weapons. Again, given the false meaning of "appeasement", you can hardly believe how this is ignored. We fulminate about Hitler, but brush over the way the arms and manufacturing industry in the United States funded and armed Hitler. Listen to this. It is the US Ambassador, William Dodd, in Berlin writing to Roosevelt in October 1936.

> But what can you do? At the present moment more than a hundred American corporations have subsidiaries here or co-operative understandings. The Du Ponts have three allies in Germany which are aiding in the armament business. Their chief ally is the I. G. Farben Company, a part of the Government which gives 200,000 marks a year to one propaganda organisation operating on American opinion. Standard Oil Company (New York sub company) sent $2,000,000 here in December 1933 and has made $500,000 a year helping Germans make Ersatz gas for war purposes; but Standard Oil cannot take any of its earnings out of the country except in goods…The International Harvester Company president told me their business here rose 33% a year (arms manufacture, I believe), but they could take nothing out. Even our airplanes people have secret arrangement with Krupps. General Motor Company and Ford do enormous businesses [sic] here through their subsidiaries and take no profits out. I mention these facts because they complicate things and add to war dangers.[xvi]

Hitler had been in power since January 1933. His aggression and hatred were obvious and a few months earlier he had put the whole German economy in the direction of war and yet he was being armed big time from America. They were powering him up for war. Big investment funds were going to Germany, especially through the Harriman Bank and Prescott Bush, to fund firms producing for the Nazis, and the money had to stay in Germany. Overall, some $475 million, at 1930s prices, was invested in Germany before Pearl Harbour. *The US was massively bankrolling and arming the Nazis through to and even after the start of the Second World War.* By this stage the arms companies throughout Europe were doing whatever they wanted and expanding like crazy as the letter above conveys. They were providing arms to Hitler more or less on Hitler's terms. I.G. Farben was evil and unprincipled, but the Du Ponts could go along with that. So, the war machine in Germany was fuelled by US arms deals. It was this that let slip the dogs of war. The problem was not "appeasement" by pacifists, but US companies selling weapons and military factories to the Nazis. The pattern carried on after Dodd's letter for another five years, and so you can imagine how strong the effect was. It was part of the reason why the US did not enter the War against the Nazis until Pearl Harbour; these arms industrialists were effectively fighting against Britain from 1939. The United States armed Nazi Germany and strongly helped bring on World War Two.

I. Peace in our Time and Hitler's arms bonanza.

As this world-wide militarisation gathered in the late 30s, once again calculations like those before World War One emerged. Who should be our ally? Stalin knew his danger from Hitler and tried to link with Britain and France, but the Tories were not going to line up with the Soviets, sadly *because the USSR, France and Britain together could have stopped the Nazi War.* The aristocratic Tory leaders, the ones who had destroyed the Geneva Disarmament Conference in 1932, now backed Hitler as their natural ally. He was on their side and the Soviets had to be the enemy. Appeasement was Right Wing militarist Tories in the UK lining up with the Nazis in a supposed alliance against the more socialist powers of the USSR and France. They hoped, as Neville Chamberlain stated when returning from Munich, for "Peace in our Time." This was not Britain not arming. It was arming as fast as it could. His choice of a right-wing militarist ally, because of the long-term anti-socialist Tory bias, was a blind disaster.

That deal gave Hitler Czechoslovakia. It also gave him the kit for War. When he walked into Czechoslovakia, as he later boasted in a speech, Germany gained 2,175 field guns and cannons, 469 tanks, 500 anti-aircraft artillery pieces, 43,000 machine guns, 1,090,000 military rifles, 114,000 pistols, about a billion rounds of small-arms ammunition, and 3 million rounds of anti-aircraft ammunition.[xvii] *It armed about half the Wehrmacht.* Alongside this great haul handed over to him, Hitler was also given control of the giant Skoda works, *the biggest arms factory in Europe.* At one fell swoop Munich completed the Nazi capacity to wage World War.

When Chamberlain came back from Munich and spoke in Parliament on the 3rd October, 1938, after the resignation speech of Duff Cooper, the response from Clem Attlee, leader of the opposition says it all.

I say we are witnessing a degeneration of the world due to two things. The first thing is the failure to deal with the political and economic questions arising out of the follies of the Peace Treaties, and arising out of the widespread injustice and maladjustments of the economic system. The other thing is the failure to deal with force, the failure to restrain aggression. The Disarmament Conference's failure; the failure of the World Economic Conference; aggression in Manchuria, Abyssinia, Spain, Austria and Czechoslovakia—these are milestones that mark the road to the abyss. We on these benches have, again and again, shown the danger of a policy which failed to restrain aggression, which failed to face the issue, which neither stood firm against aggression, nor tried to deal with causes.[xviii]

Attlee was correct. Chamberlain and the Appeasers had chosen force, as had US arms manufacturers. Both Britain and the United States helped Hitler wage World War Two. The militarists had defeated peace and slid down the helter skelter of armed force again into the biggest war of all, unless we allow another one to come along.

J. Appeasement is the world's biggest lie.

The idea that "appeasement" *caused* the Second World War because it was disarmament is thus complete fiction all the way through. It is worse than fiction. It is as bad as having a complex murder whodunit on stage with multiple conspirators who contribute to the foul crime, and they point to the murdered corpse and say, "He done it; look he's got no guns. That proves it." It is moonshine. When people disappeared into the vortex that was World War Two for a decade or so of horrors, there were sufficient militarists around at the end to assert that appeasement as lack of arms caused the War and they have drowned out the truth. It has shaped our lives for fear, destruction and war. It has wasted hundreds of trillions of dollars by falsely telling us that disarmament is dangerous.

The cause of both World Wars was the same – the expansion of armaments. The real "appeasement" lesson should be the opposite. The Second World War happened because the arms companies, the Merchants of Death, were once again let off the leash with sharpened teeth and the killing industry was dominant. Now we all do the sensible thing and systemically close it down.

7.THE WORLD'S MILITARY SYSTEM SOLVES ITS CRISIS.

A. When the War stopped.

We need to understand how militarism operates and 1945 is a good place to start. The Second World War saw the arms industry expand into the biggest industry on the planet. It was vast, especially in the United States, but also across the world. We focus on who "wins" a war, but the arms industry wins every war because of the money poured into it. Militarism dominated every area of life. Particle physics was directed towards the atomic bomb. Flying technology was dominated by bombers and fighter development, and tens of thousands were produced. Mathematics was war focussed in code breaking at Bletchley Park and in many other research developments. Weather reports were military in purpose. Sonar, radar, information, transport, logistics, communication, manufacture, food, furniture and housing were shaped around the business of war. In the United States the war economy rose to 38% of total GDP in 1945. In the USSR, poorer and more directly engaged in the War, it may have been over *half* the economy. The Soviets even moved many of their arms factories bodily back into Siberia away from the advancing Nazis. Factories were made and factories were bombed. Industrial scale bombing occurred in Japan, Germany and elsewhere. War in China and other parts of the East was fairly total. For five or more years the whole world was shaped towards a total military economy. Then it fell silent. Economies, families, factories, cities, states would take five to ten years to recover from the damage and, of course, many people, buildings, cities never would. The build-up and shadow of the WW2 economy lasted in many places from 1935 to 1955 or later; I walked to school in 1955 across a bombsite.

The Second World War ended on the 8th May in Europe and the 2nd September 1945 in the Far East. With the defeat of Germany and Japan, the Allied weapons and forces had overcome the attackers and vast stocks of captured weapons and ships were added to their own. Many

58

weapons were destroyed, the troops went home in millions and the wartime system closed down, *although it did not really*. US bases remained all over the planet. Military control needed to be maintained in Germany, Austria, Italy and Japan. The Pentagon stayed built. Work continued on atomic bombs. And something else happened. Stalin seemed threatening in Poland and the Cold War started. The politics of it has been covered repeatedly – the meetings at Yalta, the news of the bomb, the "Long Telegram" and the emergence of the Soviet threat, but perhaps it is not all quite as it seems.

B. The heroic USSR and the end of the World War.

First, any thorough historian recognises that the USSR took the brunt of the Second World War. It faced the biggest invasion in human history – Barbarossa – and fought the great battles of Leningrad, Moscow and Stalingrad, aided by the Russian winter, which destroyed the main part of the German army. It was heroic and costly. The USSR lost *twenty five* million people during the war, compared with about half a million each for the UK and US, fifty times more people than each of the two countries that "won" the War. More than this, much of the fighting took place in Russia, creating devastation in cities, towns and countryside. The front moved east and then west in continual destruction. As a result, the Germans lost about six million on the eastern front and one million on the western front and in the Mediterranean; it was the Soviets who mainly defeated them. Then, Stalin even committed to helping defeat Japan in the Far East as part of the Alliance. Perhaps, we Westerners could acknowledge that the USSR largely won the War against the Nazis and Hitler. Roosevelt knew that and so did Churchill, even as he resisted opening up the Second Front in the west. Yet, ever since, the West blanks this truth and ignores the extraordinary cost to them of fighting Hitler.

On 12/4/45 the great Franklin Delano Roosevelt died, job almost done. It had been now forgotten that he faced a Fascist plot in 1934 aiming to oust him from the Presidency, and the Liberty League had tried to defeat him, supported by military and other business interests. Now he had defeated Hitler and Japan correctly understanding who they were.

Fascism in all its wickedness had been overcome. Yet, he had had to fight the War using the military men who opposed him and gradually they had moved back in charge as he weakened. They ousted Henry Wallace, a great internationalist, as Vice President and replaced him with Harry Truman, Chairman of the Committee on Military Affairs Subcommittee on War Mobilisation. He was a small man, without international knowledge. immersed in the wartime weapons business and really out of his depth. When Roosevelt died, Truman suddenly became President, seeking to prove himself, and a month later on 8/5/1945 the war in Europe ended. Then things moved fast. On 28/6/1945 a new Polish Government is formed. On 17/7-2/8/1945 at Potsdam Stalin, Truman, Churchill and then Attlee met to organize the post-war system of occupation in Germany, Japan, Italy and Eastern Europe. Stalin was informed about the atom bomb. On 26/7/1945 Labour won the British General Election with a massive majority, ousting the War leader Churchill possibly partly because he was too militarist. But Churchill did not disappear… On 6 and 9/8/1945 atom bombs are dropped in Hiroshima and Nagasaki and on 2/9/1945 the war in the East ended and World War Two was over. What will the new world be like? First of all, of course, it needed to recover. But let us look at the USSR.

C. The USSR in 1945.

The USSR had three genuine problems in 1945. Poland had helped the Nazis fight the Soviet Union at the beginning of the War in the cruel push east, and Stalin did not want a hostile Government on his doorstep. He therefore organised a sympathetic Government with western acquiescence leaving the Polish Government in exile stranded. The relationship was bad both ways; there was a massacre of Polish officers at Katyn at the start of the War with Russian cruelty towards Poland as well as Polish aggression towards Russia. So, the relationship with Poland was a problem. Second, twice Russia had been invaded from Germany and Eastern Europe killing millions of their citizens each time in less than a quarter of a century. A base line for the USSR was therefore that military build-up in Germany and East Europe towards them should be absolutely impossible. Its concern above all else was addressing this threat to it from its West. That point, although it was mixed up in the USSR's territorial dominance in Eastern Europe, was not difficult to understand. After being overrun by German attacks in both World Wars, it had some rights to peace on its western side. Third, the USSR faced the winter of 1945 with devastated cities and housing beyond other countries, few resources for heat in the bitter cold, severe food shortages and scrambling for any resources it could get its hands on to survive. Really, we cannot understand the levels of need faced throughout this vast country. Its desperation was acute. But once the War was over, Western aid was stopped and the USSR received only hostility from the new Truman regime in the States. The USSR was both not thanked for winning World War Two, and it was treated inhumanely with regard to post-war help. Later, it was even excluded from Marshall Aid while Germany received it; that must have hurt...

D. The Threat to the Militarists.

Meanwhile, the arms companies and the militarists faced an existential threat. The world was sick of war. Fascism was totally discredited in Germany, Italy, Japan and throughout the world. More than that, in all the world's economies, except the United States, there had been so much devastation, far more than in World War One, that budgets would be absolutely unable to provide any resources for defence and the military, especially because arms and fighting were not needed. War was over and done with. Housing, food, heating, clothing, shoes, road, hospital care, rail repairs, shortages, raw materials, steel, coal, furniture, were all absolute priorities. Many countries had a baby boom on the late 40s. Healthcare needs, rationing, rushed house and flat building, recovery and reclamation were needed. People combed bombsites for things they could use. Repairing was normal; there were shoes with cardboard in them, coats turned inside out and wool was like gold. People shivering through winters. Everything was needed to help people survive after the devastation of war. The last thing governments or the public needed was more weapons. What would the militarists do? Inevitably, for perhaps a decade in the most devastated countries, they would be out of a job and completely quiescent. They knew from 1918 how bad the downturn would be in this much bigger War. They had profits, but their business was closing down and the shutters put in place.

E. We need an Enemy – starting the Cold War

The United States economy was different. It had expanded through the War and now was an amazing half of world (measured) GDP. It was dominant and rich. There was money around to be spent if the right strategy could be set up. The US contribution to WW2 had created a vast manufacturing and organisational system. Some of it could go back to manufacturing cars and tractors. A lot was the generous support given to the allied nations which would continue as a trade surplus, but much of it was military and preferred staying that way. In addition, groups of people had learned how the military worked and it had become their career. The Pentagon was the biggest office in the world full of career workers with specific skills. The military personnel, those who had not died or been injured, were also often quite committed to their work, although millions demobbed. This Empire needed a strategy to survive. What could this great military machine do in the post war world? Germany, Japan and Italy were totally demilitarized. Britain, France and the other states directly involved in the war needed recovery time. They could not afford, or see the need for, military expenditure. Therefore, as after WW1 the US armaments business and the military faced a long recession. Given its greater scale than in WW1, it would be even more catastrophic for them. They understood this. It was Grade One lesson in the weapons business. You could not say, "Give us another war." Or "How about we build some useless bombers for you." *The military needed an enemy, otherwise it was a stranded whale facing massive contractions as in 1918. The USSR was the only possibility.*

F. The Nazi sympathizers - the Blame Game.

Through the 1930s there were millions of people who were Fascist and Nazi sympathizers in Germany, Italy and Japan. But there were also many in France, Britain and the United States. In 1945 Hitler was obviously evil and the Holocaust was perhaps the most evil ever act. If you had been a Nazi or a sympathizer before the war, you could do various things. You could repent, the best way that evil shrank. You could quietly disappear or find somewhere to hide your past and that happened in many ways. The War was a suitable distraction. Or we could all be on the same side against the Nazis, and the history of the 1930s could be forgotten. That helped. It was not a seamless transition in Germany, Britain, France, Greece and other countries, but perhaps the one which really counted was the United States, now world dominant and with lots of Nazi sympathizers right up to Pearl Harbour. The way out of the problem was solved by the kid in the classroom response, asked if he broke the window? "It ain't me, Sir. It was 'im." If another suspect can be found, then you are off the hook. Remarkably quickly the USSR, who had vanquished the great Nazi forces at immense national cost, who had been our ally, taking on most of the Nazi aggression in the great Barbarossa campaign became the culprit, the problem and the new focus of evil. It was even better, because identifying the Soviet Empire as evil attacked Socialism and was thus an automatic protection for the rich capitalist US employers and money-makers. It allowed them to persecute US Socialists and write them off the map for half a century.

Some of this process was in place even before the War was over. It became a systematic long-term fixation of the American Right, through and beyond the hysterical McCarthyite era. The world was invited to forget about Fascism and the Nazi Alliance with Capitalist America in the face of *the Communist Threat* and *the Evil Empire* and largely it did. The Bush family history was covered up. All kinds of Nazi business links disappeared into near oblivion. Deals were done to use Nazi spies covertly against the Soviets and suddenly the USSR, our ally, was the greatest evil in the world.

G. The key people.

Key people in the business and political establishment stepped into this role. They included Henry Ford who had funded Hitler as far back as the early 1920s. He transitioned in the 1930s to supplying American factories to the Nazis for military vehicles and after the war into being vehemently against unions in any of the Ford plants. But he was not a politician. Several politicians moved close to the centre of power. The Harriman Bank, and Averill Harriman, had strong links into Nazi finance through the Thyssen Empire. Although those assets were seized in 1942 under the Trading with the Enemy Act Harriman had various jobs during the War and emerged from it, with his assets returned, as Ambassador to the USSR. Prescott Bush, running those accounts for the Harriman Bank, helping US investment in Nazi Germany, was suddenly a well-funded Senator. The later President George H. W. Bush was eighteen before his Dad was forced to break with the Nazis in 1942.

Alongside Averell Harriman was John Foster Dulles, working for Sullivan and Cromwell in Berlin. In his biography Hoopes describes John Foster Dulles in tears in 1935 when the other Sullivan and Cromwell partners could no longer do business with the Nazis and threatened to resign. [xix] Soon however, he had eased himself back into being a foreign affairs statesman. His brother, Allen Dulles similarly, after enjoying his war, moved smoothly into running the CIA. James Forrestal, Secretary of State at the Navy from 19/5/1944 and the first Secretary of Defence (17/9/1947) had Nazi sympathies and hated the USSR. His personal route via the Bikini Atoll nuclear bomb explosions – a clear message to the USSR - through to suicide is unclear and numbing. These figures surrounded Truman. George Kennan's Long Telegram of 22/2/1946 also pushed a hard line, though Kennan later regretted how it had been used. So, this coterie was close to power, forming the post-war political culture, and they were committed to continuing US militarism focussed against the USSR..

The centre of the problem was the new President, Truman, and his Secretary of State, Jimmy Byrnes. Truman tried to cover his inexperience with bluster against Stalin and Molotov, and Byrnes was, according to Ward's careful assessment, often poorly prepared and out of touch with Truman.[xx] At Potsdam Truman used the atom bomb as a way of dominating Stalin; it was the response of a little inadequate man. The wartime trust Roosevelt built up with Stalin was dissipated. Truman and Byrnes were ill-informed about Russia's broader situation, and so when this group of ex-Nazi sympathizers now in key roles rolled out an anti-Soviet line, it shaped American foreign policy. Even in July 1945 the USSR was set up to be the new enemy.

Truman backed his military and saw a strong armed force as basic to the US leading the world, and so disarmament was not even considered. Churchill, thrown out at home, used the "Iron Curtain" phrase in a telegram to Truman four days after Victory in Europe on 12/5/45 and then in his Fulton, Missouri speech on 5/3/46. Forrestal worked with Churchill. The Cold War stance was in place within a few months of the end of the War. Really, Poland, which is the usual justification for the supposed reaction, was hardly as important as is made out among a whole series of negotiations. More widely, the decision to make the USSR the great enemy suited thousands of militarists with a nice career. They were not necessarily thinking big, or thinking at all. Militarism needed an enemy and the USSR, minus 25 million killed by Hitler, was the only candidate on the block. And so, it came to pass.

H. The USSR "Red Peril".

Of course, the USSR had serious problems. There were the Stalinist purges, the famines, the atrocities as the Soviets pushed the Nazis back westwards. It is not difficult to see Stalin as evil. But there are explanations, even of evil. The Tsarist regime had been vicious and militarist. The First World War against Germany and then Poland was horrific for Russia. The Civil War involved another level of national trauma, not least because Churchill, appointed as Minister of War to wind up fighting after the Great War, actually carried on a vendetta against the New Communist regime. All that resulted in a long traumatic war of nine years. Stalin's agricultural revolution failed and the Kulaks suffered appallingly. Famines are catastrophes and also cheapen life. After Lenin, Stalin's fight for dominance was vicious and even deluded; his purges of his own military leaders were partly engineered by Nazi spies. Finally, the Barbarossa Campaign was one of the cruellest ever with Russian lives butchered on a massive scale and atrocities beyond recounting. A country that has gone through all these things needs to be treated with some understanding, but the USSR under Truman got none, and the US military had found the enemy that would keep it in business.

Soon it became an industry. The phrase, Red Peril, was widely about in the media in the late 40s. It was a Nazi phrase, possibly formed around the Reichstag Fire, but it came to the US post war. The USSR was the enemy, the Peril. Through the FBI Chief, Edgar Hoover a massive scare campaign was mounted of "Reds under the Bed" implying Russian spies were everywhere. Soon most of the American population were convinced that there was a massive USSR threat to the US when there were, at most, a few Soviet spies, as, of course, there were US spies in Russia and Eastern Europe. This had the added advantage of allowing all the Nazi sympathizers to hide their past and become moral crusaders against Communism. The US military even thought of nuking the Soviets, though they did not have the bombs so to do.[xxi] In 1946 Forrestal helped Joe McCarthy start his crusade. The House Un-American Activities Committee (HUAC) was taken over as a court, except not for crimes or offences, but merely for being Communist. A load of Hollywood figures were accused. Soon the simple message of the bad dangerous Commies dominated US politics. I remember hearing thus stuff on the radio as a kid and thinking Americans must be slightly loony. They said Paul Robeson, the gentle friend of the USSR, was a traitor and we could see that he was as dangerous as a bowl of fruit and a kind, wise man who lived the Spirituals he sang.

This solution met all the problems. It kept the US military intact in the new dominant Superpower with its world-wide role as the defender of Freedom and Democracy. The arms companies were back in business, especially if they lied about the military capabilities of the USSR, as they later did. It made American Socialism a pariah and kept the workers in their place. It buried Roosevelt's critique of capitalism and allowed a Republican revival. It found an enemy who was so very bad that the United States was automatically good. It got all the old Nazi and Fascist sympathizers off the hook. They were the good guys against the bad Soviets. After the War the US were world dominant and so what was decided in the White House and Pentagon ran the show.

It set up the next 45 years. The USSR, both scared about attacks and cementing its empire against the United States, continued in what came to be called the Cold War. Weapons escalated, the arms companies were very busy, most states were introduced to militarism by aid and sales, while the world ruled out the possibility of peace. From 1945 to 1990 the US led aggressively in shaping this War. People thought enemies were normal. The Cold War completely obliterated the 1932 World Disarmament Conference. To talk disarmament was to be a traitor. The militarist Fascist and Nazi sympathisers were able to lose their past by fulminating against the evils of Socialism. The United States and United Kingdom took the credit for winning World War Two in decades of historical revisionism in history, books, films, comics and world politics. Most important of all, this allowed the United States to continue the militarism which had produced WW1 and WW2 unchecked. Of course, they were not politically colonial, but this was the era when US multinational companies were spreading around the globe, backed by military support and deals with friendly states. The Cold War, with two opponents capable of destroying the planet would build and build until 1990. The USSR's militarists were behind the US in the nuclear confrontation until the late 60s, and eventually the USSR collapsed under the weight of its military expenditure in 1990. It was a Cold useless War of forty-five years. Militarism ruled, and those who could even remember the world peace movements of the 1920s and 1930s died. It need not have been, had not shallow militarists moved to the same faith in weapons as the Nazis. There was, and is, a better way.

I. Eisenhower on the Military-Industrial Complex.

As a reflection on this empasse, it is worth hearing Eisenhower's well-known warning about the Military-Industrial Complex (MIC) as he left the Presidency in early 1961. As a Republican and the Supreme Allied Commander in World War Two he could hardly be accused of being anti-militarist. Yet, this was his sober conclusion from decades of experience.

Until the latest of our world conflicts, the United States had no armaments industry. American makers of plowshares could, with time and as required, make swords as well. But now we can no longer risk emergency improvisation of national defense; we have been compelled to create a permanent armaments industry of vast proportions. Added to this, three and a half million men and women are directly engaged in the defense establishment. We annually spend on military security more than the net income of all United States corporations.

This conjunction of an immense military establishment and a large arms industry is new in the American experience. The total influence -- economic, political, even spiritual -- is felt in every city, every State house, every office of the Federal government. We recognize the imperative need for this development. Yet we must not fail to comprehend its grave implications. Our toil, resources and livelihood are all involved; so is the very structure of our society.

In the councils of government, we must guard against the acquisition of unwarranted influence, whether sought or unsought, by the military-industrial complex. The potential for the disastrous rise of misplaced power exists and will persist.

We must never let the weight of this combination endanger our liberties or democratic processes. We should take nothing for granted. Only an alert and knowledgeable citizenry can compel the proper meshing of the huge industrial and military machinery of defense with our peaceful methods and goals, so that security and liberty may prosper together.

There is one bit of background to this speech. The military lobby had effectively lied about the number of nuclear bombers and then missiles which the USSR had, multiplying the number by at least ten times to get more orders. The "bomber gap" and "missile gap" did not exist and, rather than being behind, the US was well ahead. Eisenhower, and then Kennedy, knew that the Soviet threat had been grossly exaggerated.

There is also one postscript to the speech. Six days *after* Eisenhower gave the speech, a US bomber broke up and dropped two big nuclear weapons near Goldboro', North Carolina. One dropped in mud and went deep underground. The other, when the engineer examined it, was one switch away from detonation. The other switches failed. The firing signal went to the core and then held. Eisenhower received the news shortly before he left office. The US had nearly nuked itself a hundred and fifty miles from Washington. We do not know what the speech would have been like if Eisenhower had made it a week later.

But Eisenhower, the Christian, saw the issue. The Military-Industrial Complex had its own impetus, and military power is dangerous. It believes in its own destructive might. You can believe you are a Democracy, but those with controlling power work out how to control people and voters. More than that, they control people in other countries, as the United States did, in Chile, central America, the DRC, Iran and dozens of other states through bases, CIA activity, aid linked to militarism and inter-governmental deals. As Eisenhower points out, three and a half million are in the defence establishment. That number of people cannot be easily moved. They will do their own thing. They will run their show. And so it was.

J. Permanent worldwide militarism.

So, from 1945 the US and USSR ran a worldwide military system. You had to be on one side or the other anywhere in the world. Their militaries expanded into millions of troops. Big factories grew supplying old and new weapons and the arms companies were in permanent demand. They usually hid fairly well, remembering the bad publicity around the "merchants of death". Some like Ford and the Du Ponts changed their ethos for the better. But the underlying truth was that the United States dominated in spreading militarism and did not allow it to be questioned. The USSR puffed along behind. The United States was the main world problem, but it always thought that it was the solution. Indeed, Americans became congenitally incapable of thinking they might be the problem. Militarism became normal; it was Sargent Bilko doing his harmless stuff. Kennedy solved the Cuba crisis and America kept the world safe for democracy, even though the world everywhere was steadily arming. The arms companies kept a low profile but spread their wares around the earth. It was not in your face. They did not make public pronouncements. They operated in the back corridors of power. They had systems of bribery, like that revealed in the Lockheed Scandal. The message was always that they were carrying out the necessary defence against the wicked USSR or other similar foes and their work was therefore totally uncontroversial. There was no need to think about disarmament because it was off the agenda, aside a few nutters. The whole (western) world population grew up within this ethos for half a century. It inhabits our souls. It is normal thinking. You and I have lived in this bubble. It has worked right up to the present. Weapons appear and are sold around the world with strong backing from governments, but the public rarely sees or considers arms companies or their role in military policy and wars. *Of course* it is good for us. You might as well ask, Do we need roads.

8. NATIONALIST DEFENCE KEEPS THIS OBSOLETE SHOW ON THE ROAD.

A. Nationalities and the World.

Nationality is strong. It has a vast presence throughout the world. It is normally our real community. We are Indian, Chinese, Jewish or Brazilian. We learn the same language. We take responsibility for others in that community, have a common currency, buy and sell, form cultures which address the depths and fun of life. Nations organize politically and function under the same laws. They have common institutions for education, health, faith, poverty, the arts, recreation, sport, work and family support. Nationality in these senses is a big part of life.

Nations need not be oppositional. For example, since 1957, Europe has moved into communal relationships in which all nations are open to one another and govern with mutual co-operation. National life operates with a strong transnational respect and open borders. Across Europe Nation speaks Peace unto Nation. It was a strong lesson learned after WW2 and especially reflected in the Triumvirate of Christian leaders, Schumann, Adenauer and De Gaspari. [xxii] Nationalities can be a mutual part of life we share with one another, in families and within us in the rich multi-ethnic people among us. All Europeans can enjoy Delft and Delphi and their other European homes. Paris is for all of us. We partly dwell in and learn from different places and grow through the wonderful people we meet from every race and nation. We are, as Tutu articulated with wide eyes, the Rainbow People of God. We can love the Dutch, the Ugandans, the Pakistanis, the Japanese, the Russians, Jamaicans, Jews, Iranians, Nepalese, New Zealanders and all the other rich ethnic groups of our world.

Further, through mass and social media we have all been taught to understand different nations and their peoples. They live near us. We travel. We hear international news each day – the Kenyan election today

– and we learn different nationalities – their geographies, histories, characters and more. In thirty seconds, we can be in any country in the world, whereas five hundred years ago world maps were just getting going and most of the world stayed at home. We are all internationalists, also by trade. We will probably use or eat stuff from twenty countries today. We depend on one another. We are world people. We probably talk to people each day from China, Africa, South America, India and Australia. We understand global warming, and yet we fight nationalist wars in a throwback to ancient tribalism. What is going on?

B. Nations have long seen through nationalist war.

The contrast is even more sharp. For a hundred years world-wide we have stood *against* national wars. The Preamble to the League of Nations in 1919 sets out the principles.

> "IN ORDER TO PROMOTE international co-operation and to achieve international peace and security
>
> by the acceptance of obligations not to resort to war
>
> by the prescription of open, just and honourable relations between nations
>
> by the firm establishment of the understandings of international law as the actual rule of conduct among Governments, and
>
> by the maintenance of justice and a scrupulous respect for all treaty obligations in the dealings of organised peoples with one another...."

Does anyone not understand that? Accepting the obligation *not* to resort to war? The League of Nations, backed by world statesmen and tens of millions of supporters, required all to think beyond Nation-States and National Militarism and pursue Disarmament and Peace. This policy was defeated by subterfuge in 1932 at the Geneva World Disarmament Conference, and opened the way for Hitler and the next disaster for rampant nationalism. In 1945, after Hitler, the same principles were back with the formation of the United Nations.

"WE THE PEOPLES OF THE UNITED NATIONS DETERMINED

to save succeeding generations from the scourge of war, which twice in our lifetime has brought untold sorrow to mankind, and

to reaffirm faith in fundamental human rights, in the dignity and worth of the human person, in the equal rights of men and women and of nations large and small, and to establish conditions under which justice and respect for the obligations arising from treaties and other sources of international law can be maintained, and

to promote social progress and better standards of life in larger freedom,

AND FOR THESE ENDS

to practice tolerance and live together in peace with one another as good neighbours, and to unite our strength to maintain international peace and security, and to ensure, by the acceptance of principles and the institution of methods, that armed force shall not be used, save in the common interest, and to employ international machinery for the promotion of the economic and social advancement of all peoples..."

So again internationalism, humankind, united nations, seeing the world picture and ensuring that "armed force will not be used" is the framework for world politics. The UN from 1945 until now has stood for this. For a hundred years we have known it is right to think this way. In addition, it is plonking obvious right. Isaiah was there 2,700 years ago - all nations learning from God - so we have had enough time to take it in. Why has it not worked?

C. We still do nationalist wars.

We all say, No Wars, and then we do wars, cold wars and hot wars throughout the lifetimes of all of us. Many are nationalist wars – the Korean War, the Suez conflict, Greece-Turkey over Cyprus, Egypt-Israel, Algeria, Cuba, Lebanon, Congo and so many more. In war the Nation becomes absolute. Everything is subordinated to the Nation winning, especially the truth. In national wars both sides are diametrically right. There are also Bloc Wars – NATO and the Warsaw Pact – where pan-national identities are formed. We British expected world-wide loyalty to the British Empire and with appropriate control, got it with Indians, Gurkas, Africans, Australians dying for the British Empire. Russia and Ukraine do intense nationalism now. The national militaries stay intact and grow, and the wars keep coming. Many states do unconditional loyalty in their anthems, rituals, art and buildings. Despite our global world, nationalist wars arrive right up to the present. For a hundred years we have all known nationalist militarism does not work, but it still gets stronger, and we are locked in it. We keep hitting the nail with the hammer and we are surprised when it sinks further in. Why do we still do total nationalist armed forces and war a hundred years after we saw the problem? It needs explaining. It is mad.

Wars do not just happen, especially when millions of people are damaged by them and hate them. They are caused and people and organisations cause them. There is some powerful force linked to nationalism driving the national war machine onwards. More than this, because so many national military rivalries are now dead and unthinkable (for example in Europe or between the US and Canada), this force must be extremely efficient at driving other national militarisms through to conflict. What is it? More important, what drives it?

D. It is the Old Nationalist and Bloc Militarism.

First, we all see and take part in nationalist shows. We are fed the nationalisms of war, war against other nations, war over other nations, wars which require distortions of the truth, and make a fight right, and lead to "our" heroic victories. This was the appeal of the Nazis, Fascists, and Japanese during WW2. It goes back through history and continues. The State becomes ultimate against other states. The Kamikaze pilot is heroic for deliberately killing himself while attacking the enemy. Still, dying for the nation is everywhere made sacred. The Cenotaph, Arlington Cemetery and the new Cathedral to the Armed Forces outside Moscow with six gold domes to commemorate the 25 million who died in World War Two fit this model. Those who so die are unquestionably sacred to the nation. Their death is for us. And so, often, it was, and the sacrifice is as it is, but the ultimate nation state is religion and it says killing for the state is fine. The killed were trained to kill others. Often, they were conscripts fighting against other conscripts who also did not want to fight. My country, 'tis of thee, but it is also of the one next door. Country A fights Country B, each to defeat the other, but at the end of the war A and B will still be sitting there alongside one another, so what was that all about? Most of us now have even seen through football nationalism and enjoy the way both sides play.

Everywhere it must not be questioned, and yet it should be. My country right or wrong. Deutschland, Deutschland über Alles. Well, No. "For God and country", as though God does not relate to all humankind. To die for your country. Perhaps, not. Wilfred Owen nailed the old Lie: Dulce et decorum est Pro patria mori. "If you could hear, at every jolt, the blood Come gargling from the froth-corrupted lungs.." Perhaps dying for your country is the wrong ask. Is there a better way? Perhaps Rupert Brooke hadn't seen the full picture. Mrs Thatcher fights for the Falklands and is re-elected with her son as arms dealer; patriotic wars win elections, even when there are failing politicians. From Joan of Arc to Mao-Tse Tung to Churchill to Putin, every country has its nationalist leaders who are fêted and live through into the present, but examine them closely and all nationalisms are wrong, a failure in self-criticism..

The narrative is always selective. There are honourable war deaths, but the big picture is that two hundred million do not die noble nationalist deaths. Most wars were unnecessary, even World War Two. I remember seeing a letter in the British Library Churchill wrote to Lord Robert Cecil... "My dear Bob, This War could easily have been prevented if the League of Nations had been used with courage and loyalty by the associated nations. Even in 1935 and 1936...." [xxiii] Almost all did *not* want to die for their country. Millions were wiped out by bombs without choice. Those who died nobly often killed others. Our side was often wrong or partly wrong. Calculations of territory or revenge were part of the fighting. Generals, Field Marshalls and politicians, as in the charge of the Light Brigade, thundered and blundered. There are the injuries, PTSD, the broken families, the vast areas of death and destruction caused by fighting. Though the sacrifices are real and the honour may be real, the idea of National Remembrance is also an unquestionable shroud, even a paper napkin, placed over all the failures and ugliness of war, so that we should not think, criticize or really consider the futility of the whole military process. It is all covered by smart uniforms, national anthems, memorials, Heroes, Wars Won, Conquest, Greatness, Superiority, Civilisation, Victory Arches and the achievements of our particular nation *against* other nation-states. Often, we keep silence in remembrance, because if we talked, the absurdity of the nationalist war enterprise would become evident. The silences remove the need to think and speak these different realities. Yet, we must think outside this box, this coffin of destruction, even when it is the Tomb of the Unknown Warrior. It is a toxic, dishonest excuse and we romanticise hell.

E. The Grand National Narratives are kept alive.

Military nationalism, this object of sanctity, is kept alive everywhere. There are military parades in Beijing, Moscow, Delhi, Paris or Washington. They are spectacles of power, order, colour, immaculate uniforms, unity of purpose, marching and weapons. The State is ultimate and it is against other states. It requires loyalty, and treason is its great crime. To win, victory, is national validation. "Send her victorious" is a message to God in the British National Anthem, which was recently turned down twice and disowned from the beginning. Anyone who reads it can see *Genesis* charts this wrong fragmentation of humankind aeons before modernity. We live in the lies, the false choreography. We invite foreign rulers to inspect the troops. Why? When Putin appears in Tsarist glory, he is peddling a lie. When, in Shakespeare, Henry V shouts heroically "Once more unto the breach, dear friends, once more, Or, seal the wall up with our English dead" it is a lie. Why should he be attacking French towns and is it glorious to invite your "friends" to die needlessly in a hole in the wall? We do flags, flypasts, the boredom of inspecting the troops – well the bands are fun. Military nationalism fights unnecessary wars self-righteously. This empty nationalist show is repeated in Paris art, especially in endless boring paintings in the Louvre. Washington, Beijing and elsewhere support and justify militarism in great false shows. We are supposed to be impressed, but should not be. Soldiers dress up magnificently, march to nowhere and then go home. It is keeping the nationalist military show mindlessly in our heads and otherwise it is pointless.

The propaganda is supported in the small media things we are fed every day. In 2021 the UK withdrew from Afghanistan after fighting and occupying it for nearly 20 years. We had obviously *lost* the war, but we could not admit we had lost a war and quickly withdrawn while the Secretary of State for War was on holiday, because the UK cannot *lose*. General Carter explained "The British military was not defeated on the battlefield. They showed remarkable adaptability against a very cunning and nefarious opponent." The Prime Minister added there could "never be a perfect moment" to withdraw and the UK's presence there was "never intended to be permanent".[xxiv] So any discussion of the US/UK *failure and defeat* there in a twenty-year unnecessary military occupation is discretely closed down by being just short of perfection. Of course, we could not be defeated, but we were.

The same pattern occurs around the world. Russia is right. The United States is right. China is right. All states when they fight are white knight right. Wrongs can be glossed over. "My Country, 'tis of Thee, Sweet land of liberty.." was written when slavery was in full swing in the States. Real culpability, being wrong, is painted over. War crimes disappear. Apology does not happen. To fight must be right, otherwise the war for the wrong reason has to be honestly faced, and that cannot be. Being right trumps and buries the truth, but the truth does not die. Nationalist wars are always the rotting of humanity.

F. National cock-ups.

Sometimes, the national self-rightness is bizarre. The Vietnam War was part of a process of France withdrawing from its colonial interest without allowing a Communist national government taking over. The North had fought against the Japanese in World War Two and now they were fighting against France and the United States, largely because they wanted their country back. The United States was trying to hold the line by keeping a few troops there, but not really wanting to be involved. Kennedy was warned that it could suck the US in unnecessarily.

Then Johnson became President after Kennedy's assassination and two events occurred in a sparring process between the Vietcong and the US forces. In the first on 2nd of August 1963, three torpedo boats attacked the US destroyer Maddox, or actually it fired first and sunk two of them while it was largely unscathed. One bullet on the deck of the Maddox was the only sign of the attack. In the second on the 4th August, Maddox and the USS Turner Joy set out to show the flag and were attacked in bad weather in international waters. For two hours they fired back and manoeuvred sinking two torpedo boats. Except they did not. It turned out later that it was unusually bad weather and mistaken identification of the torpedoes and boats. The sonar sound of the torpedo was probably the US ships' propellers. The same evening the President broadcast news of the attack and set in train the escalation of the Vietnam War on the basis of the mistake. Soon another 150,000 American troops were in Vietnam and it was a full-scale War. *The Vietnam War was started by bad weather.* You could not make it up. Johnson was livid, but the great USA could not back down and in public he had to defend it all the way through. As a result, some *two million were killed and two million injured.* More bombs dropped on Vietnam than the US used in the whole of World War Two and a whole nation was traumatized.[xxv] We should weep for the long suffering of the Vietnamese people. The Pentagon Papers show just how bad American conduct in the Vietnam War, *started by bad weather,* was. But, of course, the United States was right and those who leaked the Pentagon Papers wrong.

Every week the need to be right, to have patriotic justification, is upheld by all kinds of media and military groups which gather round political leaders to keep the show on the road. Always we are right and the other side wrong. As always, Jesus nails it: "you see the speck in your brother's eye and ignore the plank in your own. The Taliban walk around with guns, because the US and later the UK, have militarized and occupied Afghanistan since about 1980 dishing out guns and rocket launchers. It was our fault.

G. National Militarism must be deconstructed.

So, we must all demolish these vast constructions in our minds and hearts. Tanks in Tiananmen Square must go. The UK's Monarch does not have to troop the Colours. Hitler need not have been, or Mao's Long March, or the Cold War, or the two Iraq Wars, or the Russian invasion of Ukraine. In all out nation-states we put guns and missiles in the hands of armed forces and all of those states have been brainwashed into thinking they are right. As a result, wars happen, but they need not. We understood that a hundred years ago, but the thought police have made sure we have forgotten it. So, rather than fall for this one, we walk away from nationalist self-rightousness locked into militarism and fighting. It is small minded. The world is not like that. Patriotism is used to manipulate gullible people. Fighting for our nation is a false answer. Nationalism is often institutionalised hatred; it drives all states to evil and chases away the good, *because it is good for the arms companies*. It's a sales pitch we are invited to live inside. We are taught to focus on our armed forces. But what about everybody else's armed forces and armed conflict and seeing a better way.

We will unthink. Why do the nations rage so furiously together? Isaiah had supplied the answer two thousand years before Handel. Why do they take their stand yet again in blown up self-righteousness to dash one another to pieces. Oh, grow up, do. We will remember that our state is no more important, no more right, than other states and our attack-defence is the petrol to the flames. We will not demonize them, kill them, destroy them, because we are the right, white, might, fight knight. Even the Daily Mail will say, perhaps we got this wrong.

H. Back as Far as You Can Go: - Abraham, the Father of many nations.

Let us shame ourselves by seeing the issue worked through in early biblical history, some four thousand years ago. Abraham is a key figure in human history and obviously in Jewish national formation. The Bible narrative shows Abram receiving God's blessing and understanding that "all the nations of earth will be blessed through you" (Gen.12:3). We should be astonished at this early internationalism, when Russia and the US fail to do that now, but there is more. Abraham avoids quarrels and is shown routes away from tribal loyalties into peaceful relations with other groups. He turns down receiving wealth from other kings and peoples and therefore setting up the power battles which follow from wealth. It is an amazing narrative back in early world history– read it.

But it is also odd because God requires two inexplicable things of Abraham. First, everyone has to be circumcised. Why this assault on the male genitals, not particularly serious in the long term, but painful nonetheless? Of course, now, it is mainly interpreted as a sign of Jewish identity or a medical option, but what did it mean then? It is given at the time Abraham was worrying about having an heir and was then given Isaac. Perhaps it means the opposite of national identification. It seems to convey: Do not trust in the product of your loins, the biological line, the blood line, the tribe, your people, but look to the God of all peoples. It is a great anti-nationalist sign to God's chosen people, not to trust in themselves, to be racially focussed, but to be open to others.

This is similarly reflected in the second great requirement to sacrifice Isaac. Before God, Abraham had to even be prepared to sacrifice his blood line, Isaac. Of course, Isaac was not intended to be sacrificed. It was a graphic lesson, a test set by God. The family/tribal/national loyalty had to be broken, as it was by Abraham's obedience to God and God's provision then of an offering. This great scourge of humankind, its ties with its bloodline, its people, is relativized, but in its place the nation was born which would not be nationalist and egocentric. Later it was upbraided for wanting a king like the other nations, a national focus, rather than living before God in obedience to the law, the Torah. This stand against ethnic nationalism was only partly learned and its outworking, recorded in the Old Testament is long and painful and not really complete until Jesus arrived and broke out into the great internationalism of Christianity. Given the failure now by so many nations to move outside egocentric nationalism, it is not surprising that the Jews were slow to learn. The theme is repeated incessantly in the

Law and the prophets. Since then, the Jews have, of course, been a blessing to many nations, the great dispersed international ethnic group, contributing to states around the world, and suffering attempted genocide by the Nazis. This Abrahamic purpose is still being fulfilled, aside some failures now in the State of Israel.

Here, in early written human history, when tribes and nations were being formed, the ethnocentrism of the nation state is exposed and addressed. We should, so much later, understand God's purposes to be outside this tribal introversion of humankind, this source of incessant war down the tumbling centuries since early human history. This early, in prehistory, the lesson was there to be learned, and we have not learned it yet. The inner meaning of the Jewish nation, fulfilled completely in Jesus, is anti-nationalist. Eventually, the Roman cross did not win, and the Christ sent his disciples to every tribe and nation without weapons to pass on peace and prick the great nationalist lie. And a child shall lead us all in the ways of peace. It is so easy, when all our nationalisms are wrong.

9. WARS DO NOT WORK.

A. History Distorted.

Oh, aside Abraham, this is a depressing book. It is full of silly ideas that have not worked and people should have seen through them long ago. Now we have to face the reality that wars do not work. Or perhaps, that is wrong. World War One defeated the Kaiser. World war Two saw off Hitler, Mussolini and a load of Kamikaze Japanese pilots. Surely, it was a great success. The American War of Independence did the job it was intended to do. It seems obvious that some wars are a success. Perhaps in the past wars of conquest did work - in a certain way. Armies crossed areas they could claim as their own and then people settled, pushing aside a few local people in an act of rudeness. Empires successfully acquired colonies which helped support the people back home.

That, of course, was the character of the invasion of South America by the Spanish and Portuguese, except tens of millions of natives died, and the Spanish and Portuguese fought one another. Was that a success? The Dutch, British, Belgian, French and other European empires were dominant all round the world. The conquest of North America was similar. Tens of millions of native Indians died because there was not enough room, except in Pennsylvania. Then the whites imported a load of Africans to do their work to fill America up a bit because there was too much room. Was that a success? Well, it improved after slavery. Really, throughout most of human history populations have been so sparse in most continents that warfare has been unnecessary and has just finished up creating destruction and destroying trade. Now we are asking in a more searching way if military empires, were successful. There is slavery, opium addiction, economic exploitation, native armies, killing, taxes, mining, mineral exploitation and land grab. The winners in colonial wars were usually bad. So, success has a very bad smell.

The picture gets worse. There are the Islamic patterns of conquest. Usually, people point to a few rich, elegant buildings, as though that makes a civilisation, when actually slavery, predation and the cost of conquest usually decivilized areas and impoverished them for centuries along with a trade in slaves. No, there is little good in those wars. Then there was the Hundred Years War. First, it makes you long for a ninety minutes football match. Second, these were christian states, declaring they were for peace, but so full of self-righteousness that they tore into one another murdering. They were unbelievably cruel. I remember seeing a painting in Belgium of a poor guy being flayed alive looking at the viewer saying, "How about stopping this. It hurts." Christians have got to think why, as people of peace, they have finished up at war over supposedly faith issues and been unbelievably vicious. Actually, of course, they have not been Christians but have often been preserving their personal empires, rectitude and privilege. Jesus words, "Depart from me for I never knew you" come to mind. It is not the label we wear; we must do peace. We can try to ignore the fact that these conquests killed millions of people, destroyed generations, undid decades of building and manufacture, but all these wars did not work for both sides. Alexander the Great won a lot of wars and then died aged 32 drinking, obviously a successful life. The history of who won and who lost is hopelessly biased. Both sides lose wars. It is a blinkered way to do history just so that war comes out all right.

Or it is romanticized.

> The boy stood on the burning deck
>   Whence all but he had fled;
> The flame that lit the battle's wreck
>   Shone round him o'er the dead.
>
> Yet beautiful and bright he stood,
>   As born to rule the storm;
> A creature of heroic blood,
>   A proud, though child-like form.

So that's all right then.

B. Nobody Wins.

Let's just have another word about the winners. They don't. The Normans came here and won in 1066 and were holed up in castles ordering around a load of serfs whom they could not understand who hated them and deliberately worked badly. Their servants put unmentionables in the dinner and shat in the wrong places until eventually the Normans had to marry locals who gave them bad sex. We do not know the half of it. It is the same now. George W. Bush did Mission Accomplished in Iraq in 2003 and then carried on fighting for nearly another two decades spending billions of dollars, giving US soldiers PTSD, messing up Iraq further and setting up a long-term terrorist problem. Did he win? The boy stood on the burning deck. Did he heck. Or in Afghanistan? We won in 2003, but oops we lost it in 2021, or not lost, but rather mislaid it for twenty years and had to come home.

Nobody wins wars. They signal up the next one. They destroy the young. They make winning economies dependent on handouts for others, setting in train decline and fall. They create servitude. The winners become unbearable rulers. The cost of the war and destruction requires one or two decades of hard labour. History writes about the process of winning, but rarely addresses the who wins question in depth. Widows and the bereaved know they did not. The long shadow of trauma slants across decades. The soldiers do not remember the victory but their dead comrades. The delirious celebrations are not about winning the war, but about the end of the war. When this bloody war is over..... Nobody wins. We should close down the arrogant history flattering the victors, because it is not true.

C. World War One.

But surely, we defeated the Kaiser in World War One. The Great War was great in size, but all sides lost. As another 50-100 million more people died of Spanish flu at the end of the War among weakened populations indiscriminately, everyone knew that all had lost. All should have learned that this was the War to end all Wars, and millions did. But look what happened. At Versailles some of the statesmen wanted to be winners. The USA wanted paying for all its loans which had gone up in smoke. France and Britain had to cough up and in turn exacted from Germany. They had *won* and needed rewarding. The USSR ratted and had to be punished. So, Germany had to pay reparations to France and the Britain because it lost. Keynes in *The Economic Consequences of the Peace* and others warned about it. Because Britain, France and the United States approached the end of the War in terms of *winning*, they set up the history of the next twenty years through to 1939 and the even worse war which came along as the economic realities played out. The truth was that everybody had lost through the waste and destruction of the War, not that Germany had lost and the USA, France and Britain had won. Nobody wins. If we understood that we had not won World War One, World War Two might well not have happened. Keynes and the others saw the fuller picture.

D. What about World War Two?

We all believe that the Second World War was our great victory, as indeed it was, over Hitler and over the power crazed Fascist and Nazi powers which began it. But we delude ourselves. At any war memorial in Britain there is a large list from World War One and a short list from World War Two. We did not mainly win the War. As we have seen, the USSR did, losing 25 million people. There is a photo of Trafalgar Square in 1943 full of people protesting that we were not opening a second front, but leaving the Soviets to fight largely on their own. Really, the USSR won World War Two, but it lost and faced the cost because it had so many dead and injured, had been ravaged by invasion, bombed and flattened beyond western knowing. It had won, but it had lost and it is still lost and suffering a lifetime later.

There was a victory over the people who believed in war, who were war crazed, who were still really fighting the First World War, who were marching they knew not where, and who breathed the hate of the Holocaust. So, it should have been a victory over the belief in war which the Nazis exemplified. The meaningless Fascist march to the future was defeated after six years of disastrous fighting in 1945. Thankfully Germany lost and understood it had lost. The formation of the United Nations, united in the determination not to go the route of military confrontation again, should have principled the world. The determination in 1945 that war was wrong was strong. But that truth did not win. The United States believed it had won, but within months in 1945, a new enemy, the USSR, was in place and war went on. And the losers, Germany and Japan, who were forbidden military expenditure when they lost, became the strongest economies in the world two decades later because they were not wasting money on militarism. The winner lost and the losers won. War does not work.

E. What is War *for*?

Now, we do not even understand what war is for. We cannot answer this question. It is not for occupation, because people live where they live and the world is largely settled; Americans did not want to settle in Vietnam, Iraq or Afghanistan. Native people do not want to be controlled and can be very awkward. War cannot be a long-term business; it has to stop. When you have fifty tanks on the local town car park, what do you do with them then? What is war for? Really, they are like football matches. Once the winning-losing thing is over, there is no other purpose. You wander home or go to the pub, except the pub has been bombed. The only purpose after wars is to recover.

Even worse, wars start off and go on wrong. Wars have been a long catastrophe of mistakes from the start. Archduke Ferdinand being shot by a nutter should not have caused *a World War*. The Suez War was started by the sacking of Glubb Pasha. Vietnam was a mistake caused by the weather. Iraq One was caused by Saddam's arms debts. Iraq Two was caused by WMD *which did not exist* and because the arms people needed a war. Largely, no-one had even thought what to do when the Iraq War was "over". No-one understands the Yemen War. Or Syria? Or Libya? Or Ukraine. Putin would be hard pressed to sit down and say "What the Ukraine War is For?" He would mumble something about

NATO and the West, but he has chosen the route of not calling it a War so that the question does not have to be answered.

Let us ask why war has no purpose? The old style of victory and colonial occupation is no longer possible. We live on a crowded and settled planet and you cannot, it seems, occupy countries successfully. Nor is external slave labour, or taxation or the exploitation of resources possible. US and western exploitation of Middle East Oil has had its day. So War cannot even now be selfish. Mineral exploitation in DRC and elsewhere will shortly be held to account, and controlling populations is now so complex that it cannot work. The Chinese Uyghurs attempt may be the last; we all know what is going on and it is intolerable. War as the empty beating of another state, because the weapons are available, on the basis of some diplomatic splat which should have been avoided is not really a viable way forward in world politics. It is silly. The militarists cannot answer this simple question, because it has no answer. War should die discretely. Far better play chess.

F. The Boy stood on the Burning Bush.

Indeed, the pointlessness of war is perhaps exemplified most poignantly by George W. Bush in the war in Iraq. It was aimed against Saddam Hussein who was already largely disarmed and the American military agreed that it would be an easy military success and so they were for it.. The United States "fought" the war with Britain to root out the Weapons of Mass Destruction which did not exist. After a short period of fighting Bush appeared on the deck of an aircraft carrier announcing that it was "Mission Accomplished" and the war had been won. It was an easy victory. But what was it *for*? The best explanation offered was regime change. That's was in 2003. Because the WMD reason for the War did not exist, the US and UK did "regime change", which left them running the country through the corrupt, destructive regime of Nouri al-Maliki. Though the US continued to take a cut of the oil revenue, running a colony these days is a deficit operation, especially when the natives do not like it. Roughly 20 years later after the war had been held in place by the invading power, the United States and United Kingdom pulled out of the war largely defeated. They had spent several trillion dollars on the conflict. Many soldiers had been traumatised. In camp Bastian torture and abuse had fired a load of Iraqis into pursuing a terrorist war against the United States, requiring more defence. From start to finish the War had no purpose. The main impetus came from the military, especially the Haliburton military logistics group in the States, for an easy victory. But to what purpose? What good is winning a war? The question is now so obviously unanswered that the system has to collapse.

G. The Troubles.

We could look at the "Troubles" in Northern Ireland as another archetype of the problems with War. It has been a long armed conflict. When it started is a moot point. Does it go back to Cromwell and other Irish colonial wars? Did it start with the Independence Movements of the mid-19th century? Was it the settlement after WW1 - Churchill and the Black and Tans? Was it the reactivation of the IRA in the 60s? There has been a mixture of aggression by the UK troops and armed terrorism from the IRA through weapons supplied from the United States and then from Libya. Always arms were the problem, the irritant. Bloody Sunday followed by Bloody Monday. Neither side won. The confrontation ground on for several decades, building resentment between the communities. Problems, like those associated with Brexit in 2021, become exaggerated because of the lack of trust. Ulster is now defending the Government in Stormont, which *has not existed* for several years because the DUP refuse to serve in it. It is a long useless failure with some effective peace-making. Of course, all wars are trauma and troubles, often far more acute; this is a mild case. Does Ulster belong to Ireland or to the United Kingdom? However, much fighting occurs in Northern Ireland, it will remain geographically and in other ways linked to the South and the UK; war does not change geography. Why take the either/or, when it is both/and?

H. The Shadow of War.

War suffering is not just something that happens, but it is embedded in the very conduct of war. War trauma is experienced directly by soldiers who kill and are killed, and the shadows cross decades. There are shadows of distrust and hardness which last half a century. I have seen shadows of WW2 in the last few weeks. The shadows of male absence at war still shape family relationships a lifetime later. There are the houses that are not, the trade that does not take place, the stereotyping of nations, the envy of success, the long shadow of debt; the UK's debts to the US after the Second World War were finally paid sixty one years later. The United Kingdom sacked the V sign Churchill in 1945 because people knew they needed housing, equality, a health service, pensions, trains and rebuilt cities. Far from being intoxicated by victory and Churchill, the people voted to sort the shadow of war. Churchill lost two hundred seats in the election. Victory is always much worse than no war. People had faced bombing, the devastation of their homes, rationing, relocation, family losses and waiting for something better. Always there is the contrast between the propaganda of success, victory and conquest and the reality of bombsites and the bitter widow. In some areas most of the populations will be traumatised. We cannot think of the trauma the Vietnamese have experienced since the end of the war in 1975. A million children, now middle-aged if they are alive, suffered birth defects from the chemical agents used as defoliants by Monsanto and the USAF. War is like two men pounding bricks to smithereens with sledgehammers and then stopping and asking, "So what shall we build, then?"

Finally, now we have the Russia-Ukraine War. Both sides are destroyed. The costs are vast. They will take ten years of determined work to rectify. The point of military attacks on both sides is to destroy the most valuable part of the Ukraine economy or the Crimean One to win the war. But the costs of the destruction will be perhaps a trillion dollars on either side. Russia seems less damaged, but its military costs in Crimea, damage to its infrastructure, deaths and injuries mount and mount. Already they are about a hundred thousand deaths on each side. Russia is losing energy income permanently, financial assets, skilled personnel and more.

It has destroyed its international trade for a generation. It is en route to impoverishment. The militarists might pull back, but "We need a bigger budget" they say. You would think when they look on the horrors of yet another war caused by their system, they would think, "This is not a good way to conduct international affairs." but they do not. They plough on with their formidable propaganda system self-righteously pushing the way of weapons and war. But now is the time, the last time, to declare war on them, war on war and the causes of war.

History has played through every option. A goes to war and so B goes to war or vice versa. There is stalemate and so it carries on. A loses or B loses. If A wins it seeks to extract the costs from B. If B wins, A resents B. If A wins, B tries to win the next one. Revenge carries on. The loser gets allies, or arms more. The winner tries slavery, taxes, occupation. Occupiers face terrorism or sabotage. Winners are superior. Losers resent winners. Those who fight wars take over government. Losers develop the next best weapon. Wars stop because people have to live, but many of them are dead. The winner gets killed by his own side so that someone else gets the spoils. Murder, robbery, rape, drinking are let slip by war and ruin winner and loser. War runs on hate and hate carries on. Children are blighted. Destruction upon destruction of that which is good occurs. The only line the weapons people have is: "Well, we stopped Hitler didn't we?" ignoring the facts that weapons and War created Hitler and gave him the tools to fight. At the end of the book is an incomplete list of our modern wars with fallible but reasonable estimates of vast deaths, injuries and costs. Of course, figures are not the funerals, the suffering and the personal loss. Their witness stands. This is the way not to run the world. It is obvious disaster. It is not even a difficult to wage war on war because the debate is over. Putin is the undertaker for war, the last post, the pall bearer, the loser from whom we all learn. Obviously, war does not work and we close the factory.

10. THE MILITARY ARE GOOD, BAD AND VICTIMS.

A. Thoughts about soldiering.

We live regarding the armed forces as normal in all countries at all times, except perhaps in Switzerland. There they have few arms and many of the "armed forces" were ordinary farmers who took a gun out of a cupboard once a year and did a bit of practice shooting at hares. When I saw them more than fifty years ago, it was a bit of a game, but then they had not had a war then for a hundred and fifty years. Things may have changed a bit, but they still have not had a war. Yet when we think about armed forces, we are taught to think about "our armed forces" whether they be Russian, Australian, Brazilian, American or Indian. We think *within* the idiom of necessary defence, their place in the life of the nation and the history of wars within which they have fought.

Yet, we may think about global soldiering. There is this class of people, the military, who are trained for fighting and combat in different scenarios, on land, sea and in the air all over the world. As we have already seen, at present there are something like 28 million armed forces, an unimaginable figure. But it has been far higher. Obviously, this was the case during the Second World War. For some reason there is no available figure of how many armed forces there were then but it will probably be some 110 million of whom perhaps 22 million, or one in five were killed, alongside many more civilians. Of course, they were not all fighting at the same time, as the process went on for five years. Just think of this vast host of mainly men fighting one another. It need not have happened. Churchill, and many other sane people for the reasons already covered, understand that the war need not have happened. But it took place. One hundred and ten million men were fighting one another in what we call modern civilisation. Fighting one another is generally seen as a bad thing, whether in the playground or the streets. It is the breakdown of civilised behaviour. Jesus gave people a number of tools to avoid it: - don't get angry, sort quarrels quickly, see the others point of view, avoid revenge, "turn the other cheek" and be generous beyond bargaining. Fighting is bad, and having a hundred million men fighting one another is worse, and equipping them to fight is worse still for civilisation. Civis, the state, being civil without fighting, is the bedrock of *civilisation*, and yet here in 2023 we professionalize the opposite. However well the military behave, they will be killing wholesale sooner or later. Shurely, there musht be shum mishtake.

B. From Conscription to Professional.

After World War Two most states were left with big Conscription Armies. You did National Service. The vast armies of 1945 shrank. The US went down from about 12.2M in 1945 to 1.6M in 1947 and the USSR from 11.3M in 1945 to 2.8M in 1948. Britain's forces dropped from 5M in 1945 to about .8M through to mid-1950s. The war personnel returned to ordinary life and useful jobs. There were some professional soldiers, but the main form of soldiering was conscription, the "Draft" as it was called in the United States or "National Service" in the UK. It was normally for all men who were fit for one, two or three years of training and service. That generated a large reserve of already trained soldiers in case anything big went wrong. The rules were complex, and there were exemptions for fathers and married men and on other grounds, but it was seen as a national obligation in theory for all men and "good" discipline for them. It ended in 1960 in the UK but continued in the States through to the Vietnam War in what we could call the Sargent Bilko years. Elvis was in the US army from 1958 to 1960.

Really during the 1950s and 60s an issue cropped up in relation to conscripted military personnel. They had to join up and to fight, but what if they were conscientious objectors, who were allowed not to fight in WW1 and WW2? Should they be forced into killing? It especially became an issue in the States when the Vietnam War came along. Large numbers objected and left the country for Canada or elsewhere. There was another problem. The exemption system was complex and widespread evasion became common, especially it seemed among politicians' sons, and so it was bedevilled by a sense of unfairness as more than half of those eligible were deferred, exempted or disqualified. But more than this, as the armed forces became more militarised, a professional, highly trained force was needed and most states in the fifties and sixties therefore moved over to a professional model of personnel who signed up to unconditional full-time service. The politicians decide on war and the professionals carry it out. Service personnel were in practice not given the right to conscientiously object and that is now normal. You sign up and forfeit your conscience.

The military under international law have a variety of requirements to protect life in the context of war. Armed personnel can surrender safely and cease fighting. The Red Cross and other emergency services should be allowed access. Unarmed civilians should not be killed, attacked, raped, or abused. Many armed forces obey these laws and conduct war according to principles, but sadly, by accidents of war and by intent they were often disregarded or directly disobeyed, and war crimes occur. Throughout World War Two cities including Chongqing, London, Coventry, Stalingrad, Rotterdam, Hamburg, Dresden, Tokyo, Hiroshima, Nagasaki and dozens of others were flattened with no regard to civilian or military targets and Churchill and Truman saw indiscriminate bombing as acceptable, and so really it has continued to the present. Basra, Mosul, Baghdad, Grozny, Aleppo, Damascus, Homs and other Middle Eastern cities have all been bombed wholesale and so there is no firm control of the aggression of the armed forces, as we see again in Ukraine.

C. We respect the Military.

Yet, the military often deserve wider respect. Usually, they are smart, impressive and put on good displays, but it is more than this. Much of the time they try their best to produce good from destructive situations. They aim to contain terrorism. They tried to restore order in ravaged and fragmented occupied countries. They try to avoid escalation towards war and contain the aggressive attitudes of politicians and military dictators. They act as peacemakers, restoring stability, and with a deep commitment even to their opponents. These good aims and actions need acknowledging; they have done good across the world, sometimes at great personal cost to the soldiers. But, again, this does not stop the bigger critique. They are trying their best in a business of destruction and social collapse caused by war and aggression. Within such a gigantic failed system, there is a necessary trajectory towards war and destruction. Continuing this system is the big mistake. Sooner or later, they are compromised whether they acknowledge it or not. The United States' and the United Kingdom's militaries have tried to do good in Afghanistan and Iraq but have failed strategically and in practice. They were upholding corrupt rulers. There was even torture at Camp Bastion and elsewhere, because war is ugly and we are ugly when we are fighting. So, we can both respect the military and their attempts to do good and recognise the system will not work.

But there is another factor at work. Military commands come from the top. Partly, that is the top commanders in the army, navy and air-force. The insistence on military discipline makes decision-making quite centralised. It is even more than this. The central decision makers, involving the politicians, perhaps secret services, big arms producers and whatever the military-industrial complex might be tell everybody else what to do. In theory in democracies decisions about war involve Assemblies or Parliaments, but actually they are strongly directed by the executive, by rulers and central military decision makers. In a very real sense, the armed forces are carrying out orders and are probably quite frequently at odds with what they are asked to do. Many American service people in Vietnam had critical questions about the war. Many Russian soldiers feel the Ukraine War is wrong, would rather not be there, or have deserted. So, again, the military are, perhaps more than any other profession acting against what they believe is right. There is one further key element in this picture.

D. Military Discipline and Murder.

For centuries the armed forces have been taught to kill. This outright denial of the Sixth Commandment, the bedrock of civilisation, is brazen. It encourages what the Commandment forbids. It should shock all of us, but it has been dressed up over the centuries. Crucial is military discipline, the idea you must obey your commanding officer unconditionally, even when that means killing opposition soldiers and civilians in large numbers. The UK's Prince Harry in Afghanistan, obeying orders, killed perhaps 25 of the Taliban. Marching, military orders, uniformity and uniforms convey the idea that the killing is backed right the way up to the state, and if the state says it is right, then it is. But it is not. The Russian State should not be killing in Ukraine, Saudi Arabia in Yemen, Israel in Gaza and so on. As soon as the State validates state murder, it compromises its law and creates the likelihood of state murder, insurrection, external attack, mercenaries, revenge and the business of interstate war all the way through to genocide. Ignoring a good law, even the central law to civilisation, opens the way to evil and destruction and everywhere we see its consequences.

Ah, you say. That is just not practical. The prohibition of murder does not work when there are military states. But you do not see your problem. You do not say, "Ah, the law against murder is not practical in Beccles, Buenos Aires, Naples, Chengdu or wherever you choose to live. You know it must work in all these places because it is good and you have not been taken in by military discipline and unconditional obedience. The law forbidding weapons is because they will kill in our towns and cities. We see that. If there is a gang in your town trying to establish their right to kill, we hold them to account. The law against murder is just as good in international relations as it is in national It is international militarism *which must bend to the law* so that the killing stops. We must stop being taken it by military discipline, unconditional obedience and autocratic rule's false validation of international killing. It is bad to kill people, even in trenches or under a bomb.

How do you try to make killing acceptable? The answer usually is that it is necessary to win the war. It posits a "greater good" to set alongside the mass murders. But, as we have seen, "winning" wars is a farce, a mirage. Even the double standard does not work. Yes, we say, the killing is necessary for our national survival and for us to "win" wars. But really, every historian can see the links between WW1, WW2 and the Cold War.

Really, nobody wins wars, the killings provoke revenge, kill husbands, traumatize millions and the pattern continues. No murder is right. State organised murder, killing thousands or millions, is not right when one murder is wrong; it is a thousand or million times worse. Military murders set off other military murders. Does anyone not understand that? Why not solve the problem rather than one tenth of it by winning a war? So, we act to forbid all weapons and eliminate the mass murder of war; it works internationally as it works at home. Civilised and educated world populations can easily work out what "You shall not kill" means. An unconditional commitment to state killing, because arms companies need to make a living, is bad ethics and is really on the same side as Hitler. The false faith in the system of the military "right" to kill validated by the State needs to fall dead. Most days I hear soldiers practising to kill with high velocity rifles at a local firing range. One day, they will shoot to kill real, unless stopped, and that is not acceptable. Or the firing range stops. Jesus said, It is not only Don't Kill, but try not even to be angry, understand your enemy and sort quarrels out, but we are still at Stage One back in the Iron Age.

E. The new task for the Military.

So, the military, sometimes principled and sometimes not, are not the nub of the problem. Strangely, when you fight Militarism, the military can be your friends. When soldiers fight in wars, and may die in them, they are not cavalier. The armed forces often know the cost because they will pay it. Their training, areas of professional expertise, operational competence and good intent are frequently present and looking for good ways forward. Often, they work for unprincipled rulers. They are trapped in conflict zones. They uphold military dictatorships. Their politicians make wrong decisions. Really, they are caught in a bigger system, the system of attack-defence fuelled by weapons which generate these areas of tension, small or world-wide. Focussing on the person with his finger on the button is not the issue; the question is how did the nuclear, or other button system, come to be there? Where are the decisions really made and the systems developed? We need to close down militarism, and this generation of soldiers can do it.

The world's military personnel can do world disarmament. They can be the generation, properly paid, who firmly close down all these military systems that we have built up over the centuries which now threaten us all. They can work with the UN and National Governments during world disarmament, as the whole system is run down. They monitor the closing down of weapons and forces. They can together under law defeat terrorists and others who might evade the process, and confiscate retained weapons under UN supervision. Over the next five years there is a big job in the careful logistics of disarmament to be done by a lot of servicemen and women. Of course, the numbers of service people will shrink, but there is another burgeoning industry for them to move to funded by governments and aid. They can move over from the war-based disasters scattered round the planet to the natural disasters which we will face with global warming. They can move fast, mobilize, save lives, address famine, drought, floods and tempests and do the flood defences, international water movement, rescue and storm damage work the world, rich and poor, will need. They can make the great transition from the destruction of war to healing from disasters. They will often have pensions and other jobs, but corporately they can redeem the centuries of war, killing and destruction with an unconditional commitment to help and peace-making. Finally, it is war no more and they build rather than destroy. Finally, they will be faithful to their deceased colleagues by making sure that no-one else dies in war. That is the best profession ever and it is coming soon.

11. WE NEED AN ENEMY: RUNNING THE MILITARY-INDUSTRIAL SYSTEM.

A. The problem is not the armed forces, but the Military System.

Now we must go back and begin to close in on the nub of the issue. Militarism is not just, or even, soldiers, sailors and air force folk, but includes the arms companies, secret services, industrial, research, university, media, supply systems, local economies, local and national politics and many other related organisations and industries like shipbuilding, space, computing, communication, mental, health, civil engineering. It is big and complex whether in France, India, Brazil, the United States, Russia, Israel, the United Kingdom, China, Egypt or Argentina. President Eisenhower called it the Military-Industrial Complex. It is there. Big and Powerful. It has a brain, or several million of them, and thinks in its own terms, long before mega-computing. There are those who are responsible for important parts of the complex – maintaining and improving the quality of the air-force or navy, securing the next big contract, making sure that the CIA or MI5 is needed, keeping university contracts, setting up long research projects and they think and develop policy within a grand strategy. They do media work with expertise, making sure that their products are marketed to the public and the politicians. They keep their show on the road. They have business plans. They calculate the way forward for twenty years or more. They mean to succeed. They are big. They have become among the biggest systems on the planet. How does it operate?

B. Thinking the obvious: You need an Enemy.

This section insults your intelligence and mine. It is obvious, but we need to think the obvious which we have forgotten since the Second War. Then, we needed a vast military system to defeat the Nazis. They were defeated, but another enemy quickly emerged. The USSR, the great ally of Churchill and Roosevelt became the Cold War enemy. Then it collapsed under its military burden in 1990 and was gone. Soon another enemy appeared, Saddam the wicked, but he did not last for long. Fortunately, after a while Russia has reappeared as the enemy under the wicked Putin and already the wicked China is lined up for the next thirty years. If Militarism is to carry on it needs to have an enemy including at least one big one. It is a general principle. It is no good some children in the playground constructing a load of cannon down one side when the rest of the kids just carry on playing as usual and being nice. The cannon kids are just stranded, wasting their time. Always the military system needs an enemy, a threat, against which it will defend or attack and this now becomes industrial policy, like cough medicine needs coughs. Except, enemy creation is political engineering.

It is a mind-teetering thought that we might not have, or need enemies. No enemy and you might as well be playing a game of darts. There are no enemies in the church, the pub, the shopping mall; we understand this is a good way to live. What if we had no enemies at all? We are all globally on the same side. If there is no enemy, the whole military-industrial complex is washed up, some thirty-five million of them including troops and arms suppliers. So, it does enemies every which way. It is not just that enemies happen, but the politico-military system makes them happen. There are secret services, military think tanks, gatherings, long-term reports, embassies, alliances, military exercises, alliances, media contact systems and they are doing enemies all the time for the silly public who cannot really understand. The tools are fear, scares, threats, worry about "security", De Fence and evil. The sense of danger must be permanently there. Now, with mass media conveying the messages instantly, everywhere, to all, it is technically easy. There are no rural populations, local communities, cities untouched by the messages of *enemy*. North Korea, is scared stiff of us and we are supposed to be scared stiff of them. They are actually the other side of the globe, but also in your living room. Teresa May, justifying a new generation of Trident nuclear weapons, was able to get away with using North Korea as the only example of the threat they were supposed to meet. North Korea was our enemy, but nobody thought at the time, North Korea is not much of a threat to Milton Keynes. Or, really, it has an economy half the size of Lancashire, and is not much of a world threat. It is a really useful enemy.

Finding enemies is not so easy. Most people just want to get on with their lives. So, the arms companies and militaries have to work at it, talk it up, incite enemies, create military blocs, threaten and build the fear. There has to be an enemy. I thought I would test this out on Hawaii, sitting bang in the middle of the Pacific Ocean. When you look at it on a globe, almost all of the rest is blue water; it can only be attacked by flying fish. Surely, it does not have an enemy. But it does. North Korea is, we learn, preparing dangerous missiles and there is a US defence system for hitting missiles from North Korea which might attack Hawaii, and so local people need not worry. Except when you read the small print, the interceptor system is in Alaska and a local Hawaii response costing $747mn is on hold. But some arms manufacturer is making millions out of Hawaii having an enemy. Kim Jong Un *might* wake up one morning and decide to send missiles four and a half thousand miles over to Hawaii in the middle of the Pacific. He is the best enemy they have got. He is a useful enemy bringing in arms contracts to make Hawaii safe...

C. Selling Aggression and Militarism – the Trade.

The Military-Industrial Complex postures as defence but it is actually in the business of selling aggression. It understands that when it sells weapons, then more weapons will be needed down the line. It needs the other side. Unless China and Russia produce weapons, its demand will dry up. So mutually, they all press for wars and rumours of wars, while saying the opposite. They need regular wars for four reasons. First, its products are useless without wars; they have no other purpose. Second, wars use up its product as each side attacks the weapons of the other side; it is a double demand bonanza. Third, it is wars which really bring profits, as states pay anything for products in wars, and fourth the public and states around the world need to be kept in a continual state of fear otherwise their business is dead. Ten years without a war and everybody would relax and not buy weapons. The arms companies sell weapons but mainly they sell fear, which makes their business work.

Sometimes there are private arms fairs, but the main route to sales is through favoured politicians, admirals, field-marshals and those who work in the Ministry of Defence or the Pentagon. It is an insider business, premised on the idea We will Defend You. These people do Defence Budgets, big Budgets with a lot of preparatory work. In the US it is pushing up towards $1tn each year extracting about $2,500 from each man, woman and child in the States. It is very big business. There are new weapons, each an industry, gaps to be filled, Senators and Representatives with financial support from the arms industry, pressure groups, sales teams, media people paid to push the weapons or the manufacturer. It is a vast industry around the Budget, funded by it and coming up with the orders. We remember reports that a toilet seat cover cost $10,000 or $7,600 for a coffee pot, but it is the big extravagancies which count. Money sloshes into these budgets to fund everything. In 2015 an internal Pentagon Report suggested $125bn was wasted, but the report was (nearly) suppressed. In other states, it is no less organised, but smaller. Defence Departments co-operate. Every year when the UK defence Budget is being formed, some US General says that the UK has a "second-tier defense" or a collapsing military and needs a vast increase in the Budget. It is to help their mates get the funds. Usually, the pressure wins. The UK cannot have a "second-tier" defence system. Tut, tut. If the State can't defend us, it has ignored its primary duty, goes the budget line and so they cough up the money. Politicians then bask in the idea that they are defending us from invasion by Belgium or the Isle of Wight.

Often, arms companies employ former defence ministers and military people who are on the inside and know the system. In the United States they have strong links with politicians who represent the areas where their business is. For much of their history they have practised bribery as a way of getting orders. Sir Basil Zaharoff used to leave wads of notes on the desk. More recently, BAe Systems, among other bribes, laid on a large jet so that the Saudi Arabian princes could bring their shopping back from California; peacock blue Rolls Royces were a favourite. They were being prosecuted for Criminal Bribery by the Serious Fraud Office, but Tony Blair insisted on letting them off because it was not in the UK's "national interest" to prosecute an arms company for criminal behaviour. If you want a hollow laugh, look at the case of BAe Systems v the Crown prosecuted by the Serious Fraud Office in front of Justice Bean in November 2010. The SFO under pressure from the Government stitched up the case as poor accounting when it was clearly a bribe and Justice Bean had to go along with it. As he said archly, "I cannot sentence for an offence which the prosecution has chosen not to charge". Of course, there is much bribery that is not criminal; people are merely paid handsomely for services rendered. Bribery is endemic in the industry throughout its history.[xxvi] So much for the rule of law.

More generally the arms trade is externally sanitised. They "believe" in their products, but they do not mention killing or war. Rather they provide "solutions" and "capabilities" and will give us prosperity through exports and are "staying ahead of threats". Some of their kit is "lethal". They will sell to governments and world leaders and so their sales routes are sophisticated, often with lavish hospitality, smoothed by Embassies. Sometimes, they make mistakes. One sales dinner, at a cost of £3,000 per table, was sponsored by Lockheed Martin in the Tower of London. Outside was the great poppy display remembering those who had died in World War One a hundred years earlier. Inside the Merchants of Death were filling Defence People with champagne and fine fare to encourage them to buy killing weapons. When the news came out, people remembered the contributions of arms companies to starting WW1.[xxvii] The media saw it as "inappropriate".

The Arms Companies have a difficult business, partly because stocks of arms build. They have to sell year on year, but when they are supplied, unless they are used, they accumulate and create a likely future recession in business as all this kit is lying around. The imperative to sell is very strong, and by and large it is the arms industry which drives the military. They do not fear for themselves, like soldiers; the arms manufacturers are never killed in action. Wars just bring them profits and perhaps bonuses. They stay hidden inside most of the governments around the world, driving the Attack-Defence system. In the Pentagon and elsewhere, "the revolving door" is the process whereby ex-military chiefs get jobs with arms companies to help land contracts. Innovation and selling new weapons might open up markets. Some states are captive markets and special links grow up. Obviously in military dictatorships they are the name of the game. Usually, initial prices seem quite low, but then a lot of add-ons generate really big profits. In the UK the two aircraft carriers moved up from £3.5bn to £6.2bn on completion. The biggest contract was the US Lockheed Martin F35 Fighter which grew to a $1.1 trillion support bill in 2018. So really, they do not have it too hard and can afford a few dinners.

Broadly the big arms sales companies have succeeded in building the myth that they are indispensable, they do good, there is no alternative, the enemies are in place ready to attack us, we need the "best" arms possible, they need subsidies, they should be free to sell to almost anyone, and certainly military dictators, they are an economic asset, they keep the peace and they should have privileged access to governments. They are tucked inside the world political system, safe from democracy in the democracies. Most people do not think about them, though they rule the world, but we are thinking about them now.

D. Some examples of enemy creation.

We stay with enemies. If we do not have enemies, we do not need weapons. So, the arms companies must create enemies without being seen to create enemies. If we do not have an enemy, they must make one. It is like the old cartoon of the brick through the window with the glazier's phone number attached. They must create the problem they then solve by increasing the problem. They must generate enemies, but they must not be seen to throw the brick. The secret services help, but the main strategy is to sell arms to everybody and sooner or later something or other will blow up, especially if rivals are selling too.

Let us look at the Falklands War. So, the naughty US and France supplied weapons to the Argentinians before the Falklands War. Oh, and the UK did as well. Nobody asked, "Now what does Argentina jutting down between the Pacific and Atlantic with no neighbours at sea other than Antarctica and the Falklands want with two Type 42 Destroyer?" They were either going to attack the Falklands or some dangerous flapping seals on an ice floe. It turned out to be the former. If you sell weapons wars will turn up. We, and the US, created an obvious enemy and the war followed. The politicians in this case were asleep, but the arms industry knew what the destroyers were for. They sell cheap to start off new potential conflicts. Then the prices build.

This is a long-term problem. The case which first woke me up was around 1906 when Mr Mulliner of the Coventry Ordnance Works, out of orders for naval guns, sent a worker to Germany to report that Krupp were vastly increasing their Dreadnought building capacity so that they could turn out battleships in several months rather than years.[xxviii] It was a lie. The War Office knew it was, because they had their spies. The Germans did not build a battleship in under two years even during the War, and to their credit the War Office insisted Mulliner was sacked before they gave the Coventry Firm another contract. Yet still a propaganda machine in Parliament, the Press and Government pressed to increase naval orders by exaggerating the German Naval threat, as Churchill in the Admiralty recognised. The Dreadnought scare of 1908-9, "We Want Eight and We Won't Wait!" was a manufactured lie. The Naval yards were doing enemy threat for their order books as they had for decades back to Gladstone.

The Cold War confrontation institutionalised this pattern on both sides. It was stoked by both militaries. President Eisenhower and Nikita Khrushchev describe the process by which the tail was wagging the dog. Eisenhower is talking to Khrushchev, then Khrushchev replies.

"My military leaders come to me and say, "Mr President, we need such and such a sum for such and such a program." I say, "Sorry we don't have the funds." They say, "We have reliable information that the Soviet Union has already allocated funds for their own such program. Therefore, if we do not get the funds we need, we'll fall behind the Soviet Union." So, I give in.

That's how they wring money out of me. They keep grabbing for more and I keep giving it to them. Now tell me, how is it with you?"

"It's just the same. Some people from our military department come and say, "Comrade Khrushchev, look at this! The Americans are developing such and such a system. We could develop the same system, but it would cost such and such." I tell them there is no money; it's all been allocated already. So, they say, "If we don't get the money we need and if there is a war, then the enemy will have superiority over us." So, we discuss it some more, and I end up by giving them the money…"[xxix]

Here are the two dogs talking while their tails are wagging them… This accurately represented the process both in the US and USSR. It was more complex and devious than this, involving lies, scares and massive propaganda systems to drive through to contracts.

Another risible example, except people died, was the need of the US militarists, especially Cheney and Rumsfeld in 2002-3 to show that Saddam was the big Enemy with weapons of mass destruction and more. It is indecent to recount all that the militarists did to show Saddam as the enemy linked to 9/11 and everything else; it was a litany of lies. But listen to Cheney's scarcely articulate rant.

Armed with an arsenal of these weapons of terror and a seat at the top 10% of the world's oil reserves, Saddam Hussein could then be expected to seek domination of the entire Middle East, take control of a great portion of the world's energy supplies, directly threaten America's friends throughout the region and subject the United States or any other nation to nuclear blackmail. Simply stated, there is no doubt that Saddam Hussein now has weapons of mass destruction; there is no doubt that he is amassing them to use against our friends, against our allies and against us. [xxx]

It is embarrassing that an American Vice-President will peddle such untruth to get a war. Saddam had previously been defeated, been disarmed of all strategic weapons, subject to bruising embargoes and inspections by UN officials. He was cleaned out of WMD, and Cheney's words were moonshine to give him the War he wanted and his former company, Halliburton, their big contracts. When Saddam emerged unkempt from the bunker in which he had been hiding from his easy vanquishers and was shot, did anyone think to ask, "Is this really the great enemy who was supposed to dominate the Middle East in 2003?"

The fifth example is more recent. Where did the Ukraine War come from? NATO was out of a job at the end of the Cold War. Its enemy had broken up. Really, it had nothing to do. The Communist ideology had disappeared and the new Russia was less than half the size of the USSR and it was friends with us. Gorbachev and Yeltsin wanted to fully end military confrontation for ever. They asked that, after the unification of Germany, which they generously allowed, eastern Europe remained un-militarised. It was not much to ask. Broadly, Germany has respected that. But the US and NATO held on to military dominance aside some cutbacks. Bush, Clinton, Cheney and the Pentagon were not going to dismantle the Cold War system because they were part of it. Then, a group of very well-paid people in NATO worked themselves back into a job. They had to recreate an enemy and the only one available was Russia. NATO gradually built a military alliance of nearly thirty states surrounding Russia. It was a slow, behind the scenes process, and it has worked. For example, they carried out military exercises involving 20,000 troops in 2020 "Defender 2020" and have done the same at various points along the border of Russian influence. Putin's invasion was evil, but the long build-up to the conflict was partly because NATO has needed its enemy. In all of these cases and many more, building the *enemy* goes on ceaselessly shaping the lie into our heads.

E. The weak ruler syndrome.

Sometimes, of course, an external enemy is used by dictators and democratically elected governments to deflect from their own domestic weaknesses or to maintain their military dictatorship. Militaristic leaders tend to underperform; their spending on military resources cuts their ability to provide for the people. There is a slide into militarism which gets worse and worse. Military dictators stay in imposed power while big armed forces impoverish their people. The Shah of Iran was like this, soaking up American weapons and neglecting his people. He was a puppet held in place by the US. In another example, Blair and Berlusconi concluded big arms contracts with Muammar Gaddafi which allowed him to dominate internally until the Arab Spring when he was ousted. The West had the pleasure of bombing its own weapons in Libya, creating a failed state. It is interesting how little the West backed the Arab Spring popular democratic moves in Egypt and elsewhere because its arms contracts had a higher priority. It has been a normal pattern. Arms often trump Democracy in strategic politics. France and the States were quite happy to sell arms to Brazil as it drifted towards military dictatorship. Abdullah Aziz al Saud in Saudi Arabia is showered in weapons by the US and UK while he cuts up his enemy and puts the bits in a suitcase. If regimes have money and will buy weapons, the Military-Industrial Complex make selling weapons their priority. They supply almost anyone however dubious. Ways are found round embargoes with state connivance. The great "democratic" powers do arms deals trumpeting democracy while destroying it through militarism.

But there is another level even below this. A whole range of arms producers have grown up who have cheaper labour costs than the big boys and will sell almost anywhere. China set the trend, but a range of other states in Eastern Europe and elsewhere followed the same pattern. Alongside these transactions are those carried out by the major arms producing countries which sell on and off load weapons not needed by their forces or super-ceded by later purchases. There are also weapons traders who operate illicitly buying and selling weapons for terrorist groups, mercenaries, drugs related operations, mining operations for western multinationals and rebel groups on the "black" or "grey" market. Much of the world is in chaos because of the small arms trade operating at a sub national level. It creates another level of enemies who plague the planet and requires that normal state forces arm to a higher level than they would otherwise and so the arms companies love them.

F. Of course, there must be an enemy.

And so, the conspiracy builds. At one level the arms companies are competing, but really the challenge is to expand the market and in this they are on the same side. When one sells, they all benefit. There used to be cigarette advertisements selling particular brands of cigarettes in competition, but really all the advertisements are saying the same thing. Any handsome man or pretty girl out there will smoke cigarettes, and so should you, whatever brand. Of course, cigarettes kill, but still you smoke. For decades the cigarette industry flourished on the simple idea that everybody smoked, and a bit of addiction helped. The arms companies similarly sell the message – we all need weapons all the time and they all stream the same message and we are all addicted.

The arms companies go one stage further in self-fulfilling prophecy. There is no smoke without fire. If everybody buys weapons, then of course there must be enemies. There is unlimited suspicion; the CIA spies on everyone. There will be an enemy somewhere. It is obvious. We all buy weapons and we all are enemies. It is heaven for the arms industry, but it messes up the world. People know from the news there are enemies somewhere, even everywhere. If governments get a bit flaky, we engineer another war to bring them into line. *The arms companies and militarists manufacture enemies because that is their business.* "All those idiots out there have not worked it out. Ha. Ha. Ha. Ha. Ha. They must be so thick."

12. ARMS CAUSE DICTATORS.

A. Progress, then regress.

Let us address the military dictator problem. A few years back in the good old days we used to believe that the world was getting better. In the modern era we understood a lot more because we were educated and gradually politics would improve around the world as democracy became universal. In 1945 we got rid of Hitler and obviously military dictators were wrong and democracy would spread to the newly developed ex-colonies now governing themselves and would rule the world. In the West we believed that there was a problem with Communism, or State Socialism, because they did not espouse Democracy, but we hoped eventually they would come round in the USSR and then in China to the Western Democratic Way. There was a slight problem with this worldview in that Nazi Germany, Italy, Spain, Portugal and Japan the strongest opponents of Democracy from 1935 to 1945 were very right-wing and not Communist, but we assumed that Democracy would emerge as the modern form of government for all humankind. The Cold War was a distraction, but things would get better and better. The Modern World would be Democratic. But it is not. Military dictators are everywhere.

We have known dictators are a problem for quite a while. Shakespeare summed up the problem with Julius Caesar.

> Why, man, he doth bestride the narrow world
> Like a Colossus, and we petty men
> Walk under his huge legs and peep about
> To find ourselves dishonourable graves.

Dictators are full of themselves and use others. They are a system of political selfishness and power over. Of course, Shakespeare did not find this out. Brutus had already got the message two thousand years ago and murdered Caesar. In the Old Testament they get a bad assessment a thousand more years further back. To state Jesus' version of the critique, governments should serve people, not lord it over them, and dictators lord it. They are, *you do what I say people* - with the rider, "or else I will kill you because I have the military behind me." They have never been very popular. The question is, if we have progressed so much, and are educated, and know, especially since Hitler, that dictators are bad and democracy is good, why is dictatorship a dominant mode of government around the world? What happened to progress? We have probably known that putting your head in a crocodile's mouth is not good for you for slightly longer, but no-one now does it; we learned the lesson. We have long known that dictators are bad, but half the world has them. It is probably not that people go around saying, "Come and be our dictator." But they seem at arrive everywhere.

Indeed, perhaps Democracy is actually being undermined even now. The Arab Spring democratic revolt in Egypt fizzled and died without western support so that western exports could carry on going to the military dictators. When after the last United States' Presidential and Congressional election a group of Trump supporters stormed Congress, it was sign that all is not well even in the US. Bolsonaro at the last Brazil Presidential election intimated he might not accept the result and riots occurred against it. Many states which have elections also capture and lock up or kill people who might be an electoral threat. We seem to be regressing from sound democratic politics around the world. Why?

B. Military Dictators everywhere.

Let us try to quantify this a bit. There are queries over when a military dictatorship is firmly in place but one list includes the following: Afghanistan, Algeria, Angola, Azerbaijan, Bahrain, Bangladesh, Belarus, Brunei, Burundi, Cambodia, Cameroon, Central African Republic, Chad, China, Cuba, Djibouti, Democratic Republic of the Congo, Egypt, Equatorial Guinea, Eritrea, Swaziland, Ethiopia, Gabon, Iran, Iraq, Kazakhstan, Loas, Libya, Myanmar, Nicaragua, N. Korea, Oman, Qatar, Republic of Congo, Russia, Rwanda, Saudi Arabia, Sudan, Tajikistan, Turkmenistan, Somalia, Turkey, Syria, Venezuela, Uganda, Uzbekistan, UAE, Vietnam, West Sahara, Yemen. *That comes almost exactly to about half of the world's population.* Possibly about another 10% live in states which have been, or threaten to be, military dictatorships, like the Philippines, Nigeria, Zambia, Zimbabwe, Chile and other states. Thus, bizarrely, a political model of government which almost everybody agrees is a disaster is the majority world model or close to it.

Nor is this "ideology", the old Cold War idea of Communism against Democracy which was supposed to be the problem. China has moved on in complex ways from Mao type Communism. Russia is now run by Putin and oligarchs in a fairly extreme form of capitalist control. The idea, peddled for sixty years, that Communism was the source of our miliary problems has gone. It is not, and was not. All along the problem was militarism. In almost all the other states the best description of the system of government is probably state corporatism where the military state supports the capitalist organisations either domestic or foreign in its borders in return for financial support and other backing from them. You can't blame Communism, Socialism, or whatever the old bogy was.

Indeed, now, the links with Capitalism have become even stronger. Military states did deals with the big multinationals. You pay us and we let you exploit our resources and we spend a chunk of our gains buying weapons. Then, in addition, the military leaders, frightened they might one day be overturned, hold a lot of their wealth in western banks. So, the West profits from the weapons, the multinational company deals and the dictators' bank accounts. All over the world the poor are paying for the costs of this form of power. So how are military dictators formed? The suspense must be killing you, but we need to go slowly. Are dictators really bad? We would not want to be criticizing a system that is good for us.

C. Are Dictators Bad?

Of course, we could take on most of world history - Genghis Khan, Caesar, Herod the Great, Ivan the Terrible, Charlamagne and all the other rulers who have been surrounded by armed forces keeping them in power. Often, they are glorified while the dead are ignored, but they were usually nasty killers. European royalty fitted a similar pattern with their military might. For a while "benevolent despots" ruled in palaces but with armed forces doing death. Idiot French and Spanish kings dressed up for the worst paintings in the world, but the monarchies went backstage as the sans culotte revolted and middle classes got the vote. Then twentieth century dictators emerged with propaganda which took a lot of people in. They would lead their people forward to a glorious future with marching soldiers goose-stepping and looking sideways; you were never allowed to ask where they were actually marching to. Probably it was the future, which actually arrives whether you march or not. Mussolini was Il Duce and Hitler was Der Führer, but of course they did not really sell the idea of military dictators successfully. These days dictators have smaller visions; they just want to stay in charge. They might dress up their regime with a series of projects or buildings which will give them a good image in the future, like Ceausescu's horrible Spring Palace with its silk wallpaper and ornate furniture. The fake life of Ceausescu is summed up by the fact that bears were sedated so that he could shoot them successfully and he had to shoot more of them than anyone else. Military dictators surround themselves with fake importance, while they do the necessary evil stuff behind the scenes.

They are usually bad or very bad. This is hardly scientific, but we could mention Pol Pot in Cambodia, Charles Taylor in Liberia, Suharto in Indonesia, Mengistu in Ethiopia, Kim Il Sung and Kim Jong Un in North Korea, Suharto in Indonesia, Amin in Uganda, Saddam Hussein in Iraq and many others killing into millions. They are not good advertising for military dictators. The daily news tells the same story. Jamal Khashoggi is murdered and cut up into bits and put in a suitcase for his criticism of the Saudi dictatorship of King Salman. Prison is used in Uganda to help keep democratic opponents at bay. The idea of bumping off anyone you do not like because you have the power to ignore the law, or to rewrite it, is not very nice. So probably dictators are bad.

Really, military dictators tend to be egos sitting around wanting their own way, expecting everything to revolve around them and their wishes. Usually, they cannot trust others and defend themselves with the military because they are so bad that someone wants to get rid of them. More than that, they usually cannot think, debate, listen, be honest, self-critical or acknowledge that others are right, because they have become the centre of their universe. We all know that Putin sitting at that long ornate table is too full of himself to not do bad things. Really, it is beyond discussion that dictators are bad. Everybody knows it and the evidence is in untold millions murdered because the military dictator has the power to. What a travesty of the human race.

So we face the question yet more directly. Why in this time of progress and yet more progress do we have a system of government which is bad or very bad controlling more than half the world's population? Why do we not stop it? Why have we not invented a way of preventing dictators which works?

D. What makes dictators Dictators?

This is all so intellectually demanding for you that we need to go slowly. Let us ask what causes military dictators? Why do people listen to them when they dictate? They could dictate, but finish up at the bottom of the garden talking to themselves, rather than running the government. The clue for those who are struggling is that they are *military* dictators. In fact, most of the time people call dictators, "military dictators". This signifies that they govern because they are backed by military forces. The military forces enforce what the dictator might want and prevent the government being chosen by the people. They all have military forces which mainly, apart from quarrels with neighbours, are there to keep the rulers ruling. They eliminate opposition. It is interesting that we have a word for when the military take over - a "coup", but don't have a word for standard military enforcement because it is so normal. We see the coup, but ignore the saucer. The military do not always have to stand there with guns, tanks and bombers to enforce the dictator's wishes. As long as people know they can be shot or imprisoned, they tend to conform to the dictator's wishes. Of course, the tanks came out in Tiananmen Square, but direct confrontation is failure and normal control through heavy policing is better. The military and the police want a quiet life as long as they are well paid and have the perks of the job. So, arms make dictators into Dictators and lower their standards in relation to human life and rights; that is why millions are killed, shot, bombed, eliminated and massacred. Bashir Al Assad in Syria drops bombs on his people when they do not toe his line. Leaders appear in front of their troops. Dictators are dictators because they are military dictators. Oh, that was so difficult.

E. Arming Dictators is a failed world policy..

Let's repeat it, in case you are not Einstein. We are now clear that half the world lives under dictators, dictators are bad or very bad and they are dictators because they are military dictators. Really you are reading this not because you are learning anything, but because the subject is ignored. We could tediously point out that the military are military because they are armed with weapons, but you understand that already. Rather, let us look at the way in which dictators are armed. We in the West, or rather Western Arms Manufacturers have done it avidly. Vickers and Schneider did it to Russia in the early 20th century. Western countries competed to arm the warlords in China in the 20s and 30s. In the 1930s the US, Britain and France armed Hitler, Stalin and the emerging military dictators of that era. We have armed almost all of that long list of dictatorships. In the fifties the United States linked extensive aid to the purchasing of arms, a technique used widely since, because western democratic governments have been keen to promote arms sales world-wide. The UK used aid for the Pergau Dam to support its arms sales to Malaysia in 1988. Often loans support sales; have the weapons now and pay later. Have a laugh on us in the UK.

> Documents....show that Argentina still owes debts to the UK government based on arms sales to the Argentine junta in the years leading up to the Falklands War...Argentina's £45 million restructured debt includes loans for two Type 42 Destroyers and two Lynx helicopter which were used in the invasion of the Falklands.[xxxi]

These were sales to *General* Gautieri. He won't be an aggressive ruler; the penguins will be safe, and he can pay us when he wants...

Meanwhile arms were sold around the world corrupting regimes into militarism and supporting military dictators. The USSR and China copied the process and the intensity of the militarisation was accelerated by the Cold War. In the major weapons producing states – the US, USSR, France, the UK, etc. the governments backed this arms export business and entertained dictators galore in order to get their business. Queen Elizabeth has had to do royal hospitality to Assad, Mugabe, Putin, Ceausescu, Mobutu, Suharto and Hamad bin Isa Al Khalifa to keep the arms contracts moving. Looking at Her Majesty's face, it seemed she did not always enjoy this jollity. So, democratic governments colluded in the selling of arms world-wide, often with the additional process of bribery as with the Lockheed scandals in the 1970s or the illegal BAe Systems bribes to the Saudi Royal Family and many other states. No other conclusion is possible. Armed dictators exist across half the planet because they are armed by our "democracies". We know they are a disaster, but we, the arms selling states, do it.

Repeatedly, states armed then became a problem, as with Iraq and Saddam Hussein. Donald Rumsfeld was sent by Reagan to offer him a big bundle of aid tied to arms sales, which he accepted and then it cost the US several trillion dollars to be at war with him. That was one of Rumsfeld's "unknown unknowns". When Robin Cook tried to bring ethics into the business of arms transfers in the Blair Administration he was brushed aside like a fly and Blair then carried on to do a big British deal with Gaddafi. So, we have arrived where we are largely through western arms sales supporting military dictators from the far east to the far west, from Duerte to Pinochet. The USSR/Russia and China have also helped. Let us give another example. Sweden sells 36 Gripen combat aircraft to Brazil with a $5 billion loan/aid package in 2015. Why? Because it wants to sell its planes. Meanwhile Brazil will be attacked by no-one and moved closer towards becoming a military dictatorship under Bolsonaro. It was an irresponsible sale by Sweden, and they are one of the best governments around. It is no mystery. The arms companies and superpower governments act surprised at military dictators, or pretend they do not exist, but they have done this thing. It is so obvious.

Of course, the hypocrites brush it under the table. They do not say "There are military dictators around the world governing badly and destroying democracy because we, and those who have copied us, have been selling arms wholesale for seventy years." The System tries to make it invisible or pretend innocence. They make peace noises and sell more weapons. We have a moral protest when killing takes place, which sees us through. Oh poor Khashoggi cut up, how terrible, but we must keep supplying bombs so that Yemen can be flattened because Saudi pays us well, sorry, is our ally against Iran. *Our world-wide hypocrisy forges the world-wide problem.* We are so used to it that we do not even notice. But that is the way the world is run and it is a disaster. It is time to take stock. We come to the crunch.

G. Big problem – Small solutions?

Here is a problem which afflicts half the population of the world and we are convinced we can do nothing about it. We must just live with four billion people under military dictatorships and probably more on the way as more arms are sold. Anything we do is going to be small and ineffective. Except that is precisely the problem with our thinking. *Hitting a big problem with a small solution is going to fail and the militarists lock us into thinking about small solutions. The World is on fire. How many water pistols can we afford?* **A BIG PROBLEM NEEDS A BIG SOLUTION. WORLD DISARMAMENT MEETS IT AND PROPERLY ADDRESSES WORLD-WIDE MILITARISM.** *Anything else is just messing about.* The big solution also ends wars, mass killing, mass trauma, world poverty, and cuts CO_2 by 5-10%. We see and accept the big answer. Most of the world's population saw it a hundred years ago in the lead up to the World Disarmament Conference in Geneva. Then we allowed the big problem to be addressed by the big answer, but it was sabotaged by the militarists. This time we see it through. All cut world arms by 20% a year for five years until it is all done. We bring military dictators into line, because they have democratic populations who can vote for an end to military dictators. We do not just throw up our hands and say, "Oh dearie me! Half the world is under military dictators! How absolutely horrible! And we thought they were nice when we gave them weapons! What should we wear tonight?" We democratize the world and those under military dictators. People can vote on international petitions already to the tune of half a billion or more. All people vote to end weapons, military dictators and crack this system of soldiers marching around protecting idiots. All that is needed is for us little people to vote for unmilitary democracy. Military dictators cannot cope with even a million people who rightly say the system must be reformed. When the whole world is undergoing reformation out of militarism, dictators will want to retire quietly as we give one another peace and put fear to bed. Billions of us ordinary people know that military dictatorships do not work. We merely need to see: Big Problem - Big Solution. And Do It. We can all do it and vote for Full World Multilateral Disarmament.

F. Clear-eyed Faith.

Suddenly the issue becomes clear. Wars and militarism are a massive world problem, as we see again from Ukraine. Half the world's population live under military dictatorships and more fear war. In the face of this vast problem, we see that any small attempts to put things right are bound to fail, to be bulldozed aside by more arms, tension and wars. Little reforms are engulfed. We despair, feel helpless and especially become fatalist. This is inevitable. Until that is, we address the Big Problem with the Big Solution. You do not address a major motorway traffic jam with an ant carrying a flag. We think the size of the problem.

Christians should see this. Jesus, very deliberately said faith could move mountains. Oh, he was just exaggerating; he did not mean it. If so, he was blatant. He even said *not much faith* can move mountains, faith the size of a seed can hump over a mighty mountain. Perhaps we Christians think he is over the top, or it is wishful thinking, although we would not *say* that. But perhaps he is steady accurate, pushing us to see clearly, right all the way and offering us the true faith, the faith that will disarm the crazy, fighting world. He was insistent. "You can say to this mountain, 'Go throw yourself into the sea,' and it will be done." The mountain was to be thrown in the sea, not just landscaped. What is he on about? Militarism is a mountain. It and military dictatorships need to be thrown into the sea, freeing people up, ushering in peace. All we do is merely see that full world disarmament is the necessary big answer to the big problem. The logic is obvious. Then the moving can be done. After all, Isaiah has been going on about it for a long time. Jesus invites each of us to do a little. How much? If each of us into billions do a bucket worth of moving, it will be done. Actually, a million people doing two minutes each on a mass petition would get everything rolling. Then a billion or more others saying they do not want to live under military dictators, or as superpowers, and the world would be turned. A lot of people doing this little could change the world. We disarm the world – one piece of UN legislation – properly implemented. It is not difficult; we merely have to vote effectively. It is good, so good for all of us, the healing of the planet. We do it. In five years it is finished - the big solution to the big problem. Jesus left his peace with us two millennia ago. Oh, now we see what you mean. You did really mean that mountain moving thing. We merely take the key out of our pockets, and turn it in the lock. But first we put some more nails in the military coffin.

13.MILITARISM MESSES UP AFRICA.

A. African Militarism.

One more nail in the coffin is the way it corrupts Continents. We could easily have chosen others. Africa contains no superpowers. It is a vast continent of smallish and some bigger states with a more rural economy that others on the planet. It was largely colonially controlled through to about 1960. Aside North Africa, and providing troops, it was mainly outside the two World Wars and involved in none of the big armament confrontations of nuclear weapons, bombers, missiles, warships and tank warfare. Yet still militarism has dominated Africa. In the last sixty or so years governments have been marked by a high degree of central military organisation and we need to ask why. First, we undertake an overall survey of the evidence that militarism is tangled in African governance. Countries are presented in alphabetical order.

B. It corrupts most African Governments.

In **Algeria** General Gaid Salah is in charge of the government. He ousted the President; the clue is in the word, "General". In **Angola** a long civil war fuelled by US-Soviet military input left 4m people, a third of the population, displaced. Some kind of stable politics is emerging though with flawed elections. **Burkina Faso** has a military junta in power and has had ten coups since independence. In **Burundi** a 2015 coup attempt has de-stabilised the system. The **Central African Republic** has armed groups and mercenaries in control of areas. General Mahamet Déby now controls **Chad**. The **Republic of the Congo** has had a recent civil war, army control and a ceasefire in December, 2017.The **Democratic Republic of the Congo** had military rule by Mobutu and a civil war in which 5m died. Kabila became leader with military power vested in his office and since 2008 a major war has raged in Kivu Province. Its rich resources lead western multinational companies and militias to run much of the country in their own interests. In **Ivory Coast** militarily disputed elections and a civil war in 2011 led to President Ouattara being backed by the military, probably correctly. In **Egypt** in 2013 President Morsi was removed from power in a coup d' état. El Sisi now governs through military control. **Ethiopia** is a one-party state with no opposition MPs in Parliament, a Civil war in Tigray Province and is fighting in **Eritrea**, another totally destabilised state. **Ghana** is now a democracy with a strong regional military force. Earlier, Nkrumah was evicted from power in a coup, possibly with US involvement. There were a series of coups through the 60s to 80s. The **Guinea** National Assembly did not meet for five years 2008-13 through army control. More recently, there were doubtful elections and a 2021 military coup. **Liberia** has had two civil wars involving the notorious military figures James Doe and Charles Taylor and now has the former warlord Joshua Blahyi running the state. **Libya** was run by Colonel Gaddafi after a military coup in 1969 through to the Civil War in 2011. He was heavily armed after an agreement with Blair and Berlusconi, lost the Arab Spring conflict through western involvement and the state has been in military chaos since. **Madagascar** has had two decades of disturbance and a military uprising. In **Mali** there was a military coup in 2012 and two in the 2020s with the military in charge now. In **Mauritania** a military coup in 2008 rumbles on. **Niger** has had many military regimes, but more recently, sound elections, despite a coup attempt in 2021. **Nigeria** had military dictators from 1966 to 1999 and has moved over to more stable democratic governments, though subject to Islamic-Christian tension. In the north Boko Haram have run a terrorist campaign for more than a decade, killing, kidnapping, displacing and destroying through their weapons. They are now linked to ISIS. **Ruanda** had a Civil War involving genocidal murders. It now has elections but has effectively become a one-party state under Kigami. He outlawed the main opposition party so that he can win elections. Its army has operated in the DRC in relation to expensive western mineral extractions and Kigami is useful to rich western companies and a ruthless military dictator. **Sierra Leone** had an eleven-year Civil War. In 1998-9 a coup led to UN peacekeeping forces trying to stabilize government. **Somalia** has had a long insurgency, torrid relationships with the Ethiopian military and a substantial breakdown and fragmentation of civil government. In **South Africa** the ex-President Zuma is currently being charged with a corrupt arms deal. South Africa is the only country thus far to withdraw from having nuclear weapons. **Sudan** had a long Civil War between the North and the South involving deep disruption of the South until it became independent. Half a million people lost their lives. When the South became independent, it too had a Civil War killing a further 300-400,000 people. There have been coups in 2021 in the North and instability in the South. Civil War has broken out in the North in 2023. **Togo** has been governed by a Father-Son monopoly backed by the military in a total package of control. **Tunisia** was controlled by President Ben Ali, an ex-military man and Minister of Defence from 1987 to 2011. Once he managed to get 99% votes in re-election and ran a highly repressive regime. Presently, Parliament is suspended. **Uganda** has been a military dictatorship more or less since independence under Idi Amin and Yoweri Museveni. Parliament is highly paid and docile. The LRA in the North creates more problems. **Zimbabwe** had white colonial military control and then the military dictatorship of Mugabe and a strong military presence since he was ousted. There are other states not covered, but the problem is evident.

This is a deep pattern of destructive interference in the life and politics of Africa, and it needs explaining, addressing, and eradicating. Nothing less is acceptable. The cost is enormous. Perhaps five million children in Africa under the age of five died as a result of armed conflict between 1995 and 2015.[xxxii] Many states have been paralysed and badly ruled.

C. Forming African Military Establishments.

How are these militaristic regimes formed? There are probably several contributions.

1. **Colonial military training.**
   The colonial powers, Britain, France, Belgium, Germany, Portugal and Italy trained "native" soldiers and militias to run their colonies for a century or more. They were trained, often in the imperial country, well paid and used to being in charge. When

independence came some of them became Prime Minister or President, either through leading independence movements or as transitional figures. Links were retained with the colonial militaries and suppliers of arms, and the militaries became close to a central establishment which was well off, could exploit business deals and the wealth at the centre. Both the French and British ex-empires operated in this way, selling arms, offering loans, doing deals and linking in with continuing colonial-like military regimes.

2. **Cold War Militarism.**
    The United States avidly spread arms, often with aid, after WW2 as part of the build-up in the Cold War and partly to obtain economic dominance in the continent. The USSR did the same. The Cold War pushed arms on one side or the other in most African states and produced wars in Congo, Angola, Eritrea, Yemen, Guinea-Bissau, Mozambique, Ethiopia, Ogaden and Namibia.

3. **Corruption through multi-national corporations.**
    Africa has a lot of natural resources, especially in states like DRC and Angola. Western companies, and now China, want to extract these and are keen to do deals, either with governments or with militaries which control an area. Obviously, the commodity, geography and kind of deal varies, but often the military can be close to these deals and the money made from them.

4. **Populist politics and Managed Elections.** Frequently those in power seek to stay there, and the normal route is through managed elections involving restrictions and voting control. The military are often used to "channel" elections through various forms of military supervision, disqualifications, and fixing results. Occasionally African militaries have tried to stop this. More often they have supported the ruler seeking full control and preventing opposition. Single or dominant parties have been normal and as a consequence attempted military coups have often been seen as the way to change governments. All of these processes keep the military close to power.

5. **The Proliferation of Small Arms.** Mainly the big arms have been absent from Africa, and it has concentrated therefore mainly on soldiers, rifles and small arms. These move in unregulated transfers both from Russia and the West, and also though more production in Africa's main industrial centres. They are low cost, threaten people in large numbers and are very destructive of life and national cohesion as in Nigeria, DRC, Sudan, Ethiopia and many other states.

6. **Islamic Militarism.** The Islamic-Western confrontation in the middle east has been transposed by terrorist groups into north and Central Africa again causing disruption, death, refugees and military responses.

The effects of these processes is to produce widespread endemic small-scale militarism affecting most African states and shaping their political formation. All the attempts to address it have been piecemeal, mainly because the Russian and Western powers, multinationals and arms people *do not want reform* upsetting their profits, neither do most of the entrenched African politicians or militaries. It mirrors the issue we address later, namely that the established powers are militarist and will not bring about change through reform while they are dominant. Any sane person who thinks will agree that Africa should be fully demilitarised. So let African people and all of us do it, removing weapons and the destructive power of weapons for all Africa's people as throughout the world. It can transform the continent for great good immediately. It requires a mass popular movement which will insist on bringing it about. It will be a totally popular policy, perhaps the most popular on the planet, and the challenge in Africa, as in the rest of the world, is to merely make people aware it can be done. It can. We discuss it later. A great continent, crippled by militarism and military establishments, waits for reform....

14. ON NOT BEING RIGHT.

This chapter is mood. In the next chapter we will look at the central reason why militarism is truly worse than dead, the disaster far worse than all earthquakes. Anybody can understand why that is the case, even with a dead horse between their ears, but we all carry on carrying on supporting this mausoleum for the masses, this money eating bank, this we-can-kill-you idea. We therefore ceremonially murder militarism in the next chapter. But there must be an explanation of why we support this terminal failure, a mood that has settled on us all, zombie like, which needs removing. It will be big, a vast cultural fog, but we need to try to read ourselves before we face ending militarism straight.

A. The self-right christian west.

This might be it. It has been there a long time. For two millennia and more, since at least the Romans, there has been a feeling which has settled on Europe and the West that it is right. We are right and the others are wrong. It is deeper than thought. It is linked to conquest; we conquer because we are right. It is the right to rule and tell others what to do. It is: you must learn our language, Roman or English. It is the right to have slaves and servants. It is the enforced submission of colonies. It is the recruitment into the system of the subdued populations or the aggressive expansion of the right people into other lands. It is Caesar conquering Britain or rather Europe, because for a long while this superiority settled across the Roman Empire. The Spanish Conquistadores or Columbus discovering the New World were copying. It is sedentary colonials fanned to keep cool by sepoys. We are the people who run the show and can order you around, because, of course we are right. Probably, all the world has been like this – the Pharaohs, Babylonians, Eastern rulers and more. For much of its history China was ruled by the literati, a group of educated bureaucrats, who were automatically given deference and shaped government. The Indian caste system reflected similar accepted patterns of superiority and inferiority. It is probably a universal tendency, but it has had a Roman form in

Europe and the West which fused with militarism in shaping the modern world.

It has partly dominated Christianity. The love your enemies, growing in a small, subjugated Jewish-rooted faith, spread by walking, we-are-all-sinners, true Christianity with its toe-curling attack on self-righteousness has often given way to the established church, invade with the sword and Bible, we are always right, God will give you the victory christianity of the self-right. It is difficult to admit how compromised Christianity is, but the evidence is incontrovertibly there. Christianity, lined up with state aggression, slaves, conquest, the establishments of states and empires, came easily to churches time after time. Christianity in the West has often gone along with the establishment, as if the Creator would line up behind Brit'n or Ameerica in wars like some cheerleader. Of course, there have been other better Christian responses. Often missionaries went without aggression, learned the local languages, built hospitals and schools and became martyrs. Now that is courage. They are God's real army.

There was the enormous arrogance of the Spanish and Portuguese Empires, bringing Christianity along with organised murder to the South American Continent while looting gold and anything else to take back to their kings and aristocracy, stiffly dressed up to be painted by Velazquez in their self-importance. There are the Dutch, trading around the world with gunships, hoovering up colonies in the Far East when they had heroically "broken free" from control by the Spanish Empire and then doing blue china as their own. There are the French, glorying in the Sun King and the splendour of Versailles, then in Napoleon the Conqueror, but finding that something had gone wrong somewhere and having occasional revolutions. There are minor imperial powers, like Belgium, cruel beyond belief - chop off their arms if they do not get enough rubber today. All of them have their Cathedrals and church buildings, and, as Leslie Newbiggin pointed out, they are conquerors' churches. They say they follow the Jesus who asked that they own their sin before God, who pointed out what hypocrisy was like, and insisted on the evil done in dark places being brought to the light. Real Christianity was prostituted.

Christian self-examination, peace, forgiveness, patience, humility became self-righteous arrogance. Churches allied themselves with conquest, war and domination. Their mentors did: What sin? Kill your neighbour. Of course, we are right, and those who take the sword will bring civilisation. The rule systems refined hypocrisy and would use nice, and-also-with-you, pliable Christianity and Christians like plasticine.

Of course, other religions have replicated this. Islam was absolute right in all its conquests and if we interviewed all the petty and big dictators of history, of course they were all right. My will be done. I am good for you. It is mood. It is *we know best*, while you poor natives need to bow and scrape and do what we tell you. It is before thought, the assumption that will overarch all things. It goes along with servants, country estates and the sense of the innate right to rule. We will train you to be good soldiers for us. It was aristocratic Europe with suppliant populations, the Unholy Roman Empire.

B. Great Britain

Britain, Great Britain, was perhaps the worst. It was busy picking up colonies around the world not merely because it had aggressive naval vessels, cannon and guns but because it was better. It believed it was superior to the native populations wherever it went and it hoovered up 14 million square miles around the globe to be the British Empire. We are the British, the rightest of all, the fair's fair British who just happened to have a navy and guns so that they could civilise the world. The schools for the ruling class did Latin and Roman History, so that they could understand ruling imperial civilisation and history and also ritualised Jesus out of sight. Rule Britannia moved easily through from Caesar in Britain and straight roads to Britain everywhere else building railways. Britain aimed to rule the waves and the people over the waves. It used its navy to organise the international slave trade around Africa and America and Britain. Conquest, dealing in cheap human sales for profit and a careless disregard for life was dominant until 1807 when it became a matter of conscience and the slave owners were compensated for their "losses", but not the slaves for their slavery. Oh India, we will drink your tea while you wear our cotton goods made with your cotton while we destroy your cotton industry. Oh, and thanks for the diamonds. We confiscated Hong Kong for 150 years and fined China for *opposing* our Right to make them opium addicts, and later humiliated them further by burning down the Emperor's Summer palace. We used the vast Indian economy to our own ends and set up other colonies around the world which suited us, for mahogany, sugar, or peanuts. The British were sure of themselves. They had a stiff upper lip. They were good for everybody. Their rule brought civilisation to the countries they governed. Sometimes the natives needed killing because they rebelled, but usually they were just grateful for being part of the British Empire. All of this we regarded as normal.

We had the right to govern across the world, because we were democratic. We gave the people, or actually, until 1918 the richer men, the right to vote and had the mother of Parliaments, and so we were right in the way we controlled the colonies undemocratically. Slowly, the contradiction dawned that autocratic rule over colonies while proclaiming democracy at home was incompatible. It took a hundred years to work out the inconsistency. Then, governing all round the world slowly became impractical, and finance worked faster than logic. Churchill had not given it up on empire even in the 1950s. By then, everybody was learning our language and our talk became normal. We then congratulated ourselves on granting colonies independence, so that they too could learn democracy and English. So, for a long time the British were, and are, insufferably right.

C. The Great U. S. of A.

But Britain was not the last word. The Founding Fathers (the unnoticed myth) soon established themselves with slaves and dominance. The American Declaration of Independence was just the arrogant teenager leaving home. Then he grew bigger. Millions of Europeans flocked over and all learned nearly English, thank goodness, and the United States of America grew bigger, Europe free of mistakes, the New World as opposed to the old European World. It was moral and freed the slaves, after a very late Civil War, while keeping the ex-slaves as cheap labour. It struck gold and oil and had vast tracts of land fertile with sweetcorn, turkeys and hamburgers. The same sense of entitlement was present. It was Cowboys and Indians when really the native populations of North America were being decimated by shooting and disease in their own country. As a boy I watched the boring Lone Ranger, with Tonto, sorting things out while Mum got the tea ready. He was always right, with a gun, on a white horse. I learned that Cowboys with guns were good, because they shot guns out of the hands of baddies without killing them.

America was rich and Christian. It did Christianity its way - big churches, big rallies, conversion and membership, but the State was neutral, above everything, and America was big, brave, democratic and free. It had to rescue Europe in WW1 and then again in WW2 and then again from the USSR and planted freedom around the world as the Great Superpower. It was the Good Power. The Brits, following Churchill, became poodles, or part of a Special Relationship, and most countries were part of, or bribed into, the Free World. We were All Right. We are All Right. We are educated. Our technologies can sort everything out, and the world is made up of Goodies like most of us and Baddies like Communists and Ex-Communists. That is the world we live in. It has led the world for eighty years, dominating the United Nations, sorting states for its convenience, becoming the world currency, incurring debt and armed itself to the hilt because it must defend the free world and punishing all who do not toe its line. Its insane self-belief is measured by the fact that, in the heads of tens of millions, Christianity could be morphed into Trumpery. And so, the Younited States was all right. Of course, it has done good, been generous and melded many ethnic groups into a nation, but it was, and is, all right.

We do not even hear the multiple modulated systems of self-congratulation in other countries. The French, slightly outdone by the British Empire, do culture and sophistication, and sell arms. The Italians, lusting after colonies for a while, now do permanent Renaissance. Europe is now sane and knows how to live together. Britain, Great Britain, as we still call ourselves, in case anyone does not notice, has given up natural superiority but says we are "leading the world" through an idiot Prime Minister. Trump was a snake oil salesman for "Make America Great Again". It is all normal. We are all inside the long history of self-rightness. Our ceremonies, cities, events, media, dress, buildings, food, sports teams, civic and national life live in this self-congratulation. Of course, sometimes the British and the French are quite nice, as the privileged can afford to be, but the premiss is always that we are right and the other is wrong. For decades, global warming could not be, because Western Consumerism was right. The USSR, Cuba, China, Iran, Russia and others must be wrong and we must arm against them for the right to win. It is so normal. I and you do not have to think we are right. We Just Are.

D. The Big Hypocrisy - Killing, Sin and Truth.

Sin is being wrong. Hey, I am the problem. Christianity, especially Jesus, attacks sin big time. He went around telling everybody they were sinners and should sort themselves out, but they cannot even do that. It is surprising he is popular at all. He also did a big range of sins – lust, greed, hypocrisy, superiority, self-promotion, aggression, status, self-congratulation, selfishness, pride, not forgiving people and lots more. Broadly speaking, he nailed all of us, especially the saints. He spent a lot of time addressing those who thought they were right with rather aggressive language – you "brood of vipers", "hypocrites", "blind guides". Those are negative. He knew exactly what he was doing. In modern parlance he was deconstructing being right, demolishing it, pulverizing it, because it destroys the truthfulness of self-examination before God. He went all the way. You die to self, so that there is no self to be right. So, Jesus undid being right, and western fake christianity does it up again.

Actually, most western people ignore the vast cultural problem of self-righteousness. It is becoming more difficult because historians, woke historians we now call them, insist of naming all the bad things the west has done. Slavery, racism, exploitation, concentration camps, were then, and occasionally turn up now. Sometimes, Christians just do Jesus and a little bit of "love", without questioning themselves, while the baddies are over the ocean. Many sins are the basis of advertising appeals and dominate popular culture and so they cannot be wrong. We are hourly invited to selfishness, envy, pride, dishonesty, coveting, discord, ambition, idolatry and hatred. Seeing these as sin is completely out of fashion, because we do not need to question ourselves. We are right whether we are CEO, President, or buying clothes. Being wrong is wrapped up, kept off the agenda. In our mood being right is deeper than nationalism, as it was in Jesus' time. It is the deepest. It dwells there, under all. It is My Way. Thus, we cannot be wrong about militarism. If the State has to kill people industrially, that is unfortunate. How could all of us be wrong for a hundred years when we are right. Remember Hitler. We got rid of Hitler. Whatever we do, we remember Hitler, because Hitler shows we are right.

E. Jesus and Murder.

Jesus and murder are interesting. Of course, murder was and is wrong, arrogant, self-worship, hating the to-be-loved neighbour. Jesus looked behind murder to the anger that might generate it and that was wrong too. He insisted on putting his own upcoming murder on the table. It is stark. He is discussing with a load of respectable people, our equivalent of an academic discussion, making the point that everybody who sins becomes a *slave* to sin. It takes them over and they are no longer in charge. Yes, there are addictions to alcohol, smoking, money, gambling, fame and weapons. It is slavery; it dominates people and ends the possibility of living openly before God. Then suddenly he says, "You are out to kill me." He brings the Truth up. Jesus insists that they are running from the truth and have sold themselves to the devil, the father of lies. He is directly accusing them, standing there in an ordinary situation, pillars of society, of being evil, out to kill him and being trapped in it. Actually, Jesus was right; the evidence emerged; they did kill him. He was addressing murder before it happened. But in their view, he was merely one person and he had to go for the sake of the nation.

When we read this stuff, we are, of course, on Jesus' side and the baddies put him on the cross to save us from our sins - problem solved, but that is not where we really are. We are with the respectable people insisting that it is unfortunate that people are dying in Yemen, Syria, Iraq, Ukraine or wherever because we are slaves to militarism and we are right. If sadly, it is necessary, we will shoot them. We have been doing it so long we do not even think it needs addressing. We trust our ancestors. We believe we will not kill "unnecessarily", frequently against the evidence. We might even mumble in church about repentance, but we don't own that we are the problem. We have not really heard Jesus.

That might overall be why we carry on. We think we are right, when we are the problem. We have long come to terms with killing and the means of killing and all the other "necessary" evils. Jesus said, "what is done in the secret places, must be shouted from the housetops." Bring things out into the light and evil loses. But our guys try to keep them hidden. Julian Assange brings the US military dirty linen out into the light and the US aims to eliminate him, aided by its poodle, Britain, in a long and cruel vendetta. How dare he show the world the truth? We keep the uncomfortable stuff hidden enough not to bother us.

All of us, me, you and millions more need to stop the western, freedom, good for the world, paternalistic self-congratulation and face where we are - doing and selling militarism, worldwide, doing wrong as right, because we are right. We may not be as much on Jesus' side as some of us think we are. We may be children of the devil.

F. There are no Baddies and Goodies.

The militarists depend on Baddies and Goodies and we are Goodies. The Kaiser was bad and we were good. Hitler was bad and we were good. Now Putin is sooo bad and we are good. So goes the propaganda, propping up the system. But it is half wrong. British militarism (and lies) contributed to World War One. British militarism opened up the way for Hitler right through to the Appeasers and Munich, and America funded and armed him. NATO has contributed to the present Ukraine confrontation and War. Western weapons corrupt countless regimes. It is not Bad and Good. It is Bad and Bad. All militarisms are bad.

Stalin was bad. Churchill was bad. Britain was bad in the Boer War, in World War Two, in Africa, in Iraq, Afghanistan, Libya, Syria and Yemen because we are militarists. The US was bad in the Congo, Cuba, Iran, Vietnam, Iraq and central America. The US stoked the Cold War and in the Cold War exactly the same kind of calculations and moves were carried out on both sides for half a century. It is brain dead to say that one side was bad and the other was good. All the national constructions where we see "our" militaries as "good" in all the States around the world are false, because they are adding to the problem. That is why it has been, and is, so big. We are all bad. You would think there would be some level of self-awareness, but there is not, because at the heart of Militarism is the need to be right. We - me, you, everyone - are wretched, need to repent, unthink, unsay, un-support the killing machine we have backed. We should do it on our knees before God on concrete for fifteen minutes hitting our heads with a hammer so that it sinks in. We can try real repentance. Yes, Lord, we are all wrong.

G. Denial - Blair and Iraq.

The United States military system in 2003, led by Dick Cheney, Donald Rumsfeld, Paul Wolfowitz, parts of the military, and arms companies including Haliburton wanted a war with Iraq. Bush agreed with them. The US had been attacked on 9/11 and was stung, looking for revenge. The attack was not by Iraq. The War in Afghanistan was ineffective. Al Qaeda melted away and the US needed to show they were invincible. Tony Blair moved in. Bush was intellectually challenged and it was easy for Blair to shine in comparison to him in the United States, a bigger stage than little ol' Britain, and Blair pushed for War, the nearly world leader. He had defended BAe Systems as being above the law, done weapons deals in Libya and elsewhere and was the normal we-are-doing-good militarist. The world was told Iraq had Weapons of Mass Destruction, and therefore Saddam was breaking his agreement with the UN. The UN was told the same, against its weapons' inspectors report.

The war had to take place. Blair and his inner circle – Alasdair Campbell and Peter Mandelson – swung the Cabinet, Civil Service and Parliament round to his view. We must go to War. The Military was cautious, even against. The Secret Services were used to present false evidence of the central claim that Saddam had Weapons of Mass Destruction – nuclear, chemical and biological. The weight of propaganda across the world media was vast. It was the dominant story despite widespread dissent. But it was untrue. More than that, it was a deliberated lie.

Glen Rangwala of the Politics Department here at Cambridge helped expose it. He put up on the web an interview conducted by a number of UN experts interrogating General Hussein Kamel. Hussein was no ordinary General, but had been in charge of Iraq's full military system since the First Iraq War. He was also Saddam's son-in-law and had defected to the west in the late 1990s - hence the interview. He explained that because of the thoroughness of the UN weapon inspectors work, the Iraqi WMD had *had* to be all thoroughly destroyed. They were gone. He explained the process, evaluated information and points raised by the UN experts, and answered their questions with strategic, military and executive expertise. In the transcript, Kamel states bluntly: "All weapons — biological, chemical, missile, nuclear, were destroyed." The evidence fitted and the conclusion was accepted, although the UNSCOM weapon inspectors carried on with their work. Kamel had other written evidence. It meshed with the inspectors. Clearly, he was telling the truth. He was murdered 23/2/1996 by Saddam while returning with his family to Iraq; he was hardly a Saddam stooge. Meanwhile, UK Government propaganda was saying the opposite. Yet, the Hussein Kamel evidence had to be available to Blair, Bush and the others before war was declared. It was unthinkable it was not known by them. Meanwhile, Campbell was constructing a "Dodgy Dossier" from a student paper and using any statement that helped create the illusion that WMD were there. Blair was lying, not mistaken, inside the being-right western bubble. A million marched through London protesting the War. The lie carried the day.

The other main actors were given false scripts to present. Watching Jack Straw and Conan Powell carefully on TV, it was evident that they knew they were lying when they gave evidence to the UN, acting being right. So, the US and the UK went to war on the basis of a known lie in defiance of international law and the United Nations. Saddam, because he was disarmed, was an easy foe to defeat and *we were right*. Blair and others never admitted the lie but acted right, wriggling in a slough of duplicity for years to come. We were not right, but deeply wrong, to the death of a quarter to a half million people, but to the world public we have insisted that we were right because we are always right. Still, the fiction rules. We were not wrong and Blair is heading for the grave where he will lie and no longer lie.

H. The Self Rightness of Militarism.

Self-right military power is a religion. It has corrupted much of world history and Christianity since the time of Philip the Great, Genghis Kahn, the Caesars, Ivan the Terrible, Napoleon down to Adolf. They have all done conquest, mowing down the natives with spears, swords, rifles, cannon, charges, tanks, bombs and destruction. It is My Will Be Done, an iron will which must be right. Barbarossa was Hitler's great imposition of his Will on Russia. It is religious and ultimate. It goose-steps. It is not just the will of conquest, but the faith that, through conquest and control, all the world's problems are solved by Me. Might is really right. When we are in charge, things will be OK.

The mighty centre is worshipped. That is why Nebuchadnezzar had a great statue of himself made and the Caesars had big statues all over the Empire and Hitler had the Nuremburg rallies. He wanted people to worship him. He was right. The Führer was marching into the future and the Aryan Volk were the pinnacle of civilisation. It was why Victoria was made Empress of India and feted in that extraordinary Durbah in Delhi in 1877. This militarist faith belongs to us all, because weapons blow up the sense of self-importance. That is why rulers surround themselves with cohorts of smartly dressed soldiers and Jesus didn't. Anyone who commits to the idea of being in control through military might, is worshipping the same god - themselves. The evil of fighting and war is the ego constructed on destruction.

134

This self-rightness tends to be unquestioning. One of the three planes which bombed Hiroshima was called Necessary Evil. Of course, the evil was necessary if the West said so. President Truman did not even question it. We are asked *not to doubt* all the military failures of the past century of more and believe that the problem is individuals like the Kaiser, Hitler and Stalin. But honest history shows military self-rightness has been wrong time after time. Weapons kill. Enemies are created. Both sides threaten. Arms escalate. When you are inside militarism, it enslaves you, as Jesus said. All systems of control are evil, and there is at the centre of militarism a hell which it cannot erase. It will always fail.

I. We read the Old Testament.

We need to change the mood. We need a perspective bigger that the great killing system, one which questions it. We need to walk away from the long history of western superiority into steady realism. Think for a moment about the Old Testament, part of the greatest book on earth. A Nazi might read the Old Testament and see that the Jews were to blame, but of course that is completely wrong. The Jews in the Old and New Testaments and throughout history have been no worse than anyone else and often far, far, better. Rather, instead of endless books down the ages praising the great conquerors, the lording rulers, the Old Testament shows people and rulers serially messing up. The same truth of failure is told to David, Solomon, Rehoboam, Ahab, Hezekiah and Nebuchadnezzar so that they might even understand how they have gone wrong. Always the empires of military power are criticised by the prophets, because they are wrong in their view of power. Daniel does it wholesale. "Then a mighty king will appear, who will rule with great power and do as he pleases. After he has appeared, his empire will be broken up and parcelled out towards the four winds of heaven... the king of the South will wage war with a large and powerful army, but he will not be able to stand because of the plots devised against him... the two kings with their hearts set on evil, will sit at the same table and lie to each other, but to no avail, because an end will still come at the appointed time..." (Daniel 10)

God has them in derision. They build themselves up with weapons from chariots to nuclear weapons and posture across the globe, but what does it amount to? They defeat and are defeated. Always there is another way than the stupidity of evil and conquest, and the captive children of Israel are invited to see beyond the futility of fighting. Alongside the long, depressing evidence of rulers big and small failing to do their job, the good news also emerges. Isaiah is helped by God to see eventually the world will not learn war any more. The swords and chariots and the arrogance of military man will be brought low. We still face the same pointless militarism directly, but perhaps in truth we can see that we have gone astray by reading the Old Testament. Here is Nineveh. "Woe to the city of blood, full of lies, full of plunder, never without victims... flashing swords. "I am against you, declares the Lord Almighty.. I will treat you with contempt and make you a spectacle... " (Nahum 3) It is the same for Berlin, Tokyo, London, Paris and New York. The blood that we spill comes back to us as judgement. Time we wised up...

15. SELLING DEATH AND DESTRUCTION IS A FAILED SYSTEM.

A. The god of Destruction.

Now we go for the centre of the failure. Militarism fails because its god is Destruction. It puts its faith in Destruction – chariots, swords, guns, millions of shells, carpet bombing, Hiroshima and Nagasaki, chemical destruction in Vietnam, the dereliction of cities and threatening the destruction of the planet. We stop and accept this simple but profound truth. Killing and destruction is a false object of worship. Militarism *invests* in destruction to shape the future. Both sides destroy in wars. If you have faith in destruction, it cannot come good. Nobody buys a television set with a label saying, "This will blow up." Jesus put it clearly. "Those who take the sword *perish* by the sword." It is a kill and destroy system and cannot be anything else. When you are banging your head against the wall, stop. That is why we must disarm the world. Weapons are not goods, but very, very bad. They are worse than bad; they destroy goods including the most precious we have. There is no way round, over or under that problem. It is just the case and we must acknowledge it. We have been deluded wholesale by propaganda systems better than Goebbels into believing that destruction is good, but it is not, especially as a world system. Buying destruction is silly. It goofs the planet. Gently, we depart this faith.

B. The Economics of Destruction.

There is the subsequent question of why we have bought these bads of killing and mass destruction for so long? These economic bads are so bad. Why would anyone think of buying and using them? If next time you went shopping you came home with a kitchen trasher, a leg slicer and an eye gouger, the kids would think you are mad, but that is what we do when we buy weapons. We buy what destroys us. How can we be so irrational, so deluded? The world economy works through selling goods and services which are usually good for people – food, shelter, clothes, beds, chairs, windows, taps and flowers. Weapons only destroy. They kill people, make houses and flats rubble, injure and maim, devastate cities and trash goods. A carpenter makes a good chair; a bomb vapourises it. A house may be worth $100,000, but a bomb is worth minus $1,000,000 because it destroys ten houses. We buy goods, but states buy bads - weapons, which do this level of destruction. Weapons kill, and that destruction is beyond economic calculation. They injure, physically and mentally, and those costs are crippling beyond payment. They destroy goods; in the example above their product is minus ten times, but it can be far higher destroying a hundred or a thousand times what the product costs. Already in Ukraine perhaps a trillion dollars of damage has been done, aside the human damage. Right up to the present we do madness.

The evidence of destruction since 1914 is indisputably bad – two hundred million dead and towards $1,000,000,000,000,000 destroyed and wasted (at today's prices) since 1914. Think of that cost as five hundred years of US GDP or a quarter of a million dollars for every family on the planet. None of us can imagine the riches on earth absent war, destruction and military costs. Poverty would not have been.

There is another level of irony. One of the main pitches of the arms companies is: "If you buy our weapons, you will not have to use them because you will not be attacked." Of course, as Switzerland attests, if you do *not* buy them, you might also not be attacked for two hundred years. You might even get on better with your neighbours. But concentrate on the arms dealers' pitch. The absolute best the arms companies offer is that we shall *not have to use* their products. Try selling teabags, or bikes, or cars on the basis that you can hope they will never have to be used. And, of course, often they are not used in a war and finish in military graveyards of interminably replicated pointlessness. If they are bought, the claim that they prevented the war cannot usually be disproved, although it can in one case. Saddam bought lots of weapons in the 1980s, including from France, who insisted on payment. Saddam asked for some money from Kuwait, who were reluctant to give him all he asked for, so he invaded them. In that case arms sales obviously started the war. Many other wars result from states buying more arms and hoping they can win, and so the claim is probably bogus, but if the best you can offer or hope for is that your product will not be used, you should pack up shop. Please buy our fish and chips and we hope you do not have to use them. The arms companies have learned to sell and package their wares through fear, supremacy and the illusion that this is power so that we will not question their sales pitch. But now we recognise that buying destruction is bad for all of us, the biggest economic disaster imaginable, and so we have to stop. Usually, wars do not happen because we have weapons, but because people do not like war.

C. Destruction does not work.

We can think. If we take the time to do this basic thinking, the world can easily understand that manufacturing arms which kill, maim, and destroy on a vast scale is wrong, is wrong for all humankind, and can be stopped. The lesson is free, does not take long to absorb, can be understood from the age of about six onwards. We, ordinary people can understand worldwide destruction does not work. "Can I have a very big hammer to smash up a lot of cars?" the man asked in the DIY shop. "That's not a good idea," said the man behind the counter. "Here take a seat and I'll get you a drink." We can act to replace War with Peace. We can disarm the world of death and destruction. We can all understand this truth. It is a failed system. Really it failed with WW1, WW2, Korea, Vietnam, Iraq, Yemen, the Cold War and the Russia-Ukraine War. All the evidence we need is provided. The war dead and the survivors show it has failed. The preposterous system of nuclear weapons aimed mutually across continents has failed, used or unused. We can all recognize that worshipping destruction with a quadrillion dollars is dumb. World militarism needs closing down for all of us. And the worst thing is that it will leave us all safe.

16.THE FINAL OBSCENITY: NUCLEAR WEAPONS.

A. Destruction and Nuclear Weapons.

This key point about destruction is not abstract, but embodied in the whole venture of militarism, most obscenely in nuclear weapons. Rightly, those seeking disarmament have gone for this weapon. In the Manchester War Museum, they have one, I suppose the casing, displayed on a stand. It is about the size of a human body. Your eye pans up to the map on the wall behind of Greater Manchester. The nuclear bomb would destroy Greater Manchester, people and everything, and the radioactivity and damage spread into Lancashire and Yorkshire leaving dereliction – those whom millions of us love. This is what it does.

Perhaps the biggest industry in militarism is that which surrounds nuclear weapons. It includes not just the weapons themselves but systems of missiles and nuclear submarines which can keep the location of the weapons safe from external attack and vast systems of delivery and calculation which have gone into the development of this industry. It started as we all know in 1945 with the dropping of two lesser atomic bonds on Hiroshima and Nagasaki. They had been developed during the war in the United States with the help of British and European scientists led by Oppenheimer. It was to be used against Nazi Germany, if necessary, on the understanding that's Germany might also be developing the bomb. It turned out that German progress was weak.

B. The First Bombs

Events moved fast. Roosevelt died (12/4/45) and Truman became US President. The War ended in Europe (8/6/45) after a big Soviet push through Berlin. Stettinius who worked with Roosevelt and Stalin as US Secretary of State was replaced by James Byrnes (1/7/45). Byrnes, apart from being at Yalta had little foreign affairs experience. The Polish National Unity Government formed in Moscow (28/6/45) was recognised by the US and Britain (5/7/45). The Trinity Nuclear test of the first bomb occurred (16/7/45) and the Potsdam Conference in occupied Germany was 17/7/45 to 2/8/45. On the 26/7/45 Churchill lost the election and was replaced by Attlee at Potsdam. The Potsdam Allies agreed the post-war occupation of the Axis powers and the destruction of the German war machine. Stalin was informed at Potsdam by Truman of the bomb and its use in Japan, but probably knew of it already from his spies. A week after Potsdam the US drops the first atomic bomb on Hiroshima. The horror of it must not be forgotten. One account talked of a girl screaming carrying her eyeballs in her hands. The USSR declared war on Japan (8/8/45) and invaded Manchuria. The second bomb on Nagasaki was dropped (9/8/45). Japan capitulated 2/9/45 and the Second World War ended. Churchill had hoped that the US and Britain would share the bomb and thus rule the world benignly, but the Truman Administration decided it was to be a US only weapon.

Many of the scientists involved in developing the bomb were uneasy about the weapon, especially Oppenheimer. It had been developed to defeat the Nazis, but perhaps Japanese Fascist oppression was as bad. The scientists worried about killing hundreds of thousands of people. It was not "fighting" but civilian destruction. This problem did not worry President Truman. When asked about it later he said that he made the decision more or less on the spot. Civilian destruction had already become a normal part of the Allies War in Germany, eastern Europe and Japan, "necessary" to win the War. Yet, here was a weapon, the most destructive ever. It would only destroy and kill, and Oppenheimer was against murder and the instruments of mass murder even those that he had helped make with clever science. There is discussion about whether Japan would have capitulated anyway. Many commentators now see the insecure Truman as more determined to show Stalin who is boss than assessing Japan. Some see Oppenheimer as chicken. He made the bomb, but couldn't face using it. Yet, perhaps he was and is right. The War was nearly won. Human beings should not make weapons which mass kill, maim and destroy because they are bad and eventually damage even the people who make them. Those who take the sword perish by the sword. Nuclear weapons have cost the US $10-15 trillion since, say, $90,000 for every US household. Perhaps this was a great false step. Perhaps, like

Oppenheimer, we should think again. Although the number of nuclear weapons has been as high as 70,000, none of them has ever been used. They are so destructive, they cannot, we hope, be used. None used and the cost of $10-15tn means a real cost of infinity…

C. The Long History.

We can go through the long history of these weapons. Roughly, the US and the USSR, the two superpowers, stockpiled nuclear weapons, bombers, missiles and nuclear submarines in a continual bonanza for the arms companies; it was their business plan. The levels of weapons were ridiculous – 30-40,000 warheads on each side, alongside the other nuclear "powers" playing bit parts. A fraction of a percent of these weapons used would end all food on earth. It was catatonic madness, the apotheosis of destruction, living with unused evil, because, of course, while some human decency remained in the right places (and there are not many places), they would not be used.

There is a long litany of accidents and near tragedies. They are of three kinds. Several dozen nuclear bombs were dropped all over the place from bombers, missiles and submarines, causing contamination but no nuclear explosions, although many subnuclear ones. We looked at the Goldsboro, North Carolina one, where the final safety device held, the near nuke as Kennedy came to power. There was our local Suffolk one, at Lakenheath, where a bomber with two nuclear bombs on board overshot the runway into a hanger and caught fire. The locals were astonished at American cars fleeing the site at breakneck speed before it might explode. "Whera they a going of?" they say, and found out later. Then plants making the weapons had frequent malfunctions spreading radioactive material, and the people manning the area often suffered. Suddenly the world realised that the long series of nuclear tests might be endangering us – cancers, bromide, infertile women… There were also the scares associated with possible attacks either from the USSR or the US. Because first strike gave such an advantage, the response had to be quick and a number of near accidents occurred. There is the Russian military hero who did not panic when a swarm of western missiles came up on his screen and insisted there must be some other explanation. Of course, many of these scares only emerge decades later. If one goes off, we will know immediately.

The direct confrontation everyone remembers is the Cuba crisis. Boats from the USSR sailed to Cuba with missiles on board which would be aimed at the Great US of A. It was an obvious face to face nuclear threat. Kennedy and his military men were prepared to face it out and attack the vessels. As Kennedy consulted, there were discussions about the logistics of confrontation which do not give you great confidence. Then someone at the back of the room suggested that US Jupiter missiles in Turkey with nuclear warheads aimed at Moscow might be a problem with the USSR. If the US was threatening the USSR, that might be why the USSR was now threatening the US? Kennedy listened. Then they saw that perhaps the Turkey missiles could be traded for the Cuban ones. Discussions took place about losing face with allies and there was worry that world public feeling on the USSR's point about missiles attacking them was reasonable. Eventually, the solution was that the US withdrawal of missiles from Turkey would not be publicized by the US or the Soviets, and Kennedy could be seen as winning. It was not negotiation of the highest quality. The military personnel in the US and probably in the USSR were not really up to the job of sorting out a potential nuclear war.

Nuclear weapons became a long game of competitive technological development carried out by the US and the USSR military manufacturers. In the early years the US had supremacy. For example, in 1965 the US had five times as many nuclear warheads as the USSR. Between 1975 and 1980 the USSR overtook the US and had nearly 40,000 in 1985. Really, those numbers just reflected a vast industrial system of production. They were militarily meaningless because they could destroy the whole world many times over. Disarmament was discussed in the Kennedy/Khrushchev era, but failed, *because the military stayed in charge and made sure they collapsed.* Turkeys… Eventually, the USSR imploded under the weight of its military expenditure in 1990. The Cold War ended and the supposed ideological confrontation. Still nuclear weapons did not close down and we have drifted through to the present.

It is strategically called Mutually Assured Destruction, or MAD. Actually, that assumption may be optimistic. Yes, the knowledge of retaliation may deter, but with two sides, unpredictable leaders who can do strange things, there is great danger. Once the situation arises, it is too late. It is even worse than that. Because first strike and first destruction, offers such an advantage, the ballistics people increase their readiness to trigger to stay ahead. It will happen before we know. The decision will be made, either by the ruler who is not reliable or the one who must strike fast, because of knowledge received. What the hell? The assumption is that we will not think about it, because if you actually think, you know it is dangerously mad and this could end humanity.

India and Pakistan are nuclear. The US and Russia are. The UK and France are, but nobody knows why, except to convey a certain self-importance. Israel is, but isn't saying. Iran might want to be. China is. The Non-Proliferation Treaty tried to stop new nuclear powers, but the existing ones reneged on their promise to work towards disarmament. The NPT does, however, show that we can know who is developing nuclear weapons; the policing works, and we know exactly what is happening in Iran. Yet, overall, the system makes no sense, is unusable or disastrous, but keeps the arms companies flourishing.

D. Do they know what they are doing?

We do not really know what is happening inside this industry in the US, UK, France, Russia, China, Pakistan, India, Israel and elsewhere. People are thinking, planning, designing and working out the logistics of nuclear weapons. Mistakes occur in most industries and they also come to trust themselves too much and inside the bubble they can become weird. Listen to this account of the things they get up to.

In early 2003, AFMC, AFSPC, AFRL, and the Product Center Commanders established an Enterprise Leadership (EL) Long Range Strike (LRS) Task Team (LRS-TT) whose charter is to build roadmaps to describe the integrated development of LRS capabilities/solution options. Task teams uniquely bring together expertise from across enterprises & MAJCOMs to attack horizontal integration issues &

produce integrated solutions in response to identified shortfalls. ACC had conducted several studies to research, assess and define LRS options. AFSPC has initiated the Operationally Responsive Space lift (ORS) Analysis of Alternatives (AoA) as part of the drive towards responsive space capabilities. A Prompt Global Strike (PGS) AoA is planned by AFSPC in FY05/06. USSTRATCOM has a newly defined Global Strike mission to provide Global Strike forces/options as a supporting or supported Combatant Commander. The Air Force needs to develop integrated air and space LRS capabilities to present forces for JTF/CC-directed Global Strike missions. LRS solutions must be developed to address shortfalls in current LRS capability. Operationally responsive space enables rapid access to space and power projection, space superiority, and enhanced intelligence, surveillance, and reconnaissance (ISR) capabilities. [xxxiii]

Do not trust people who write sentences like this. "Prompt Global strike" might involve some problems. They are lost in the system.

E. Dominating the United Nations.

We must recognize that the way this world works is mindless. The god of destruction must have a malfunctioning cortex. It does not make sense, but it has happened. The United Nations, especially the *Security Council* of the United Nations is dominated by the Nuclear Powers (Ha, ha, ha, ha). Let's all call it "The Insecurity Council of the UN" until it changes. The five Permanent Members are all nuclear powers – France, Russia, Britain, China and the United States, the biggest. Historically, it was more or less the ticket for being a permanent member. The places could have gone to states that are peaceful, just, or have avoided wars, but instead they go to states which can destroy the world. The implicit threat all the time is that because the big three (Britain and France do not count) are so powerful, they can do what they like on the Security Council. If they want to, they can ignore the United Nations and promote its irrelevance. Really, in the last two decades each of the Superpowers has done that: - the US in Iraq, Russia in Ukraine and China over the Uyghurs. It is the UN Insecurity Council.

Can the United Nations be rescued from the superpower domination which entrenches nuclear weapons? We remember that in the 1920s through to 1932 ordinary popular democratic support gave the League of Nations its global power. The same direct popular democratic support can disarms the world now. All the nuclear superpowers play at democracy, but really, they have faith in power and the threat of destruction. We must undominated them and the United Nations.

F. The Prohibition of Nuclear Weapons Treaty.

Most of the world's governments are already outside this mushroom cloud bubble. The United Nations Treaty on the Prohibition of Nuclear Weapons was passed in 2017 with 122 states in favour and one against. It was ratified and became United Nations Law, to which we are all subject, on 22nd January, 2021. It is completely clear. They must all go because they are evil. We will all be far better off when they do. The big boys pretended that the Treaty did not exist, thereby ignoring international law. The only *justification* given for French, UK and US non-compliance is the following:- "Accession to the ban treaty is incompatible with the policy of nuclear deterrence, which has been essential to keeping the peace in Europe and North Asia for over 70 years."[xxxiv] Read it carefully. We assume that nuclear deterrence is supposed to produce no *conventional* wars, because full nuclear abolition, which the US and UK could achieve tomorrow if they wanted to, obviously closes down the possibility of any nuclear wars. We note that "Europe" and "Asia" carefully misses out the Middle East where these countries have been happily fighting for two decades undeterred by nuclear issues. We see that Korea, Vietnam, Arab Israeli Wars, Suez, Algeria, Congo, Yemen, the Soviet-Afghan war, Bangladesh, Kosovo and lots of other wars have continued without nuclear deterrence. We see that the Big Boys have not withdrawn this statement now that the Ukraine War *in Europe* has not been deterred by nuclear weapons. We note that only Russia and the Arctic Icecap occupy North Asia and Russia is unlikely to fight with itself. So, this sentence is blah de blah, a fiction, constructed to ignore this UN Treaty, mere empty words to cover the fact that for no reason at all these leaders have sold out to the god of destruction and won't do the obvious good. The big boys, without reason, stop the UN doing ratified international law to which they are subject. It is time to put the big boys in detention.

G. Bullying.

Throughout this time there was a longstanding campaign against nuclear weapons. In the UK it was CND, preceded by the women of Greenham Common and the range of other principled people who stood against this blatant denial of the commandment, "You shall not kill." Others stood against it around the world. At times they gathered a lot of public support; this is a world threatening weapon. The military/secret service retaliated with bullying, arrests and intense attempts to discredit the people involved. They charge the anti-nuclear people with being traitors and working for the other side. Anybody against nuclear weapons was working for the Soviets and trying to destroy the British or American state. It is not surprising that militarists should be bullies and not protect democratic speech, because they live by their stock in trade.

I used to meet Bruce Kent occasionally on Finsbury Park Underground Station. We would chat while a few trains went through. Once, he had just been charged with being paid by the USSR to campaign against western nuclear weapons. It was in all the papers and on the news. We were chatting, and I brought up being funded by the Soviets and asked what he said when he was accused. It was unthinkable to anyone who knew him. Aside his character, I never saw Bruce not in his old jacket with elbow patches because he couldn't be bothered to get a new one. He spluttered into laughter and said, "I invited them to come and have a look at my office". He worked in a poky office with very few resources to run CND, and anybody who saw it would know the whole idea was preposterous. We both heaved. It was part of the standard bullying in the US and UK. Nuclear Disarmament had to be discredited because it was right. Michael Foot, leader of the Labour Party and anti-nuclear, was partly kept out of power by focussing on his baggy jacket and his thick glasses. Assange is held in prison for publishing the truth. Corbyn who dared to talk peace was trashed by the military-dociled media. The lambs of peace are hunted by the dogs of war, our dogs of war.

H. Mutually Assured Destruction is not a good idea.

Nuclear weapons are the final expression of the god of Destruction, the Attack defence System, the worst embodied evil. Aside the first two, they have not been used, because even a small bit of humanity makes them unusable. The attack logic is embodied in tens of thousands of warheads and delivery systems which have cost $10-15,000,000,000,000,000 minimum at today's prices in the US and a smaller amount in all the other nuclear power states. Fifteen trillion dollars spent on nothing, no outcome, not used. We are told that is good, because if they were used, we all die. They might be used. For the first time since 1945 we have a ruler who has little to lose. If Putin does attack, the reprisals are already primed to devastate Russia. We are committed to Mutually Assured Destruction. Nuclear Abolition has been turned down, and until now, we have accepted it. No more. Now it all goes, because it is dangerously mad. It is not that this chapter convinces you. It has merely given you permission to decide the obvious.

17. WORLD WAR TRAUMA.

A. We see Trauma.

Slowly the picture builds. You hear of shell-shock in World War One - men reduced to gibbering wrecks by the pounding in the trenches. After World War Two men are silent, locked in on stuff that has happened in submarines, convoys, deserts, bomb flattened cities, areas of conquest and retreat. The horror of the Holocaust dwells, even at a distance, spread through all the relatives and down generations of dear Jewish people, too evil to know, always present to the whole Jewish and human race. Rape, anger, gratuitous violence, the defenceless gunned down happens hidden and large-scale. Death ends marriage, parenting, friendship, chat and the building of years. Grandfather was killed when Dad was six; his wife, Grandmother, went to an asylum and Dad was brought up in an abusive children's home and his daughter knows it. So, trauma travels down generations. Suicides occur, unaccountable but for the stuff in the head. There are social problems – aggression, depression, drinking, fighting – which gather round war and the armed forces. A kind and lovely ex-soldier friend commits suicide. An Iraq veteran tells what it was like, puzzled, probing depleted uranium and his sickness. Nobody really understands. There is something big going on here.

B. How big is it?

Then the figures begin to roll out. Twenty US veterans a day committing suicide. You read of the horrors of the big wars, what killing, injury and being killed in large numbers actually means.

Let us try to face it all honestly. Trauma is experienced in war often by whole populations. Then it dwells in people in Post Traumatic Stress Disorder, as we call it, in different ways. The trauma may affect 10, 20, 30, 40% or more of the population who experience it, though many more will have difficulties. There are the effects of sleep disorder, anger, drinking, rage, murder, aggression, depression, withdrawal, violence, rape and suicide which may occur over several decades. Among much of the population these effects may be background, and the traumas differ. They come from bombing, advancing fronts, full mobilization battles, food shortages, occupation, fleeing, becoming refugees, killing, losing parents, children, spouse dead, being injured, facing cold, manning weapons, being in bombers, warships, tanks and much more. People are changed. They struggle. They lose personal peace.

It seems reasonable to say that the whole populations of the following states were traumatized in WW2: - Japan (92m), China (268m), Korea (24m) Philippines (16m), USSR (169m) France (42m) Germany (72m) Austria (7m) Netherlands (9m) Italy (58m) Poland (35m) Belgium (8m), Norway (3m) Egypt, North Africa. Obviously, the world Jewish population (15-20m) was traumatized beyond description; we cannot know the depths of it. That is, say, 800m. Other belligerent states like India, the United States, the UK, Egypt, North Africa may have had lower levels because they were not occupied, but war death, injuries, bombing, famine, including the Bengal famine, meant at least another 200m experienced the war as a cloud on their lives. So, it is entirely likely that a billion experienced trauma in that one War.

The First World War was more local in one sense, but more of the world population was found in Europe then. Sixty million troops were involved of whom 8 million died, seven million permanently disabled and 15 million seriously injured; they were mainly young. As well as the horrors of the trenches, shelling, gas, barbed wire, flame throwers and lurching tanks there were multiple conflicts. Austro-Hungary attacked Serbia under the slogan, "Serbia must die." 30,000 were hanged.; many more burned and raped. After atrocities there were a million Belgian refugees. Russia fell apart into the Civil War and 5-10m died in the 1921 Russian Famine. The Ottoman Empire perpetrated the Armenian Genocide. Most of Europe with a population of 500m was engaged in the horrors of conflict. The war spread disease. "Spanish" flu was transmitted among the troops, then taken home. Estimates of deaths, especially among the young, go either side of 50 million. In 1923 13m Russians had malaria. Encephalitis killed 5m. Round the world health, food and trade breakdown spread suffering. Labour from China and elsewhere was drafted in.[xxxv] It is not difficult to see another half billion experiencing various levels and kinds of trauma.

Then there are the other wars. Bigger states with considerable periods of unrest and war include Afghanistan, Algeria, Angola, Argentina, Bangladesh, Benin, Burkina Faso, Cambodia, Chad, Cuba, DRC, Egypt, Eritrea, Ethiopia, Guatemala, Hungary, Iran, Iraq, Kazakstan, Laos, Libya, Madagascar, Malawi, Mozambique, Myanmar, Nepal, Nigeria, Korea, Pakistan, the Philippines, Rwanda, South Africa, Sudan, Syria, Turkey, Uganda, Ukraine, United States, Vietnam, Yemen. This list contains perhaps another billion who have suffered in war and conflict one or more times right up to the present. It is not even appropriate to try to work out accurately what the figures might be, because we are dealing with so many different kinds of trauma, direct and indirect, over different time periods and with different causes.

In addition, when half of the world's population lives in military dictatorships, where often opposition is suppressed, killed and tortured, we have to recognize this additional source, and then areas of terrorism present another. *This is not an attempt to find big numbers, but to recognize this is really the biggest source of mental instability on the planet lasting a generation or more. It is not difficult to conclude that a quarter of those who have lived since 1900 have experienced war related trauma directly and half indirectly, down the generations or laterally. Perhaps, even, most of us have because this is the world we live in. It is this, too, which comes from the perpetuation of conflict and strife.*

C. The Military in Trauma.

A few months back a man was shouting across the road outside. He took his shirt off and waved it about. He had a finely chiselled physique and walked among the graves in the churchyard looking for something. He probably had a military background, was aggressive, but could be talked with and sat on the church wall before walking back into town. We do not know what was wrong, except it was probably war.

The Military have tried to hide this. The problem will not go away because attacking and being attacked traumatizes all. Soldiers suffer, although how many is not clear. It may be up to 30% depending on their war situation. There is "Combat Stress", but really it is much wider. The MOD and other militaries talk it down, but it is real and substantial. Many of the armed forces are in trauma. A study reveals 13,000 soldiers sleeping on the streets in the UK, homeless, with PTSD.[xxxvi] The hero soldier commits suicide, and what a hero, and how tragic. Secondary PTSD continues the problem for spouses and children across generations into seemingly inexplicable patterns of behaviour. Of course, civilians also suffer. Their homes are destroyed. They have fled and become refugees. Their cities are flattened. Parents die. Children die. Women are raped. People have nothing. And the others live with it all. But the military are in charge of all this business – shooting, bombing, attacking, defending, addressing destruction and death, hospital work, being hated, dealing with casualties, being injured. What can they do? The military cannot directly say, "This killing business is traumatic, and so now we do it at a distance" or "drones cut down on direct killing experience", but that is going on. Often the military have high standards and try their best to save life and prevent injury, but in conflict the standards slip as they have in Ukraine now. The business of attack-defence, of manning the weapons, of shooting and being shot at, is fear and institutionalised hate, and it damages. There is no escape for the military; they suffer. They are in it as white crosses or nightmares. Dress it how we may, it is not good.

Part of it is the long process of subservience to the machine, the killing machines. The sword and even the bow and arrow and early rifles remained tools of the soldier to use with discretion and even chivalry, though that too was a mixed-up concept. But then the machines took over. The cannon on ships and torpedoes, and then missiles, already targeted strategically. The Navy were labouring to fulfil already prescribed tasks, So, too, with rapid fire rifles. Death and destruction and trauma come at a distance and zones of fear expand…

D. Men do War and then do Women.

The horror of rape as a weapon of war is inescapable, and goes across generations. Genghis Khan advocated it as one of the prizes of victory. Over hundreds of years it was seen as a reward for the soldiers and slowly the principle that this is as wrong in war as it is in peace has been established in international law. But the horror has gone on and on and recurs across the world even now. It happened with the "comfort women" in Korea, with Isil (Isis) abuse of Yasidi women in Northern Iraq, with the fighting in the Democratic Republic of the Congo, in Northern Nigeria and some occurrences have happened in all the wars and also in revenge patterns. As the Nazis swept east raping women in WW2 so the USSR soldiers did it when the frontier moved the other way. It is a phenomenon which is obviously gendered – men disrespecting and then abusing women in the way which most directly conveys evil. It is clearly, often fuelled by ethnic hatred, but at its heart is the arrogance of militarism. Because I can do whatever I want with a gun, including death, I will control you with My will to do whatever I want. Thus, the evil is loosed. Humans become bestial. It is one of the Scars across Humanity. [xxxvii] The power to control through weapons drives through to madness. This too we must admit is part of the culture of war.

E. Jesus and Roman Military Trauma.

You do not see it at first, but then it is obvious. Luke 8 26-39 reports, at the other side of the Lake Galilee, a man living among tombs, crying out, naked, shouting loudly, cutting himself, who could not be controlled, calling himself "Legion" after the brutal Roman soldiers, isolated. There had been hundreds of crucifixions in Galilee by the Romans for people to look at and know they should not revolt and this a man had clearly had a dose of Roman unbending cruelty and it was inside him. It is personified as a demon, as it is - evil inhabiting a person to destruction. We merely now call it PTSD.

Then occurs an odd process. The evil demons, speaking through the man, beg Jesus not to send them into the Abyss, presumably the place of destruction, but to go into a herd of pigs, presumably to survive. Jesus gives them permission and then the great herd of pigs rushes down the bank and into Lake Galilee. You can imagine the noise. What the pig hell, we might say, is going on? Is Jesus just wasting pigs? It is not just us, because the locals were scared stiff and asked Jesus to leave. But Jesus does parables and shows what this stuff does until the cruel demons, driven by destruction, drown in the Abyss. Wherever this torturing drive is, it will lead to destruction and you have seen what it is like. It is pig suicidal waste and hell. The man was healed, and Jesus asked him to return home and tell people what God had done for him.

F. The Centre.

It is one confrontation, but it is not the big one, for as we all know Jesus died on a Roman Cross, not through Pilate's intent, but because the system of control had to kick in against the one who claimed to rule on God's terms. The Cross is the greatest military trauma, the exemplar of what the conqueror can do at will, the Threat tying and nailing to a large wooden cross the screaming rebel so that everyone can see. It was clear all through that Jesus ruled differently – no compulsion, always treating people peacefully, refusing control, not acknowledging the power of weapons, no threat, no violence. He insisted on turning the pattern of the masses serving the ruler through compulsion, or slavery, into the model of the ruler serving the people. Not so with you, he insisted to his friends. "Those who are regarded as rulers of the Gentiles lord it over them, and their high officials exercise authority over them.. But not so with you." (Mark 10:42-3) Democracy is the people's *service by the government*. It works. We have a Civil *Service*. Only when a government serves and is accountable are we safe, and it all started here with Jesus washing feet, so that the lesson would stick. It has changed the world; it underpins all democracy..

But we have to go where it centrally happened. The cross is the Roman's ultimate fear machine – they kill you on display so you will comply with Rome. Jesus finishes up there because the control people in Jerusalem need the Good Man to go. Pilate squirms not to crucify him. The three crosses are set up at Golgotha, the place called the Skull. They are tied on and the crude nails are hammered in, screaming and blood, and hoisted aloft. They are left to die, with the people watching around. It is the victory of military control. Then he takes over.

"Father, forgive them they know not what they do." Of course, we don't know what we do in defiance of God throughout history and in all areas of our lives. Jesus names the failure of Rome, the Jerusalem leaders and all militaries to understand. Beyond the trauma, which it undoubtedly was, is the truth that this is ignorance. We do not understand. Still, we do not understand now. Even here his enemies are loved. There is this big peaceful place before God outside the weapon fear machine. It is defeated even as it seems to be victorious. It is unjust, because this Man had done no evil at all. It was misplaced, because he was also no threat. It was the result of a failed legal system, because the trial was crooked. It happened because of fear among the money-making Temple party and the militarists that this man was destroying their system. Jesus was asking forgiveness for the vast systems of military control that have dominated human history then and now. "They know not what they do." Leaders and nations stomp around armed and killing, like the Roman Empire, right down to this year thinking they know what they are doing. Now it is obvious Putin hasn't a clue what he is doing – lost, vain, with only vindictive control. So wrong, wrong, wrong. They, not Jesus, are in judgement on the cross; he remains the gentle ruler. Yet not in judgement. "Father, forgive them." We need forgiveness first, we need openness with God, to be outside it before this garbage can be junked. This trauma can die, and we can be friends with the Lamb of God. Now that is good news.

18. YOUR GENTLE POWER.

A. The Weakness of the Superpowers.

What power do you have? First, the deconstruction. Because military power is only destruction, really it is no power at all. The big boys think they are strong, but really, they are weak because they bend to their destructive notion of power. Real power is the power to do good – to create, build, feed, help, clothe, house, educate, befriend, play and the things we try to do in life. If we knew how good the world can be without military expenditure and wars, we would see this, and so would the big states. But they are locked in their defective notion of power, of control, of winning by fear and they cannot do what needs to be done. It is Julius Caesar about to be murdered by his mates, or Napoleon strutting about pretending he is tall, or the British Empire bureaucracy not realising how completely boring Pomp is, or Mussolini reducing a great culture to his small strut or Hitler believing he has to invade Russia so that he can lose the War. All the time the power to destroy self-destroys. There is only one message. As Sassoon said, "Out of the nothingness of night they tell, our need of guns, our servitude to strife."[xxxviii] Even now, Putin sits at his long table in servitude to strife. The weakness of superpowers is that they can't escape the false god they have invested in.

Let us therefore turn the page. It might be like this. Oh, of course we will close down all our nuclear weapons in full co-operation with all the other nuclear states, because nuclear weapons are not good for us. Yes, and our military bases can become holiday centres for the world's poor. And the military budget can be split four ways for poverty, green energy, hospitals and education. And we apologize for trying to dominate the Middle East; we have allotted $500bn recompense. How would you like it spent? We have behaved like spatting children all over the globe, but now we will grow up, or grow down. We will have a friendship year in all strained international relationships. We will build a retirement home for old military dictators. We will turn aircraft carriers and submarines into fresh water carriers from estuaries to the areas of drought. No, actually China is an amazing manufacturing centre that many of us depend on and we need to change the western relationship with China. Our weapons have really messed up the world; we must end all weapons exports and make more useful things. Football matches are much more fun than going to war. The gentle way does not rule at present. Domination may be a male thing, or top dog, or needing to fight or because the "glory" is victory over others, rather than the sunrise. We need to learn a lot more from women. The good way, at present, is closed because the military-industrial complex is spinning towards the black hole of destruction absorbed in the gravity of militarism. Domination requires evil, of course it does. Now we close the black hole and open the good way. The gentle way is there, is here, is everywhere, and it rules among us because the good works. Each of us has a little gentle power. We, doing the good way, are powerful.

We are nearly there.

Ordinary peaceful common sense is there all around the world. You probably have some in your pocket. It showed up with the United Nations Treaty on the Prohibition of Nuclear Weapons coming into force in January, 2021. It was passed in 2017 with 122 States in favour and one against. The abolition of nuclear weapons is undoubtedly good for everyone; they are unusable, unless some world leader goes mad, which is world-wide destruction. They are evil in intent. But the nuclear powers could not admit they are wrong it and so they have pretended that the good Treaty does not exist, frozen in their own militarism and unable to let go. But the gentle way is still there, nearly world ruling. It could be world curing in six months and so we do the Treaty. Meanwhile, billions of us getting up in the morning, dressing for cold or warm, having coffee or water and greeting our neighbour are for gentle power. We like to help. We are, as they say, live and let live people. Even the militarists are quite nice. We could toy with the word "gentle man". The task is to turn on gentle power.

The Big Boys are stuck. The sheer level of organisation of the military-industrial complexes in each of these states makes it realistically and logistically impossible to transpose from high preparedness. They are so locked into their military systems – arms manufacture, secret services, bases, communications networks, allies, detailed reconnaissance, strategy, alliances, fear generation techniques, promotions, assessing strengths and weakness, weapons systems, new weapons systems, logistics, service personnel, budgets, rivalries and so much more that they cannot budge. They are a stranded whale. Of themselves they cannot understand disarmament, let alone do it. They are a hole in the road and we need to find a way round them. The underlying truth is that the power of destruction is no power at all but they will think and act in their system. They will derail disarmament every which way – lies, fears, misinformation, going after the organisers, creating crises, starting conflicts, trying to run the show and more. They will be cunning, use systems of control, try to distort what we will do. What will we do? Use gentle power, democratically. We will be the tide coming in so that the whale can swim away. We do not even need to hate them, or challenge them. They are stranded leviathans. When the tide comes in, we can re-float them and they can enjoy the new roles they will be given.

Politics, Sheep and Sheepdogs.

What is the way round the superpowers? If we look at the long history of democracy it is surprisingly evident that over the past half century or more ordinary people have become relatively impotent in politics. We have moved from being voters to being sheep. There are many elections not worth the name with the dominant power being elected through eliminating opponents, closing down debate, dominating the media and cooking the results. Or we have a bipolar choice. Elections are quite heavily controlled. One party might dominate publicity through spending large amounts, as in the UK. A slogan wins. A good politician's reputation is trashed. The election lie lasts long enough to win. Many elections are personality centred so that issues of policy get little place in the process; either you like one leader or another. Strangely, in this world of incessant media much of the coverage of elections is superficial and certainly could not address a major change in direction like world disarmament. Voters are manipulated and monitored by opinion polls. It is surprising how many political systems become establishments with those on the inside protecting the status quo and incapable of any big change. Nor is there much room in electoral discussion for big ideas or major reforms. The expectation is that people will be passive. More than that, we are treated like sheep. Always there are sheepdogs barking one way or the other about dangers, enemies and necessary confrontations. They bark, whichever side they are on, and we run one way or the other. Unlike the Good Shepherd, they despise us. We are to be fed lines and given suitable rhetoric so that we will go along with the show.

We will not do reform, especially big reform, because we are ordinary people who just watch television and receive politics. So, what do we do? *We stop being sheep.* Or rather we hang out with Jesus who just talks with us. Gentle Jesus, meek and mild, named the brood of vipers, but always left people free to do good or bad, even Judas going out to sell him to the rulers. He does gentle power and waits. So, stand up and do your bit of world disarmament. You have gentle power; for each of us it is a little bit. But what can we do?

The Big Democratic Rethink.

These little shifts are irritating. Why doesn't the book get to the point? But there is a lot of debris in the river. Most politicians think we vote for them or not vote for them. Often, they are in parties which present as Government. Vote for us and we will govern you well. Some states in Europe and elsewhere are more complex with multiple parties and nuanced positions, but mainly it is a popularity show, a popular vote for Putin, or Museveni, or Trump, or Bolsonaro. Issues get lost. The people are sheep who are allowed to bleat once every four or five years.

The alternative is seen as revolution, either the old Communist style, or the overthrow of the existing ruling government by some rival. Really, as we have found repeatedly, the organisation of governments, civil services, militaries and the media mean that the show must go on and, in relation to militarism governments, only think of moving deckchairs on the Titanic. Despite government changes, often the main direction carries on.

We need to create a democratic process which will steam through establishment politics. It is international mass voting. Remember, in the 1930s majority world opinion was for world disarmament, and they presented it at Geneva in petitions of tens of millions of votes. The politicians then knew they were being asked democratically to do world disarmament, and they went to Geneva to do it under popular pressure. They wriggled out, just, but nearly world disarmament nearly happened through popular pressure from all those we do not quite know. They did house to house signatures, spread the message through the bush telegraph. We have an instant World Wide Web with mass petitions. We can do it in weeks. The slow bit is people realising militarism does not work. It has killed itself. At first the realisation is slow, mainly because of fatalism. Yet, the case is easy to make. World wars were not a great success. The Ukraine War is not popular. Nuclear annihilation is not the answer we want. Having 28 million troops marching up and down in no useful employment is not a good sales pitch. So, we have to get this recognition show up and running so that people can see the obvious. It does not require geniuses. Most of us have not seen it for most of our lives because we are asleep. We just notice now that there is a big refuse dump in the middle of our garden creating that appalling smell. Then we realise that we can vote for full considered world disarmament to create a world consensus.

Fortunately, the process is there. All kinds of sites do popular petitions and thousands and millions vote for them. The discussion media are there. Good journalists see the points already and open them up. Suddenly, we all realise that peace has been sitting in a chair in our living room all the time. Oh, that is what Gandhi, Albert Einstein, Mohammed Ali, John Lennon, Gorbachev, Vera Brittain, Tolstoy, John Pilger and all the others were on about. Two billion Christians now wake up to the fact that Jesus has done peace for them, taught the lesson and we have not really listened in class and skipped doing his homework. Strong, spreading public opinion does not create an enemy. It is not dangerous. World disarmament is not against anybody and so it does not polarize; it is merely the response that addresses the world problem of disseminating weapons by removing them. Principled reform to disarm the world is precisely what all we, the people, have to do. We vote in thousands, millions and then billions around the globe deliberately and actively so that world disarmament is unstoppable, and this time we do not allow the deference to politicians or the military which defeated the 1932 Geneva Disarmament Conference. The terms for disarmament will be decisive, simple and beyond contention. It will be done, because murder is wrong and weapons which do murder are wrong for everybody across all nations, we can love our enemies and we no longer need to live in the worldwide fear of weapons or weapons people. We are grown up, or rather, as Jesus requires, we become like children. We can do all of that. That is not blind faith in people, but a recognition that globally we can live in peace and trash the weapons that divide and destroy us. We can have the gentle power to do this thing. You have gentle power. First…

19. JESUS AND THE TRUTHS OF PEACE.

A. We need help.

We need backbone help from Jesus. For thousands of years the truths about militarism and peace have not been really told. The conquest people have written history. Wars have been "won", not reported as disasters. Military egoists headline eras, not the dead, the recoverers and the subdued. The waste of destruction, the traumas of suffering and useless hate, the costs of domination and the making evil normal are written up as triumph, empires and "civilisation". The blood red story of war becomes normal to us, the only way to think, the 1066 and all that, "their greatest hour", the jaw jaw of war war. You will not hear of peace, or how it is made; "peace" is merely the end of war event. Peace is invisible. In reality we live by and in it when life is worth living, but we do not see it or understand it. In the popular mind it is a sentiment.

Even more astonishing, Jesus has told and lived the truth of peace, but we have not heard it or really bothered to work out what he is saying. There are two billion Christians worldwide who read his words but are partly dominated by the militarists and we Christians even do not hear peace. We pass the peace in church as though it were a plate of biscuits and not something more. He is acknowledged as the world's greatest teacher, but probably on this one we glaze over because it does not seem practical. Perhaps we leave the classroom with a vague idea that he is a nice peace guy, but we are daydreaming, not real. We church people, "and also with you", put peace on Christmas cards and make it into flat lake scenery. Theologians can drown peace without trying.

But the big truth to face is that peace has been rejected in the history of Christianity. Popes and Bishops have blessed their nation's wars in nationalistic Christianity down the ages. From the Crusades to Patriarch Kirill of Moscow in 2022, obscenely blessing the Russian invasion of Ukraine, it has done God on our side. So, peace is a bit lost, as Jesus warned his teaching would be. Sometimes it falls on stones, or the birds

162

eat it up, or the weeds get it. (Matt. 13) Jesus is light years beyond us in thinking, so we need a bit of awareness and depth listening to this guy. This is high grade education for ordinary people. We go for decades without seeing the point, as he said we would. Jesus' peace is partly political. We need to hear Jesus on ordinary life and politics. So let us, inadequately, look at where the Prince of Peace seems to be taking us, because we need his help.

B. The Superpower Temptation.

Early on Jesus goes out into the desert to sort some stuff out. One of the issues is what we could call the Superpower temptation, the big one. He was offered control of all the kingdoms of the earth and their splendour – the whole lot. (Matt 4; 8-10) If you wanted to put things right, surely this was the way to go; you just take them ever, do the right things and the world is sorted. But it was not the real truth. The cost was evil, probably military evil, bowing to the devil. Jesus flatly turns it down. They were already all God's kingdoms, not a matter of human ownership, and this idea of control was false politics. Jesus was being offered a lie and quickly put it right. "You worship and serve only God." Thus, right at the beginning, the Superpower Temptation was defeated.

Of course, Alexander the Great, Julius Caesar, Genghis Khan, the European Empires, Napoleon, Tsars, Hitler, Mussolini, the Japanese Empire have gone the false way and killed their millions to establish their right way. Really, many world leaders now are inside this same superpower temptation and stay in control, when control of people blights the earth. Freedom to live a good life is complex, but it is certainly not a gun in your back. So, Jesus turns down the superpower temptation. Then he tells his disciples (his students) of this temptation (otherwise how would they know?) so that they, and we, could understand it. Control over states is out and fails through human history. It makes politics about forcing people, rather than just living, public service and an understanding of good law. It's a pity Nero, Ivan the Terrible, Pol Pot, Stalin and a whole train of world rulers didn't see their problem. They worshipped the Devil and evil ruled. Lesser dictators like Amin, Marcos,

Gaddafi, Duvalier, Putin, Pinochet and dozens of others who traded evil for control similarly lost it. Even rulers in democratic countries fixating on their own control, election victories, public image have also got it wrong. The issue is not being in control but living before God. Before he really started, Jesus had this central basic issue sorted, and sorted for us. He just said, "No."

Yet, wasn't Jesus a bit full of himself to even be tempted with the possibility of having all the kingdoms of the earth and isn't this a bit political? We shall see.

C. Jesus Christ.

There is something a bit weird about Christ in the Gospels. Jesus wanders around Galilee, Samaria and the Jerusalem/Jericho area meeting lepers, fishermen, low grade tax collectors and local water collectors, and yet he seems to call himself the King or Ruler. Most Christians accept this and do the three wise men stuff at Christmas, but do not see the problem. In England it would be like a bloke from Garboldisham in rural Norfolk declaring himself king. Hoo dew he think he is, callin hisself King? they might ask.

Even the word, "king" is misleading, because in Jesus' time, the king was effective ruler. We are not talking figurehead, but the person in charge. Herod the Great was King, but his sons were not, because they were not up to it. So, this is not Christians getting romantic about their leader - crown jewels and sitting on thrones. Jesus claims he is in charge. Is he deluded about who he is? Why does he not behave like normal rulers? And what does he mean by ruler? What is he going on about? It is a gigantic obvious problem.

And what is this about not having anywhere to sleep? (Luke 9:58) It is even more pointed than this. Jesus says, "Foxes have holes and birds of the air have nests, but the Son of Man has no-where to lay his head." He says it to a potential follower, implying that there are no perks for disciples, but he says it in terms of the "Son of Man". Really, this is incomprehensible. The Son of Man in Daniel 7:14 is described in these terms, "He was given authority, glory and sovereign power; all peoples, nations and people of every language worshipped him. His dominion is an everlasting jurisdiction that will not pass away and his kingdom is one that will not be destroyed." Jesus knows exactly what he is saying. The Big Man, the biggest man of all, has only temporary accommodation. If Jesus title is remotely correct, it is like saying that Queen Elizabeth can't find a place on a camp site. Everyone knows that a king isn't a pawn and a pawn isn't a king. So, what does, or doesn't it, mean to say that Jesus is a/the political ruler?

We sometimes fail to see the full weight of Jesus' temptation and response, because we do not see that he was/is King, President, Prime Minister, the Supreme Ruler or whatever you call it all the way through. The Name, Jesus Christ, is real or it is not. Christ, is Jesus the Jewish Messiah, the definitive Jewish leader, generalised into the Christus of the Roman Empire because he should be running that ancient world-wide show as well, and rivals the Roman Emperor. He is the Roman Emperor. So, the conundrum is that big. We have Christmas bringing the baby in a manger who is somehow running the whole system. It seems to me odd that everybody does not say, "This does not make sense. What is the explanation of this?" for the issue goes right through the Gospels.

That he makes the claim is not even controvertible. Jesus identifies as the King of the Jews, Messiah, Son of David, Son of Man, Son of God all the way through. At his birth he is rival to Herod the Great. He is born King of the Jews, Messiah. He is presented as king, political ruler and that is what he understands himself to be. He is *the* ruler. He jokes that merely being Son of David is a bit infra-dig. He embraces the Son of Man theme forged as greater than the Babylonian Empire as his own self-description. He is asked by Pilate at his trial whether he is King of the Jews, when Pilate expects and wants him to answer, "No, of course not" and even presumes that he will answer, "No", and moves on from the question, but Jesus insists on answering it with a strong "Yes, it is as you say". The answer will kill him, because it makes him the rival to Rome, but *Jesus insists on telling the truth that will kill him*. That suggests he meant it. On his cross were the words, "The King of the Jews", not "He said he was the King of the Jews." On dozens of other occasions the same truth is hammered home. Jesus is the ruler. In Isaiah's words, "The Government is on his shoulder."

So, this is the problem. Clearly, we cannot understand what is going on with Jesus, the world's greatest teacher, unless we see why thus guy, going round talking with disreputables, healing people, meeting lepers, respecting prostitutes, consorting with foreigners, with no-where regular to sleep and upsetting everybody important understands himself and is understood as a political ruler, a king. We have just had the funeral of Queen Elizabeth in the UK, a devout follower of Jesus, but surrounded by stately homes, jewels, soldiers in uniforms, pomp, servants and the trappings of monarchy down the ages. He is not like her, though she was partly like him, following his principle of service as her central calling. He was definitely a bit low on gold and ermine. What is Jesus' understanding of political rule? How can he rule *and easily get crucified* and where does peace come in it? It has to be a massive problem; this Man is not easily understood.

D. Turning Down the Fight.

It is odd how we ignore what is going on politically in the Gospels. They recount a crowd of five thousand men, and Matthew adds, "besides women and children" (Matt. 14:21) heading round north Galilee trying to catch up with Jesus on a boat. This is a sudden emerging crowd, football crowd size in a remote place, and the event is dramatic. Why did they come out there, then? They are not just hoping for a good lunch. If fact, the feeding of the five thousand, the miracle, is at first misleading. It takes the focus away from what caused the event. One verse and Josephus supply the reason for this event. John 6:15 says, "And Jesus knowing they wanted to make him king by force, withdrew to the hills." What! This is the massive political event - the Uprising. The crowds stream from the towns on the northern shore and race round the top end of the lake to begin the Revolution against Herod Antipas. The location is important; they are gathering away from Tiberias and Sepphoris, the strongholds of Antipas to then march back in control. The Gospels and

Josephus supply the background. John the Baptist, critiquing Herod, has just been murdered at Machaerus by the Dead Sea because the daughter of Herodias, his wife, had asked for his head on a platter at the behest of his Mum; John had been critical of Herodias. She wanted her own back. Herod has lost a war in the South East at the edge of his Perean territory against his Nabatean ex father-in-law and was weak. John the Baptist was very popular, and so Herod was facing a bit of a crisis. John is now murdered and perhaps Jesus will lead the uprising against this tyrant. John had pointed to Jesus as the figure far greater than himself. This could be the crystallizing moment in the politics of Galilee for a generation, the rekindled hope of the Zealots, the Jewish nationalists, to throw off the Roman and Herodian yoke. Jesus needs this show of determined support and he can overthrow the tyrant by force. Of course, if you back a leader and he is then also able to supply you with copious food, you are with him all the way.

Although these uprisings were endemic to the Zealot history of Galilee, Jesus' answer was not even in doubt. He, literally, had them eating out of his hands, but to the person who had faced the temptations and who never sought victories *over* people, this way was wrong. It is wrong for the whole world. The terms of God's rule are different. If you are to love your enemies, you must not attack them. The way of peace cannot be paved with war, and Jesus has been teaching peace-making to his disciples. This Ruler has seen through the self-glorifying leader complex, and will not do armed revolution. The last thing these harassed and helpless people needed was a leader who would take them to death. So, he just walks away and becomes unavailable. The disciples don't even know where he is. They look and probably cuss a bit and then get in their boat to go home and the vast crowd straggles back the way it had come.

Some thirty-four years later Galilee did indeed rebel. The battle was finally fought out on the same lake and the resultant slaughter was described in horrific terms by Josephus.

> A fearful sight met the eyes - the entire lake stained with blood and crammed with corpses; for there was not a single survivor. During the days that followed a horrible stench hung over the

region. The beaches were thick with wrecks and swollen bodies which, hot and steaming in the sun, made the air so foul that the calamity not only horrified the Jews but revolted even those who had brought it about. Such was the outcome of this naval engagement. The dead, including those who had earlier perished in the town, totalled 6,700.[xxxix]

Notice, the figure of those dead about matches those who came out to meet Jesus. For one who sees the end from the beginning, mere rebellion was out. Jesus understood the bloody point. Its inner consistency with the third Temptation is impressive, and he is unequivocally right.

E. War or Food?

Jesus does Parables. They are Now you don't see it. Now you perhaps do. Or perhaps you never will. Events are parables. They point to bigger meanings – healing can happen, faith does work, money gets you, the humble are lifted up. The Feeding of the Five Thousand is a massive parable. You came for a Revolution. You wanted me to lead you in fighting, and here I am healing and feeding you all with the aid of a lad with five loaves and two fish. You came for a fight and I gave you fish. You came for war and I gave you bread. You came for revolution and I gave you a picnic. And, by the way, there are twelve fishing baskets full of leftovers; we do conservation here. Do you want Fighting or Food? It is the same question that faces the world in 2022. Ukraine is a massive food producer. Do you want war or food? Famine is coming. Do you want War or Food?

Later, Jesus taunts the rebellion people back round at Capernaum. (John 6: 25-71) Oh, you just came out to get fed. Of course, they didn't, but he is trying to take them and us on a journey. You were not even looking for miracles… Then, as now, he talks what could not be understood. These are simple folk. "I am the bread of life", and then he takes them on the journey away from the each-day bread and hungry business to feeding on the bread which will last for ever, the truths which reside in this Man. They can have free access to God the Father and to life before God the Creator. This is the centre of life and then of peace, not a stupid uprising.

The issue hangs in the air, as it does throughout history, and then a sense of zealot failure returns. A rebellion has gone flat. They have had a bad night. This is just Jesus of Nazareth. They begin to crowd grumble, struggling with the depth of what Jesus is saying, stumbling at the person who will not take up what *they* have to offer. Jesus pushes them further, teaching which they could hardly comprehend. He claims the astonishing prophecy, "They will all be taught by God." as a possible extant reality. Could people sit around and just be taught by God? There is quite an atmosphere as the sheer difficulty of Jesus' teaching is tossed about among the people. They want a Deliverer. Jesus' larger concern for their life before God will not square with their wants. In these terms, he lets them down and "from this time many of his disciples turned back and no longer followed him." (6:66) At the same time, as a friend and healer of ordinary poor people, he was the one to whom people flocked, and all who touched him were healed. (Mark 6:53-6) What do you want, you people, war or the bread of life? It is still the same question.

F. The Gentle Rule of God.

Even now we do not get it. We live with and in power, competitive power, winning and losing, top and bottom. Governments are *in* power. Superpowers run the show. Great theorists from Max Weber onwards do power as control over the will of others. We number crunch popularity, economic power, military weight and getting things through. We intelligent, educated, sophisticated, war-weary, modern people think power is normal our-will-be-done. We do the weapons and power calculations the earlier chapters describe wall to wall, every day in the media. We effectively discuss whether the Zealots or Herod Antipas can win in Galilee on today's news. Actually, in about a decade Antipas was removed by the Emperor Caligula because he was thought to have weapons for 70,000 men and be a threat to Rome. So, the Zealots won, or did they? They rose in 70AD and Jerusalem was sacked, and so they lost and so too did long-term Roman cruelty. But we study and practice controlling political power as normal. We, like the crowds by Galilee, do not see why Jesus turned down all the kingdoms of the world and overturning Antipas. Despite WW1 and WW2 and the litany of other wars, we do power as control and militarism. We are as thick as Galilean peasants with pitchforks.

He teaches the Kingdom, or Rule of God. We can live life before God on God's gentle terms. It re-orders everything. It is the whole of life, including politics. It is the good way. The parables of the Kingdom show this way of living can grow. It is the pearl of great price, the place where all workers get respect and pay, where lost people count, where humility is the rule of the game, where children have full membership and more. It is where we are all rich. It is the place where, if you listen, grain produces a hundred-fold and the weeds are kept in their place. Power is God's goodness, is meekness, is lifting up the lowly, is what is good for all, the wealth of commoners. Actually, of course, we really know Jesus is right through and through. Love your neighbour works in our street, town, nation and planet. Non warfare makes the world go round. Peace is basic to economics. But you have to see it as Jesus sees it, as God makes life. You have to go after the pearl of great price. You have to be a bit single-minded. Peace will not just turn up on the doorstep.

The rule of God dwells in people's hearts. They/we are to be poor in spirit, meek not assertive, merciful, honest, to meet false evils steadily and to make peace. Jesus sets out to reconstruct humanity into nice people. He rows us back from the garbage of war and militarism. It seems untidy, but there is no other way, and it involves a big mindset change. You avoid World Wars, Cold Wars and Ukraine? Quarrels? Look out for the quarrels people might have against you and sort them quickly. (Matt 5: 23-26) Murder? Don't even think about being angry. Revenge? Instead of paying back evil, tit for tat, look to show the other a more generous way. Hate your enemy? Love your enemy. God is generous to all humankind – good and evil – there is no selective sun and rain, and so you be the same. Having your own love group and hating outsiders is third rate; allies against enemies is part of the problem. Don't go after money; it will corrupt your heart. Wise up; watch out for *wolves in sheep's clothing*. And think about the kind of world you are building. If you build on cardboard foundations, it will come crashing down. Of course, Jesus' teaching touches all areas of life, but peace is in there. "Blessed are the peacemakers, for they will be called sons and daughters of God." Peace *making?* You need to actively make peace? What is going on here? The reward is to be children of God playing happily in the sun. Oh, perhaps we will take that.

How do you *make* peace? Roman soldiers went out two by two to collect taxes. Refusal to pay or opposition would be cut down viciously, because they were in control and extorting by intimidation. The ultimate threat was crucifixion. Jesus sent his "soldiers" out two by two. You go out two by two visiting people and let your peace rest upon a house. Don't be silly about it. If they are not peaceful, move on; their failure to be at peace is their problem. Don't be afraid. There will be persecution. If it comes flee. Especially, don't be afraid of those who can kill you and live in the power of weapons. Fear God who looks after sparrows and knows how many hairs you have on your head. This peace stuff will not be placid. It will provoke division. But take up your cross and follow me. The cross is big in the Christian life – grace, mercy, the release from judgment, dying to self, but Jesus is also saying to his students: Take up the you-fear-because-we-can-kill-you-control-system-of-the-Roman-Empire. Pick it up. Carry it. Of course, it is big. There are the martyrs, the dying steady people. There are those who really suffer for righteousness and justice. And we are pathetic. But Jesus' words vibrate like a cello. Maybe if we are all steady for peace and pass it on, martyrs will not be necessary. Be fear-less. All the defeats, the fleeing refugees, the sack of Jerusalem where the blood ran so thick in the streets that it put fires out, the peace destroyed by cheap, shallow leaders, the revenge, all of that can be beaten. You, perhaps, and I have read of the suffering, the heroes and heroines of peace, the mourning people, the people who really did peace across the nations, and we are asked to do a few hundred e-mails.

And so the Patient One sees the long game. He weeps over Jerusalem. "If only you had known this day what would bring you peace, but it is hidden from your eyes." This will be no instant history. It is people poor in spirit, able to question themselves, see their sins, renounce the roots to power, fame and fortune, the little people, the nice people who will save the world. They will come in from the highways and byways. They will bring peace, the healing of the nations through Christ unlocking God's good way to us. It is not without theatre. I want my subjects to be my friends; the Emperor washes feet. But when? Jesus is open-ended about the history. There will be wars and rumours of wars, catastrophes, persecutions, false prophets and false leaders. There will be times to flee. Many will falsely claim they are the leader, the Fuhrer, the world ruler. So be wise. Learn to read the times and make peace.

H. The Confrontation of Peace.

Jesus had travelled to Jerusalem when it was humming at Passover with perhaps a million visitors. It was going to be an event. We need to be aware that Jesus was miles ahead of everyone, including us, and playing with them much of the time. Earlier he had cleared the Temple the first time and then said something seemingly daft. "Destroy this Temple and in three days I will rebuild it." Of course, nobody was intending to destroy that Temple. It was the unquestionable centre of Jewish life, but what was it? Eventually, it was destroyed, and neither that place, nor churches and cathedrals, were where God dwells, because God is everywhere with us. Engaging with Jerusalem was engaging with the Jewish leaders, the supposed God hub, the Roman Conquerors and the human condition. What might happen in Jerusalem?

At Jericho, the Roman tax citadel for Jerusalem and Judea, the chief tax collector Zacchaeus, very wealthy, was converted to Jesus' way and handing money back to the exploited. The Roman system rocked a little. People were being healed. Something was stirring. A million people city, aside Rome, was awesome. The Festival was big - crowds flowing, eating, talking, assessing what was going on and prepared to do direct politics. The Romans were wary of uprisings and the Jews had factions and conspiracies. Festival Jerusalem was great, but a danger point. In AD 66 the Great Jewish Revolt was centred on Jerusalem and the Temple, and Josephus reports 1.1 million dying. Now it was not so intense, but the problem was there. Zealot nationalists hated the Roman invaders and wanted to attack them, but the Temple Party wanted offerings and the Temple taxes like normal. The Pharisees were stronger out of the city and had their synagogue system rivalling the Temple. Jesus had come. He was well known, a potential national leader of awesome teaching and healing.

He came as Peace, quite deliberately, in an act beyond theatre, calling up the prophet Zechariah. In Bethphage, just before Jerusalem, he stage-set it. Crowds massed. He borrowed a donkey colt and its mother, lest it be scared, to sit on and began the descent. He knew exactly what he was doing. This was the peace event done to the written script, the donkey for the warhorse, set up so that we all can understand.

Shout, daughter of Jerusalem!
See your king comes to you,
Just and having salvation,
Gentle and riding on a donkey,
On a colt, the foal of a donkey.
I will take away the chariots from the North
And the war horses from the Jerusalem,
And the battle bow will be broken.
He will proclaim peace to the nations
His rule will extend to the ends of the earth" (Zech. 9:9-10)

The message was obvious. The people cheered, knowing beyond knowing they needed this king. He was peace coming to them. We need him. But the moment passed. They could not understand. They saw him weep over Jerusalem because it would not realise what peace required. They could not see it, like we could not see it. He knew he was going to die. This was not ego, but putting down the long marker in case we also do not see the way of peace.

Then the confrontation occurred with the driver of evil. Paul's "the love of money is the root of all evil" applies to militarism too. The modern arms companies since Krupp have been out to make money. Jesus identifies the problem and for the second time in the Temple, he turns over tables and creates chaos for the money collectors. The Temple was stacking up gold in its Treasury. All Jews were encouraged to pay the Temple Tax and the High Priest and Temple Party were rich and protecting their system. When the Temple was destroyed by the Romans in AD70 there was so much gold around in the Eastern Mediterranean that its price fell by 50%. He put the desire for money on the stage. The issues are out in the open. Money and power – the same today.

Read the texts, especially Matthew 21-26:5. They are packed. Here we just give the gist. Then Jesus moves to the Temple Courts, effectively the Jewish open-air Parliament, the centre of government, with questions, parables and direct truths. The parable of the tenants unfolds. It is God's vineyard. You try to take over, wanting everything for yourself, and attack and kill those rightly seeking their due. You will even kill God's son. But you are thieves and robbers. The crowd see where this is going.

Then there is Rome, the trap. "Should we pay taxes to Caesar?" Either way he seems damned. Yes, and he is a stooge of Rome. No, and Rome will finish him. But he dances past their outstretched legs and scores the goal, the clinching truth. It is often misunderstood. "Render to Caesar what is Caesar's and to God what is God's" Half and half, isn't it? No. Jesus knew their hypocrisy, the pathetic trap, but this was not evasion, as the crowd knew. "Show me a denarius" he says. Everyone sees a denarius all the time. They push one forward as if he had never seen one before. Four grams, poky little thing there in your hand. I won't even take it from you. Give *it* back to Tiberius and render to God everything. Everyone knew Tiberius had been put down. It was even worse than that.. We know Tiberius, the tax collecting Emperor, hoarded *675 million denarii* obsessively in Rome; they were his comfort blanket. Probably everybody in the Empire knew that Tiberius had this great heap of silver coins which he counted when he couldn't go to sleep. It was an international joke. So, Jesus cashes the joke. Give Tiberius one more and see if he notices it, but give to God what is due to God. Perhaps Pilate's wife, with her guard, stands at the back of the crowd spluttering at the joke – this guy is sharp.

The Jewish leaders then face the great political onslaught (Matt. 23) where Jesus exposes the self-centred nature of their leadership. He tells the crowd to their face: They burden you with heavy loads so that they do not have to lift a finger. They do not practice what they preach (that is the one that nails us all). They do performance for your sake. Don't you defer to them or seek status. They will try to get you into their party, but then they will milk you. They will shut off God's ways of justice from you. The really great among you will be your servants. This ruling group will work hard to make you support *them*, and the Temple, but, really, they are cutting you off from what is good. They will give you words, make you loyal to the Temple, but, really, they are after your money. Don't put the Temple or anything else between you and God. He turns to the leaders directly. You, leaders concentrate on minutiae, but ignore the big issue. You strain at gnats and swallow camels. Outside you are clean, but inside you are full of greed. Outside you are right, but inside you are hypocrites. You claim good history finds its fulfilment in you, when you are murderers and killed the prophets in the past. You kill the good and destroy the young whom God cares for.... It is a devasting confrontation of the system that is running the Jewish state and of all states. The politics of selfishness down the ages are laid bare.

Basically, the Temple establishments led by the High Priest, Caiaphas and his father-in-law, Ananias, the former High Priest, were appointed by the Romans and allowed to run a national taxation system as long as they kept the volatile Jewish population compliant to the Roman system. The Temple Tax brought in a great deal of money and operated throughout the Jewish region and the Temple Treasury was loaded. The Temple group and the Sadducees were thus a rich establishment, seen critically by the synagogue-based Pharisees, and hated by the Zealots. They, too, wanted to lever some Roman power aside. After all Roman power was quite a long way away, mainly in Caesarea, and already Jerusalem was largely their fiefdom. They decide Jesus has to go, be killed, "for the sake of the nation". The truth has burrowed into their darkness and exposed them. "We have to get rid of him, in secret away from the crowds." "Not during the Feast", they say, "or there will be a riot." But they change their minds on that. He is too dangerous. He has said, "You are trying to kill me" and it is true. The temple people want legitimized murder, using the Roman military system, and they get it. They are fixers.

I. The Domain of Peace.

The tempo builds. Jesus holds his disciples/students in the final teachings about love, showing its character by washing their feet as a servant. He knows that God has put all things into his gentle power and he requires his students to love one another. He will lay down his life, but not one of them will be lost. Their lives are sacred and good. They will be holy before God. They will live obeying Christ's teaching, not through compulsion or control but through being taught by God, making mistakes, but growing.

Then he dishes out the big one, as easy as that. "Peace I leave with you; my peace I give you." (John 14: 25-31) The mistake is to see it as some kind of magic, but it is not like that. It is the peace in which no-one is an enemy, no fear, no aggression, no threats, no driving from Mammon, no revenge, just ordinary shake hands peace because God sends rain on good and bad. "I do not give to you as the world gives." You can say that again – no armies, weapons, military control, fighting, conquest, control, taxes. This is for you, no strings attached. Peace I leave with you. You are my friends. It's free. It costs nothing. You just live it and do it. It is the condition of a good life, of good lives lived together. The oppositional stance, the threats, attack, the ambition of control and dominance is all false. It takes you over, but it is false. God gives you peace. "Do not be afraid." Do not let the weapon of fear and the fear of weapons dominate you into false responses. Bear fruit that will last. Do not let the false powers of this world impress you or shape you. They will go for persecution and hate so that they can stay in control. Remember they hated me without reason. But the Ruler of this world stands condemned; this military show is a perpetual disaster.. " I have told you these things , so that in me you will have peace. In this world you will have trouble. But take heart, I have overcome the world…" So, this little band has been given peace and passed it on so that there are now some two billion of us, though sometimes they have fought one another. "My prayer is not for them alone. I pray also for those who will believe in me through their message, that all of them may be one...May they be brought to complete unity to let the world know that you sent me... So you and I are given peace and the question for each of us is what we do with it.. Peace is planted and the trees have grown and will grow.

J. The Arrest, Pilate and the Truth.

He is arrested at night, illegally, with weapons. He forbids the attempt to resist his arrest with the unforgettable words, "Those who take the sword, perish by the sword." If you go for weapons, they will get you. Really, that is the precis of all subsequent history – WW1, WW2, the US arming terrorists and 9/11 right down to Putin twitching nervously. Quietly, Jesus goes to the false night-time trial and then before Pilate to validate his death. "Yes" says Jesus to the Jews, "I am the Messiah." "He claims to be King of the Jews" say the chief priests and rulers because the Romans have to exterminate all rivals to their rule; it is the knife to the throat for Jesus.

Pilate knows the Jews are his enemies, out to get him and lever more power over the Kingdom, and he begins the interrogation of Jesus knowing his reputation and that he is a good man. The charges against him fall away and Pilate asks whether he is King of the Jews. Everyone knows that to say, "Yes", is death and so Jesus will say No. But he does not. He asks Pilate a question about meaning like some linguistic philosopher. "Is that your own idea, or did others talk to you about me?" Whose view of king are we discussing here? Pilate wants his, "No." so that he can flog Jesus and let him go, but Jesus insists on discussing the meaning of political rule, his political rule and on affirming that he is Ruler. My kingdom is not one which involves fighting and my system is centred on truth and truthfulness. What? Truth in politics? Truth shaping politics? Where did that come from? We all know Pilate's later response, "what is truth?" but perhaps we do not see the chasm between the Roman system of militarism, conquest and rule through fear, the same system used down the ages through to Hitler and Putin and the kingdom of non-fighting and truthfulness as the foundation of democracy. Rome

or Christ? War or Peace? Here, captive, knowing it will kill him, Jesus
sees the Kingdom of Peace through into reality because it is true. The god
of destruction is destroyed.

Pilate tries his best. Ironically, Pilate, having just heard Jesus say, "You
are right in saying I am a king" but knowing that Jesus' meaning is
different from the Roman demand for allegiance, goes out repeatedly
and says "I find no basis for a charge against him." It is ironic, because
what he says is true, though he is lying through his teeth to the Jewish
leaders. Time after time he tries to block them or find a way out. "Here is
your king" he eventually says, hoping to appeal to their nationalism, but
the big lie comes back, "We have no king but Caesar." from those who
hate the imperial system. They lie through clenched teeth, burying truth
in expedience. Militarism won and Jesus Christ died on the Roman cross,
the fear machine of the Empire.

K. Doing God's peace in history.

Of course, resurrection is not too big a problem for the Creator of the
universe. God is on our side. The mixture of militarism and intrigue
which had killed him was undone and the Son of Man was with the
dusciples again. No undue drama. It is real, they learn, as he eats fish. He
recaps so that they begin to understand all they had been through and
slowly see the big picture. Go and tell people these truths to learn and
live. You are through fear and know the gentle kingdom is here.

The resurrection was followed by local dramas in Jerusalem as the
disciples, obviously now fearless, had a go at the leaders who had tried
to get rid of Jesus. They were learning from a fairly low base from their
Teacher, conveying the teaching and beginning this business of walking
the Christian faith around the world without conflict, a unique human
history. Peace worked all over the place. Sometimes patterns of conquest
would carry on alongside ordinary people seeing to some extent the
gentle rule of God. This kingdom slowly infused the Roman Empire,
though the outcome was mixed up. Constantine became the first
Christian Roman Emperor, but remained partly militarist, fighting
through to his death. Then the Holy Roman Empire knew something of

what peace was. Sometimes Christianity was domesticated – people lived in peace locally, gathered round a church building – while the bigger structures remained castles and fighting. There were breakthroughs as Anglo-Saxons converted marauding Vikings. Around the first Millennium a big move towards ending armed conflict was partly broken by William the Conqueror and others. We do not know the extent to which peace people have stopped using weapons, refrained from war, created zones of goodwill and re-scaped their souls with love, forgiveness and service through Christian faith, because most history ignores it. A lot of this Christian history is good, but buried. Missionaries learned local languages, did schools and hospitals and loved the locals without conquest. People repented of their wrongs. There were some martyrdoms, lots of peaceful people, godly living, lovely music and diminished aggression. It is the great untold history of the world. I remember buying a Methodist Yearbook for 1899 in a charity shop and it recounts how two women missionaries that year walked into China and disappeared. We do not know what happened to them, but now there are perhaps a 100 million Christians in China.

There are many Christian failures. "What about the Crusades?" the dismissers rightly say. There are the Church establishments which have supported the state in return for privileges, perhaps using the myth that God is on our side - the Crusades, the Reformation Wars, the South and North American and African cruelties, and the mobilisation of churches to our side in the modern wars. Bishops may not have blessed battleships, but were happy to do nationalism when it was required of them. Now we have some American Christians who mindlessly follow Trump, Orthodox who support the Russian Empire, and Westminster Abbey which is prepared to "bless" Britain's Continuous At Sea Nuclear Deterrent, as though the missiles give a damn.

Historically there are the giants of peace, perhaps a lot of Saxon, African, Chinese ones we do not know. We journey with these giants of peace to learn from them. My favourites include Edith Cavell from Swardeston, near Norwich. As a kid I cycled out there on my little bike, lay down on the Common, probably outside her house, before the journey back and much later discovered she lived there. She nursed Brit and Hun. She did peace. She was killed. Her white statue is near Trafalgar Square in London. It says, "Patriotism is not enough. I must have no hatred or enmity towards anyone." Yes. But the Nationalists would not take it. Above her head on a huge square plinth it says, "For King and Country". Another is Tolstoy, the world's greatest novelist, who then followed Christ and became far greater. Out of his pen came a sharp two-edged sword. Tolstoy insists on going past all human triteness into goodness, truth and peace. He saved the Doukhobors. He wrote to the young Gandhi and set him off. Put the late Tolstoy in your soul. Then, there was the great gathering to the World Disarmament Conference at Geneva in 1932 with purposeful giants like Lord Cecil, Arthur Henderson and my guide, Philip Noel Baker whom I heard speak in 1962 and didn't really understand what he was on about. We all depend on others to see.

L. Now.

Now there are two billion or so Christians around the world who should have some kind of grasp of peace. Many of us are passive or dormant, not really setting out to make peace. There is nothing special about organised Christianity, or Christians, and other world faiths and perspectives all have their input on peace. All peacemakers are equally good, but on this one, given they follow Jesus, Christians should come up with the goods, not just mumbling liturgical peace, but doing real-world healing truth in unison.

The Church as an instrument of peace has been a tribe of unfit athletes, not thinking, or strategic, not ready to act or mobilize its vast personnel spread across the globe. Two billion people steady for peace, fighting militarism, showing the futility of war after war could slay this dragon in a year. Two billion people can hold hands several times round the globe. Christ has got his troops, but sometimes the troops are merely doing stuff in church buildings and ignoring real world Peace and War. This is the challenge to ordinary christians, churches, bishops, preachers, popes, archbishops and priests. We have failed, cocooned peace, lost disarmament and do not act decisively. Christianity is for the peace, and disarmament, of the nations and we must actually make it. Anytime it could be too late. We need to be out of church buildings and making peace in the real world which Jesus inhabited. Be ready, Jesus said. Understand the times. Move the mountain by faith. It is not the label you wear, Christian or otherwise; it is what you *do*.

Christians, despite vast international connections, remain often nationalist in thinking. Yet, they could quickly be global – two billion Christians fast for full world multilateral disarmament. Catholics are a world-wide communion. There are links from church to church. Christians travel and relate across national boundaries all the time. There are few nations where Christians are not found and have not worked with other faiths. All that is required is to persuade Christians to stand for full world disarmament, to support the peace they are already committed to on the world stage. Past failures can be forgiven. What matters is that we do it now with some sense of urgency and a little faith. Jesus just asks us to see the point and walk the walk on a large scale. We have received peace, and it is time to do something strategic with it.

20. WE DISARM THE WORLD – THE ROUTE.

A. We Know What to Do.

People will do this. We will see it clean and simple. When people go to the shops, they normally know what they are buying. We ordinary people fully disarm the world because it is good for us. War is dumb; therefore, we do *not* arm for war and we *do* disarm for peace. Everyone understands clearly where we are going, the basic rule. You cut all military forces and weapons by 20% a year for five years and then they are gone. You could go faster or slower, but that is about it. Full world disarmament is on the tin and 80%, 60%, 40%, 20% and zero does it. All states do it, and all states then face no threats and have no reasons not to do it. Any state not co-operating would be about as daft as 23 The High Street insisting on having a machine gun to keep them safe when everyone else is unarmed. All states do it equally at the same time and all the threats we live with diminish and then clear. We all understand that. No war. No weapons. If arsenic is bad for you, don't sell arsenic in shops. The whole world disarms through the United Nations in an orderly way with open access and full surveillance. That is what we are going to do. We know where we are going. The maths is not challenging; five fifths make one. We do not leave the military people to work something out, because turkeys do not vote for Christmas. They would complicate things, move back to competitive militarism and say it is too difficult as they did in 1932, the 1960s and the 1990s. The militarists obey our orders. We know how to disarm. All disarm. That is where we are going, because it makes sense.

B. We Know Why.

And we know why. We realise militarism kills millions, traumatizes billions, spends and destroys trillions through war. Militarism is failed policy, at odds with a global economy. It is no good hoping the next war will be a success. War must end to address global warming. Militarised leaders need putting out to grass. We know where we are going. It is not "intellectual", but common sense.

We know *all wars* do not work. Wars fuck up the world. Did the Vietnam war work? Does Nuclear War work? Did we sort out Libya? Is Syria coming to a final neat conclusion? Has Yemen been a great success story? Does a war against China make *sense?* Most of the world has nearly understood that wars do not work; they are 90% there, perhaps 98%. The music still plays, but they now know they are on the Titanic. The Ukraine coverage is horrific. We see a trillion dollars of waste and destruction and dear people derelict and suffering. A cross eyed rat hanging by its tail can see the Ukraine War has not worked. The military-industrial complex is sitting in front of a house of cards. "Hey, we have this system where you might be killed, they might be killed, and bombs are falling all over the place." It is not a good sell. The cards will fall any time when we put the full war history on the table. As the Old Testament puts it, "The Lord has them in derision" and we have them in derision too. We know the arms companies are selling holidays in prison, empty plate meals and rebuild-your-knocked-down house real estate. It is a dumb deal. Their stuff destroys everybody for everybody. That is why we disarm the world.

We change the mood. Who needs enemies? Buy a bomb or a hospital – not sure where to go on that one. We, ordinary people, realise that the present military holes in the ground are not a good way to live. We will all come up and look at the other people just like us who are supposed to be our enemies and we want to disarm. We can get on fine with Mr Wolfeschlegelsteinhausenbergerdorff and Mrs. 嘉木样·洛桑久美·图丹却吉尼玛仁波切.

C. We want fast Political Action - National Legislation.

This is not some vague movement. We want decisive political action where Governments pass legislation and will act on it. Any Government can legislate for Full Multilateral Disarmament proactively, as most states have now for the Nuclear Abolition Treaty. It is enacted when all have adopted it, and so there is no "unilateral" problem. Each Government adds to the overall weight for all to disarm. Voters apply pressure because they will only vote for a party or leader who accepts full world disarmament, and therefore as the petitions and public debate build, they are under pressure. All round the world we will press for States to accept and pass this legislation. It is a different challenge in each state, but in each the petitions, debates built towards the national assent legislation quickly taking place. Why would any state NOT want to pass and commit to it? So that we can know where we are going, this is the kind of document it would be:

National Assent to Full World Multilateral Disarmament.

Preamble.

We, the national Parliament, recognize here the failure of the world-wide pattern of national mutual arming against one another. It produces wars, millions of deaths, injuries, poverty, refugees, destruction, waste and contributes to global warming. Weapons destroy and are a world-wide policy mistake; we admit this and lament our part in these wars and tensions. We accept that the world can fully disarm to become united and friendly nations and the model of having national enemies is dead. We can make world peace to the inestimable benefit of everyone.

We realise that arms companies and some militaries have a vested interest against disarmament, because turkeys do not vote for Christmas. We recognize the need to prevent them from shaping this process, though value their good contributions to making it happen, and wish them well.

We give assent to this proposal to disarm, conjointly with other nations. We understand that when states representing 70% of the world's population have given assent, it will become international law at the United Nations. Before then no requirements exist. After then, all states comply. If any do not, they will be subject to a 30% import/export charge on all trade to cover the cost of any necessary remaining defensive stance.

Broadly, we agree to eliminating all arms and armed forces by 20% a year in five years, putting in place all that is needed for peaceful and lawful living among the nations. Effectively we accept the normal domestic national model of no arms and law abiding, non-aggression for all our international relations and look forward to a peaceful world.

Main Clauses.

1. DISARMAMENT. All states cut all forms of weapons, military forces and military budgets by 20% a year from the assigned date until in five years, they are gone. Weapons are recycled. Military personnel have appropriate pensions. Military facilities are repurposed by international agreement. In each state this is supervised by an international team under the UN disarmament commission. Each state should view this as an unproblematic procedure not involving picky disputes.

2. OPEN INSPECTION. To guarantee this is done, open international inspection of all sites is allowed, and all national governments and information gatherers are free to continue with visiting, surveillance and other procedures and to report to the UN and world-wide media.

3. ENDING WEAPONS PRODUCTION. All weapons and military production ceases on the assigned date. The arms producers are subsidised by their national governments 80%, 60%, 40% and 20% of annual income to repurpose to other products and services. The UN international commission monitors that the transition to peaceful production is complete. Weapons production and sales are immediately a criminal offence.

4. TERRORISM AND POLICING. Terrorist groups are offered weapon buy-back facilities for three months and then, if they do not surrender them, their weapons are confiscated through armed territorial sweeps. The

United Nations has an international military/police force to address any non-disarmament which declines in size as the weapons' threats diminish.

5. MILITARY DICTATORS. Military dictators are offered open democracy or pensions and retirement. Military Governments disarm and have supervised transition to democratic politics or face the 30% tariff.

6. INTERNATIONAL LAW AND COURTS. Clearly, the end of weapons will reduce many international tensions and threats of war. Strengthened international law, justice and courts will address issues of justice between nations in principal and practice. Any military damage anywhere faces full reparations and criminal punishment.

After a year of preparation and five years of implementation all military systems are closed down and their resources made available to good uses including global warming disaster relief. We finally make world peace, recover from wars and the damage of world militarism. Nation can now be at peace with nation. We learn war no more and become united rather than divided nations. We assent to this reform and encourage all other governments to do the same. We look forward to being fully at peace with you.

Every government thinking soundly can sign up to something like this, properly drafted, once they have been pushed out of their current mindset. There are millions of people competent to mount the pressure for this to come about, probably including you.

D. We do world opinion again.

Let's have a bit of nostalgia. Hear from a hundred years ago when they did the same world disarmament. Everyone who counted was for it, because four years of World War One was a disaster for everybody. They had fought a nationalist/patriotic war, but then saw world-wide the military system was dumb. It was, as everybody knows, The War to End All Wars. Let's drop some names. The Pope, President Wilson, Leo

Tolstoy, Keir Hardie, Mahatma Gandhi, Albert Einstein, Ramsey MacDonald, Bertrand Russell, Jane Addams, Archbishops Cosmo Lang and Temple, Lord Cecil, Arthur Henderson, Rabindranath Tangore, Vera Brittain, Augustus John, H.G. Wells, Aristide Briand, Frank Kellogg, Karl Liebknecht, Rosa Luxemburg, Sir Edward Grey, King George V were for world disarmament and you don't get much bigger than that. But so too were millions of ordinary people who collected signatures, went on marches and talked disarmament. We, the little people, do the same again.

Then, probably well over half world opinion was for world disarmament. It did not require great intellects, although great intellects understood the issues. Einstein probably had a lot of mind left over when he realised war did not work. Really the need for world disarmament was no more intellectually demanding than basic school algebra. If they did it then, with horses, postmen, door to door petitions, open top buses and cars at walking pace, then we can do it now with the web, television, mobile phones and everybody linked around the world all the time. All we have to do is refuse to stay inside the militarist box with its scares and talk to one another. Seeing through to full world disarmament for all states in the world-wide web is big, but we order the biggest meal, because it is also unbelievably cheap, for everybody.

So, the same discussion goes round the world. Wars kill millions, traumatize billions. Weapons cost trillions. Destruction costs trillions. We by-pass established politics. Pope Benedict, Pope Francis - same message. Suddenly it cracks open, as it did in 1931. There is a point when you know the game is up. It happened in 1931 with Field Marshall Wullie Robinson, British Chief of Imperial General Staff during the second part of WW1 in 1916-18. He was the soldiers' soldier, the first up through the ranks to CIGS, the top job. He was Mr. War. This is his conclusion in the great Albert Hall Peace rally addressed by three Prime Ministers – MacDonald, Lloyd George and Baldwin – in July, 1931.

> Ten million lives were lost to the world in the last War, and they say that £70 million in money was spent in the preliminary bombardment in the battle of Ypres; before any infantry left their

trenches the sum of £22 million was spent and the weight of ammunition fired in the first few weeks of that battle amounted to 480 thousand tonnes …..I do not believe that this represents the best use the world can be expected to make of its brains and its resources. I prefer to believe that the majority of people in the world in these days think that war hurts everybody, benefits nobody - except the profiteers and settles nothing.

As one who has passed pretty well half a century in the study and practise of war, I suggest that you should give your support to Disarmament and so do your best to support the promotion of peace…[xl]

Yes, Wullie, you have nailed it. The British wartime CIGS says the game is up then, and it is now as well. The conclusion has not changed.

This time the Russia-Ukraine War which much of the world has seen can be the War To End All Wars. World public opinion then and now can roll through to full world disarmament. We move from Russia bad, West good, arm for another War against Russia to: We all disarm to end all wars. We change our views democratically without indoctrination, we face down partisan propaganda and back world disarmament.

Probably what will swing the door is seeing and sharing with all of those who suffer now and have suffered through militarism as they then suffered in the trenches. Yes, it is really listening quietly to suffering which will change world opinion. The old armour of we must be strong will be removed and we hear the suffering people of Ukraine, Yemen, Syria, DRC, Libya, Myanmar, Cambodia, Vietnam, China, Japan, France, Italy, the USSR, Poland, Iraq, the 100 million refugees, the soldiers and civilians suffering PTSD. We will hear the 200 million mute war dead and not much debate will be necessary, because we have heard the quiet and the silent. World opinion will change and we will end all wars.

E. The First Few are You.

How do we get the operation rolling. It's your job. The start is hard. Big organisations - states, multinational enterprises, propaganda machines, opinion formers, advertisers, media companies are used to shaping the minds of billions of ordinary people. Often the messages are quite trivial, like "buy this" or "go on holiday here" but the drift is towards making people passive. It is difficult to get things moving. Groups like Extinction Rebellion organise to address climate change and overcome the passivity which prevents change. They are sometimes seen as "extreme", but actually that is the exasperation and the huffing required to move a massive, embedded stone which prefers to do nothing. It seems difficult to go against the flow of the big organisations, multinationals and economic establishment, because it is. They are the Amazon of world selling and decision making and going against the big flow is tough, very tough.

The problem is moving from the passive model where they do it to us to an active model of world change mobilising millions and then billions of people, who do it. How do you organize it? Money probably helps, but not much. The Militarists have billions; peace groups have tens of thousands. That inequality skews the outcome. But how does the flow go the other way? Who can do it? Each person counts. You count. You persuade people that full world disarmament is practical, successful and do-able. It is person to person. It needs ordinary intelligence, not artificial intelligence, asking people for some commitment to sign petitions and also share. There is no sales pressure and no false appeals. It is one by one, but in communion with families, friends, neighbourhoods, churches, schools, universities, cities, media networks, newspapers, political parties, workplaces. Will you do it? It is ordinary, one sentence arguments, but unless you make peace it will not be made. We start. We contact. We set the ball rolling. We debate. We all hear the arguments and pass them on. We question. We show war does not work, that weapons destroy. We show that peace is good, practical and safe. Soon it will be downhill all the way.

Then hundreds and millions of people can be disarmers. They need some honesty, to be people of peace, not self-promoting, to see through to results, and later to hold organisations and institutions to account, but they/we can mobilize millions of us to do this thing. Governments will turn (why should they not?). The United Nations will be given authority to act. We will all transparently see what is going on. Nothing will be hidden. We will *make* peace. We need some good organisers; we are the bricks and you will build the house from us.

F. Speed and Treacle.

The need is to move fast and get jobs done. The publicity out to a billion or more can happen in weeks if we understand multiplication sharing. When a job is done the next stage must be ready. Families, churches, social centres, towns, cities, peace groups, political parties, states, media outlets do their job and implementation gets underway. People can move fast or go slow. Many people stuck in jobs, self-importance, incompetent or thinking about trivia are as slow as glaciers. They are treacle. They bog everything. This movement must avoid treacle. It must be a mighty river in flood to do the business with no distractions. The right people will emerge with the right, humble view of power, and then the rain will fall, and Ol' Man River will swirl along to get it done.

G. Looking after our Enemies.

Jesus said, "Love your enemies." Look beyond polarisation to when you are friends. Have empathy with those who seem on the other side. Most of the people on the other side are like us. They are earning a living in a system that requires them to fit in. They are soldiers or manufacture arms, or have a military base in their constituency. They probably do not particularly like what they do. Not everybody in chewing gum factories likes chewing gum, and usually there is someone else who will make the ethical decision to go to war or sell arms to this state. Maybe I, given different circumstances, could be part of the military system. If this is so, then 90% of the response to militarism is not hating it, blaming it, shooting it down, but providing a different job. This is not difficult for fine scientists, technicians, competent soldiers, air personnel, logistics people to find other good work. What might initially seem a fight, and will be, until the military opinion formers who have ruled the world in all our lifetimes find they have been overturned, turns out to be a friendly football match. So, we build in the transition to a peaceful world economy and to using these fine people.

H. Most of the World's Population are for Peace and Disarmament.

Most people do not want to fight them on the beaches. They want a holiday on the beaches. They want peace. War is only remotely popular until it happens. Then it is horrific and most people have seen enough on their screens to know it should not happen anywhere. Billions of people want world peace, but have not yet had the chance to say so. So, we ask. "Do you want world peace?" and when the billions say Yes, it is given to us. Military elites now hide the choice so we cannot say yes. We take disarmament out of the shoebox. "You can support full world disarmament and this is how you do it." We are a vast group of people, who when we see peace can happen, will be for it, as was the case a hundred years ago. Football across no man's land *is* more sensible than going back to the trenches and shelling your new friends.

The truth will out. As President Eisenhower said to Macmillan some seventy years ago, "I believe that the people in the long run are going to do more to promote peace than any governments. Indeed, I think that people want peace so much that one of these days, governments had better get out of their way and let them have it."[xli] All of these leaders, or most of them, say they believe in democracy, one vote each. Well. We have voted and voted for full multilateral world disarmament. This is not an opinion poll. It is a full intentional vote to get it done.

I. People, Governments, United Nations.

Much support is already there. We assess our governments and parties everywhere. We see the allies. Norway does peace and reconciliation. Belgium seeks to keep disarmament high on the international agenda. China in 2021 pledged unwavering efforts to work for disarmament. There are the nuclear abolition and prohibition states, the TPNW states. This is a great Disarmament Law and 122 states voted for it. There is the long Indian history of peace. There are peace and disarmament organisations in most countries often squashed by the State. There are academics, thinkers, leaders who are there. This is no new thing. Martin Luther King, John Lennon, UN Secretary Generals and many quiet leaders saw through to it. The Pope, Dalai Lama, Bob Dylan, Greta, Bernie and others will back it. Many times, world leaders have talked about and sought world disarmament, but the turkeys stay in charge. They have not seen a "full solution" to the problem and so we stay where we are. But there is a full solution. Big problem – big solution. The policy is obvious. It is without danger. It exposes no state to threats. It is merely a policy which awaits full world and UN approval. The likelihood is that parties and governments will be swayed to back it when it looks like commanding sufficient domestic votes. Nationally, that may be half a million votes expressed in petitions, opinion polls in a medium sized democracy or more in a bigger state. It's a matter of numbers. Once the ball is rolling it will go down the hill. Of course, the UN will back it; its very name requires it. We live in a web world. Ideas can travel faster than jets. Militarism is busted, if we stand and are counted..

All that is needed is for sensible people to spread the message: We want world disarmament. It saves trillions. Wars don't work. Weapons generate wars, military dictators, failed states, a culture of scares. We're running out of enemies, and the planet cannot take the military CO2 budget, or its costs in poverty and destruction. Use your own arguments. Suddenly the way the stupid megalomania politicians have been talking for decades about military power will disappear in a puff of wind, and we can all discuss disarming carefully and thoroughly. There can be a world-wide pattern of understanding that disarmament is practical and militarism is unrealistic and dangerous. The national disarmament motion is easy for governments to accept and so they do.

We need a global referendum clock which adds up all those who vote for disarmament. Someone can set it up, Perhaps, it can be built from national petition sites and national peace and disarmament organisations. Soon it grows a million a day. When the world disarmers reach a billion the issue is pressing all politicians and it goes on to a world majority when it is unstoppable. At the same time governments face pressure to support it earlier. The moral authority grows as it climbs through 10, 20, 30, 40, 50%, and it would be clearly understood that a majority opinion in particular countries should be accepted by their governments as a valid decision for world disarmament.

When one state does it, especially a bellicose one, then all States can do it, even the United States. The time has come for most of the two billion world Christians to mobilize for it, and countless other organizations could contribute to the democratic weight. Women did it in 1932 and could now, for militarism is largely a male enterprise. The female half of the world's population can lead against male military dominance and war. As governments vote support in the United Nations, resisting becomes meaningless. There is nothing to defend against. Disarm or be a hypocrite. Of course, in some countries the government and the military will try to thwart a process which by-passes their power, but it will be clearly evident they are militarily controlling their own people. There is no other answer to the question, "What are these armed forces for?" The vote climbs to a world-wide majority of countries and government, goes to the United Nations and is implemented by them. Now we probe what seems to be the last impediment.

21. ENDING THE BIG BOYS' RULE.

A. The Vested Superpower System.

There is one final know-your-enemy issue. The Superpowers, the Big Boys, think they rule the world. We confront, and complete world disarmament confronts, an intense replicated system across the world of superpowerdom. Really, since the time of Napoleon and shortly thereafter when Krupp got going, industrial militarism has inhabited the main world powers as the normal way of seeing the world. It carries on. Napoleon was a Superpower, although a bit short and he finally fell off his horse. The Napoleonic Wars were a massive failure in terms of loss of life and economic blight, but industrial militarism then grew back after several decades. The Crimean War and the United States Civil War were similar failures, yet they began shaping up the "superpowers" - the Russian Sense of failure, the Light Brigade succumbing to cannon and the United States gun industry all led to more weapons. Colonialism, and colonial thinking, shaped navies and international strategy and linked the new corporate multinationals to military policy. Imperial powers sparred in South Africa, the Far East, South America, the Middle East and elsewhere, before the armed race into World War One. After the War to end all Wars, world disarmament was again defeated, quietly, by the military interests. Then there was Hitler, U.S. military capitalism, and despite the Great Depression the world entered into the greatest conflagration of all, World War Two. Still Militarism was able to assert its dominance again in the Cold War and since. There are now powerful systems in the United States, China, Russia, India, Japan, the UK, France and elsewhere committed to big world militarism.

The Superpowers do not necessarily win. They carry on in spite of direct failure, waste, and irrelevance around the world. The US failed in Cuba, Vietnam, Iraq and Afghanistan. Japan failed in WW2 but is back heavily armed. Russia failed in Afghanistan, collapsed, rearmed and has now failed in Ukraine. The UK fights as the US poodle, because really it faces no external threat, and fails in the Middle East. Nuclear weapons are a failed farce. Yet big militarism ploughs on. The systems are so powerful in their propaganda, so well-funded, that they do not stop. They live inside their intense strategy and keep moving the furniture. It is like saying before 1789 in France, "We do not need the Palace of Versailles". Of course, you need Versailles. The establishment stays. It has links everywhere. Even though it does not work, is totally unsuitable for the world, wastes and destroys, it carries on. Can it ever be defeated?

Ah... I slipped in the Palace of Versailles there without you really noticing. Of course, real Government took place then and now in Paris, and Versailles was a stranded whale with a lot of overengineered furniture. Militarism, busy with its many servants and uniforms, is surplus to world requirements. We do not need the violence of 1789, the storming of the Bastille, to move away from militarism, we merely take a horse and carriage from Versailles to Paris where we treat L'Arc de Triomphe as a museum piece. And Paris is such a glorious place to be. We do the revolution, but quietly by signing up to world disarmament and seeing it through, and get on with real living and government in Paris and our other cities. Real Government is in Washington, not the Pentagon. Real Government is in housing, food, education, addressing global warming urgently, addressing poverty and the construction of good lives for all.

There is no need to confront the great military establishments head-to-head in their terms, to hit those who govern through might. We turn the other cheek, while getting on with world disarmament, while the militarists try to scare us. They have fixated on keeping "our" people safe through aggression. They still try to live the Battle of Britain, or the enemy out there, but the end of waste and destruction is a practical necessity. We need a Big Boy demolition job. When the sun finally comes out the vested interests will take their vests off and sunbathe.

B. The Arms Trade.

First of all, let us show the arms manufacturers respect. The business motive has been to defend one's people against aggression and death and gradually the armour has developed. It is a mixed motive, mixed with counter aggression and money making, but all of us struggle with and fail with mixed motives in most areas of our lives – we are partly dishonest, selfish, lazy, self-promoting and falsely proud of ourselves. Moreover, a large part of the economy promotes goods and services which are not really good or do not do what it says on the tin. We are all really the same. More than this, the arms manufacturers have pursued professionally with outstanding science and engineering the business of designing and manufacturing weapons with the support of the superstates of which they are part. If the wheels fall off Russian tanks because someone has done a bad job, they do not fall off other tanks because lots of others have done a good job. And the demand for the products is there, coming from elected democratic politicians. And profits and accumulation drive many multinationals and firms. So, this is not the hounding of a scapegoat.

Yet, they have been driving the military car and so it requires some honesty. Basically, they have to admit that their product is a world-wide catastrophe and we will hold them to it. What use is a nuclear bomb? On a scale of 0-10 it is minus 10. The more they sell, the more wars are generated. Their products only destroy, and they wreck large areas of the planet. Therefore, production has to stop. It is cigarettes, only worse, cigarettes which shoot people. They also have to admit that they have built insider status direct to government to ensure their privileged position and buttressed that with a media scare system. For a while we must bring them out from where they are hiding onto the stage, and focus on what they do. The Merchants of Death have screwed up the planet and must admit it under the spotlights.

Then they have to get out of this business and the World Disarmament Treaty will help them to do it. They have two choices. They can deny, as the big energy companies and others denied climate change. They can try to lie. Saying "Our products are not a problem", as another bomb goes off, lacks honesty. Or they can maturely co-operate in the transition to a disarmed world. The skills, engineering, technical competence that they have is urgently needed in many areas, like low energy flying, air and sea transport, mobile aid, catastrophe management, as well as the transition to an unarmed planet. They can do that and more well and they will be friends and we help them to change, subsidize their repurposing. They are subsidized 80, 60, 40, 20% to become good companies.

C. Russia.

And so, we come to the first of the Big Boys, and perhaps the easiest, because it is in a bad way. Russia has been poorly understood. In the early 20th Century its Communism was rubbished to protect American Capitalism. Its contribution to the great 1945 victory was, and is, unacknowledged. The way the US drove the Cold War and its costs to the USSR are not recognised, and the failure of the West to demilitarize and the pressure of NATO towards militarization unacknowledged. The west could apologize to Russia for some of this.

At the same time Putin, a product of the Cold War, has remained locked in an imperial view of Russia and fought this dreadful war against Ukraine. It contains the contradiction that it invites Ukraine to *join Russia* even while it bombs it, destroying housing and infrastructure and killing and injuring people. It is the most absurd tragedy, the worst proposal of marriage ever.. We hope it will not lead to nuclear level responses and the war will end in defeat. Few Russians will have much faith in militarism when it is over, especially because of the cost. Just as the Cold War expenditure on the military destroyed the USSR, so the Russian economy will now decline, and many young lives have been lost. Several times militarism has destroyed Russia. The Russian military is also discredited at home, for international arms sales, and in superpower politics. It is isolated, and lost. Its militarism is already dead and full world multilateral disarmament will merely give it a decent burial.

Russia does have another side. It has the great Tolstoy, the spiritual root of world disarmament, and he will rise again. In 1932 the USSR Government backed the Disarmament Proposals of President Hoover and urged faster action. Similarly in the Cold War, and especially in the 1960s the USSR pushed for disarmament but was denied by the United States. This disarmament background can return, and really Russia should welcome world mutual disarmament. It needs a peaceful, open relationship with Europe. It has suffered from its own militarism and that of others beyond understanding and it knows the failures of 1990 and 2023. Whatever the ideology, militarism fails. Russia can disarm.

D. China.

China similarly can be understood. It has been subjected to the hundred years of humiliation by the colonial powers which included the Opium Wars. It suffered acutely from extremely bloody wars, and poverty and famine went along with this chaotic history. Around the turn of the century, it faced the Boxer Rebellion with Western military attacks, and then began an extended period of civil war among warlords until, beginning in WW1, the incursion of Japan became its biggest problem. Throughout the 1930s and 1940s it suffered acutely under the Japanese invasion and then through the Civil War between Mao and Chiang Kai-shek. Really there was not much time during the first half of the twentieth century when this great country was not struggling with conflict on its territory. Mao's rule was also disruptive and always reflected his military background.

When he went, a far greater degree of co-operation opened up between China and the West. Trading, financial movements and strong industrial development were carried out in part through links with the west, it has become the world's largest manufacturing country. It creates large amounts of greenhouse gases producing goods which are exported around the world to us, and its performance in converting to green energy is thus one of the crucial challenges on the planet. It has shown signs of integrating more fully with world politics.

Yet it remains, though it would dispute it, a military dictatorship. It has the second largest military budget in the world, although at about 2% of GDP it is not a great military spender. At about 3/8 of the US budget, it is obviously not a close rival. It is a nuclear power, and has contributed increasingly to the arms trade, sometimes selling to dubious states. Its military has grown in recent years, though not faster than GDP. It also has an aging population as a result of the one child policy who will not want war.

Recently, military tensions have appeared between China and the West, especially in relation to the South China Sea and Taiwan but not further afield. There are also some 3m Uyghurs held in near concentration camps in Xinjiang Province because they are seen as some kind of threat. Yet China's military threat is ambiguous. The question is how much of it is engineered by western military leaders looking for the big enemy that will keep them in business. Actually, perhaps China is, like the Great Wall, mainly defensive in its orientation. There are some issues around economic expansion, similar to those of the US, but my suspicion is that China would look kindly on full world multilateral disarmament. Someone should ask them fast. If they are for world disarmament, it will save a lot of time and trillions in destructive weaponry.

E. India.

India has a large army and nuclear weapons. It is becoming the most populous state on earth. After independence it pursued a policy of neutrality between the US and USSR and obviously Mahatma Gandhi and Hinduism have contributed to a culture of non-aggression which still marks this great country. Yet it also has the third largest military budget. Its military is largely geared towards Pakistan with whom it has a long irritable relationship, partly focussed on disputed areas in Kashmir and partly linked to the military build-up between the two states. India developed nuclear weapons in 1974 and Pakistan then followed. Another part of this rivalry is that India has largely bought its arms from the USSR and Russia while Pakistan has bought mainly from the United States. Often the arms suppliers help stoke antipathy for obvious reasons. The Hindu-Muslim rivalry sits well with Narendra Modi's Hindu Nationalism, but, if that confrontation were demilitarised, this great democratic country would not be too wedded to militarism. India and China have lived successfully since 1954 within the Five Principles for Peaceful Co-existence.

My perception of the Indian state is that, given the offer of full world disarmament, it would support it. Indeed, it has a long history of looking for disarmament, and, aside the Pakistan problems, has seen disarmament, neutrality and peace as its underlying policy all through.

F. France and the UK.

France and the UK are similar, old colonial countries with nuclear weapons, large defence budgets and an established place in world politics and on the UN Security Council. Their governments are committed to retaining their nuclear weapons and are large arms sales countries with the governments backing the companies often in ways which are illegal or immoral. They sell highly engineered kit to states which cannot make it themselves with little concern for the consequences. Actually, neither country faces a military threat. The National Front in France has also kept militarism in situ. France has learned much about making peace with Germany and framing peace in the European Union. It is half peaceful, but then does weapon exports and nuclear weapons. Perhaps the biggest half is the peaceful half and the French think peace carefully. They would perhaps back full world disarmament and even modify the sentiments of its national anthem, although the tune is great.

The United Kingdom is different. A string of weak prime ministers, Thatcher, Blair, Cameron, May, Johnson and Truss have done a pathetic "Make Britain Great again", and we are taught, since Churchill, to believe we need strong armed forces. For twenty years the UK was the US poodle in Afghanistan and Iraq. The UK departed the European union in 2020 in another nationalist move. So, it seems not to be a good candidate for backing world disarmament. We have much to unlearn. We also have a problem with truth. As we have seen, it goes back a long way. The Tory Party seemed in favour of world disarmament in the 1930s but it was not. You can say you will back world disarmament, as Sir John Simon did in 1932, and then you do nothing. You say you are for disarmament, and then fudge in committees, by making statements, by hiding information, by delay, through "problems", by generating crises. This management of the truth has continued down the decades. Without a big change, even with strong disarmament movements, Albion might be perfidious. Everywhere some rulers will say, Peace, Peace, as many times as it takes and do nothing, or nearly nothing, or will say we are a special case, or will insist on retaining military expertise or any number of moves which are nationalist and militarist, and not global. Governments are slippery. They evade. Getting honest responses out in the open is difficult. Prime Ministers fib. We can hope for more truth and peace-mongering. Scotland might help. So, we will try. Fortunately, the UK does not matter as much as it thinks it does.

But now we come to the big Big Boy.

G. Can the United States of America Disarm? No way.

The United States has ruled the world for all our lifetimes. In 1945 after the WW2 devastation, it was half the measured world economy - rich, vast resources, educated, industrially dominant and able to rule the devastated 1945 world. It has ruled for Democracy with real content worldwide. That was and is important. I love the country and good, really good, friends there, yet it has deep problems.

It is nationalist – America, America. Oh, say can you see, by the dawn's early light, hand on heart, nationalist. All should take second place to your loyalty to America. It is a land of immigrants becoming American together, but America is inside itself. Elaine was asked in the mid-West, "Do you speak English?" "Yes, I speak it like a native" she said, but the joke was not heard. Being *really* global is most difficult for America because it is global by its own power, language, fast food, capital, control of the UN, the dollar, movies and ads. Therefore, it is *really not* global, but ethnocentric, the measure of all things. Of course, it has many fine analysts, academics, politicians, reporters, but they speak to an audience with a prior introversion, and truths remain partly hidden.

For all of us the problem is being right, and the United States tends to see itself as right all the time. It is deep, as deep as the Lone Ranger. Nuclear weapons were right. The USA was right and the USSR was wrong. The US was right in South America, Africa, Europe, Afghanistan, the Middle

East, Asia, everywhere. Even when it was wrong, in Vietnam, Iran, Congo, Cuba and elsewhere, the tide came in and washed the sand flat, and there was no problem. Even in Iraq it was not the bad guy. America is defending Freedom. Of course, that is modulated in all kinds of ways by debate, an understanding of worldviews, ethnic differences, area differences, religious perceptions, individualism and world-wide empathies and awareness, but when the tide flows, America is right.

Its military commitment is reflected in domestic guns. There are nearly 400 million guns owned by American citizens who see that as the best form of domestic safety. So locally and among voters the orientation towards militarism is very strong and often unquestioned. Americans cannot even address shooting themselves in the head through their gun policy; it is not very promising. Washington is the same for Republican and Democrat Parties; there is an automatic link to the Pentagon. Really, Clinton and Obama were quite loyal to the military establishment, though Obama tried to do something different. The Pentagon is at the centre of the biggest military system in the world with both Democratic and Republican Presidents. That is the permanent system in the US throughout all our lifetimes. It seems unshakable. Even now they are developing vast US weapons systems for the decades ahead. Militarism dominates science, engineering and technology employment; it is jobs and careers. The US rules the Attack-Defend system. After 1945, for forty-five years, the two Big Boys propped one another up in the great armwrestling competition which cost trillions and had us all shouting support. Then the US won, and the USSR collapsed under the weight of its military system. Since then, the US has dominated the world as the superpower, the One Big Boy. Can it be convinced that its militarism is wrong? Surely, it cannot democratically convert to full world multilateral disarmament. It is the centre of power that will not give, and without the US nearly nothing happens.

H. The other United States narrative.

Yet there is a narrative which points the other way. The burden of militarism on the USSR through 1945-90, with a much lower GDP than the United States, led it to crumble. Arms did for the USSR. The United States, rich beyond measure, carries on with its vast military system. Except the United States is not rich beyond measure. The cost is vast. The cost of the immediate military budget is about $800bn year on year, and wars in Iraq and Afghanistan have cost some $6tn. Other related military costs are big. That is easily $2,000 per head, or $5,000 plus per household, each year. Really, too, most of US Federal Government Debt at $32tn is attributable to past wars. External debt of $31tn are substantial too. These are not crushing figures, but when the economy begins to struggle, they are very difficult. Domestic weaponry and its policing costs add to the burden. So, the economics are not straightforward. A cost of 3.5-5.0% of GDP drags on the economy and the people suffer.

More than that, the US loses wars. It lost in Vietnam and it has now lost in both Iraq and Afghanistan. Many Americans see, If the US can lose wars, do wars work? Its image of invincibility was also pricked by 9/11. Since Vietnam millions of Americans see through its militarism. More than that, Iraq was a bogus War which trashed the United States' reputation worldwide. It lied, supported a corrupt administration and ignored the United Nations. It forfeited its right to defend world democratic values and the rule of law. Mission Accomplished was not. The greater exposure of patterns of US bullying around the world, and of domestic racialism, reduce US claims to moral authority and many Americans see that. The US merely have their view. Other states have legitimate views too and they can now be debated and questioned. Maybe if the US sees China as its economic threat, that does not require the rest of us to see it as the enemy. Recently, Trump was obviously a vain bully who did little for America's principles or reputation; US Presidents can obviously be wrong. There are thus big questions around the America's Superpower "moral" authority. Moreover, these questions are forming deep roots in the younger multicultural generation as the old white Republican base shrinks. The United States is becoming far more self-critically aware.

And crucially, United States Christianity is changing. Several generations back many Christians allied in a rather unthinking way with Republican politics. It was there with Billy Graham and many tele-evangelists. President Carter, obviously Christian in his thinking, was outvoted by Ronald Reagan who scarcely knew one end of a church from the other, partly because Reagan courted the evangelical vote. Since then, the Republican leaders, the Bushes and most superficially Trump, have done the same, knowing that promises on abortion and a few appropriate gestures will pull in the votes. But many Christians have realised now that they have been used. Now the tide is in the other direction and lots of educated, black, evangelical, reformed and Catholic Christians are seeing that their faith does not sit so neatly with present day militarist Republicanism. Many are even more critically aware, and see that principles of peace and American guns do not fit. They are changing. The question is how quickly and what articulates the issue for them. That we wait to see.

Can the United States take part in full world disarmament? Of course, it can. Initially, it could be difficult, especially given the media exposure of the average US citizen. Much of their lives has been spent in front of television and other screens usually fairly uncritical of the American Way. We are talking twenty *plus* years of their waking lives absorbing this stuff. It entertains, excites, flatters, absorbs, elaborates, engages and much more, but it does not think. Thinking involves coming to a tested and sound conclusion. Yet millions of Americans can and do think, well, academically, following principles and seeing issues. They have travelled and engaged around the world with goodwill. They can easily follow these arguments. If all countries disarm, none threatens the others is a conclusion. Weapons have been destructive on a vast scale around the world is a conclusion. They know war failures. They have radical, good, Christian thinkers and Americans can understand disarmament. Many already have. Millions of American Catholics understand what peace is. People have learned from Martin Luther King. Maybe the United States knows that the long era of defending the world for freedom and democracy through US military power is coming to an end. If freedom and democracy can flourish everywhere without military power, would that not be the better way?

The United States has hosted the *United* Nations. Perhaps they can be united without war, weapons and the Pentagon. Full World Disarmament is even the real completion of the American task, the one that Hoover nearly did in 1932. If wise Americans see through to this vision for the world, the task will be easy. The clear conclusion that the suffering and death of millions through weapons and war is wrong and should be stopped can take root again in the States.

I. The Big Boys can change.

So, the Big Boys can respond too. They really know that at present they are not doing too good a job. They stand on chairs telling us all what to do, but the chairs are wobbling and they are getting old. We invite them to think about it. Look at the mess, your mess in so many different countries. Things can change. You are acting all the time to feed the arms companies and their lobbies, but it does not need to be so. Enemies can be friends. We live globally, not locked inside national states. You have supervised the deaths of millions. Look at your record without propaganda support. Does it not give you some remorse? War does not work and your system generates them. Arms destroy wherever they go, insanely, to no purpose – and you send them round the world. Should ordinary people help shape politics or just be sheep? What is happening to Democracy world-wide? Why are there so many military dictators? Why do you always feel you have to rubbish disarmament when your system works so badly? In response, they may attack to defend or they may listen. You make disarmament seem impractical, but it is you who make it impractical – Look at your response on Nuclear Abolition. By the way, your attempted validation of your non response was low grade garbage. We can show full world disarmament is practical and safe, if you co-operate. We have done disarmament with classes of conventional weapons (landmines, chemical, biological) without people even noticing. Why not do it fully? Are you in favour of ending war, cutting global warming, preventing trillions of destruction and bringing peace around the world, or not? Maybe, the Big Boys can change, or be different big boys cut down to size, or just fall off their chair. Or maybe, they can agree that we all got it wrong.

So, we build a worldwide popular vote penetrating fatalism to determined action. Once the issue is discussed throughout the media, the militarists will wilt, because at present they mainly hide and feed the media from the dark. People will see that orderly disarmament is possible, even easy. We build to several billion people saying, "We want full world disarmament in five years." The superpowers will be in the spotlight. What will they do? You say you want peace. Here it is. Comply, or lead, because the world insists that the instruments of death be collected up and the merchants of death redeploy their skills. We require international law to punish military murder and end the hypocrisy of the phrase, "war casualties". You big boys merely come off your blown-up thrones and become good neighbours like the rest of us. You can even take some credit for the move. You will enjoy peace so much. Peace is going to win.

22. WE FULLY DISARM THE WORLD.

A. We all go for total world multilateral disarmament.

So, this is it. Full World Multilateral Disarmament is to be clear, safe, ordered and transparent for everyone. The central rule is that all arms and armed forces are cut by a fifth each five years until they are all gone. It diminishes threats equally, is clear, gives time for accountability and does the job it sets out to do. Still there will be doubts.

World political leaders sometimes say, We cannot disarm while others are armed. Of course not, we say. It is no good having a no gun policy in Reading and Basingstoke, if guns are retained in Newbury and Andover. Far better and safer to get rid of all guns everywhere in the UK. Oh, we have already done it. Well, you have answered your problem. Most world leaders say repeatedly that they are in favour of peace. The problem is other belligerent states. Well now all these statesmen can be in favour of peace because there will be no other bellicose states. We are all going to disarm. We are all in favour of peace. It is practical. Everybody will destroy and recycle their weapons in an orderly way, and then there will be no weapons.

What if one state sticks with the right to bear arms? Consider this parable. Millions in the US, where there are guns, go on about their right to buy arms to defend themselves prompted by the gun lobby. Yet, *never* in the UK, which is free of guns, does anyone argue for their *right* to bear arms. That is what full disarmament does. Suddenly, all the excuses for not disarming are gone and we can actually do it, and no world leader can really disagree with it, because there will be no-one to attack him or her. We might allow an ex-weapon theme park. "Daddy, can I have a ride on the missile roundabout?" We get rid of all weapons, because we have finally recognized they are useless - destructive of life, limb, property, infrastructure and livelihood. You shall not kill does not do exceptions. Killing is bad. Guns are designed to kill. Hands up world political leaders who think killing weapons are bad. We disarm multilaterally, together, at the same rate, reducing threats, with full access, policing, buy back and then forceable disarming where necessary. You want peace. Now everybody is going to get it. Do you have a problem with that? Everyone understands what is going on. If you don't disarm it will cost you a great deal, and the world will remain armed against you; you will pay the world's costs of you not disarming..

B. The Five Year Full Disarmament.

Let us review the central process. All states cut military budgets and arms by a fifth a year for five years until it is all gone. A child can do the sums. Fractions can be rounded up. It does not really matter. They all go. All states are accountable to do it, and the requirement can be backed by open inspection by anyone in the world, help from other states if progress falls behind, and by heavy sanctions. If you are worried about Iran, go and have a look. If they are worried about BAe Systems, they can do the same. All arms go, aside a diminishing UN policing force. The Destroyer is destroyed. It will be undertaken by all states, with the co-operation of defence organisations like NATO and supervised by the United Nations, with required public international systems of inspection and accountability and the best recycling of materials. With open inspection and surveillance, we can be sure it is done. This is not new. The UN inspected Iraq thoroughly in the 1990s and were right and effective. Here there should be good will and co-operation plus, plus, from all states. Chemical, biological and landmines have been eradicated by similar processes. Big mutual reductions in nuclear weapons have been made. Actually, there are massive graveyards for old planes, tanks and other weapons which have been used for decades to end the life of arms. We already know roughly how to end armaments.

Some of the militarists might try desperately to slow things down by making everything seem difficult, but it is not. Undoing militarism is far faster than doing it. They are resisting what is easy. Weapons can usually be made unusable quickly and open inspection guarantees the process.

Recycling is easy for metals, but quite difficult for nuclear weapons. Yet, we have been decommissioned them for decades, so it just needs careful planning. Because the process is predictable it can easily be seen through and as threats decrease so confidence increases because all want peace.

Clearly, there needs to be even accounting of the contractions by a fifth each year in national military budgets and in real personnel and equipment, so that the process is completely transparent. With required co-operation, military pensions, open access, all the means of surveillance now available and the vested interest that each state has in the others disarming, the process can be without problems, especially if the major players agree to co-operate throughout.

C. Ending the Manufacture of all Weapons.

Obviously, with full world disarmament there is no need to manufacture any more weapons anywhere and the UN legislation therefore requires all manufacture of arms to stop immediately. The Merchant of Death business dies. *A massive, highly skilled industry needs to repurpose its business in a rich variety of ways.* Really, the possibilities are quite exciting. They extend into communications, weather, disaster relief, logistics, tree planting, flood defences, space exploration, civil engineering, agriculture in difficult terrains, mobile care and rescue systems, transport, trade, rescue systems and many specialised systems of engineering. Probably, they would be well positioned for a range of changes involved in addressing global warming, both in terms of extreme events and large policy options, like planting trees, drainage or flood defences. My favourite is the possibility of naval vessels getting fresh water from estuaries and moving it to areas of drought and pipe terminals for inland flows.

But it needs doing in an economically ordered way. If companies involved receive subsidies of 80%, 60%, 40%, 20% and zero from their national governments to repurpose and redeploy their production, they should have a smooth transition to other work. Because they move over to producing real goods and valuable services, the economies of all the countries involved benefit from the new investment and focus. It is the peace bonus, the new good economy.

People might worry that weapons could be produced illicitly. Really, it is not possible at many different levels. First, producing weapons becomes a criminal offence with heavy punishments, as does buying weapons, so it would be dumb to try. Second, active policing and surveillance is now so sophisticated that nothing significant can hide. These days anything can be spotted anywhere and the CIA and other secret services will move over to ensure there are no infringements. Third, how would weapons sell, as all governments become democratic, peaceful and open, rather than militarily controlled? Fourth, surveillance, business links, suspicions of motives, purchasing history and other factors makes it difficult to hide what any business is doing and fifth, the information flows around today make it possible to react to problems quickly. Finally, full world disarmament makes illicit arms production purposeless and just stupid. So, it really is a fear that can, with this approach, be fully laid to rest.

D. The Military must not be in charge.

There is one constant prerequisite to this process. The military must not be in charge. They do what they are told, because otherwise, at first at least, they will complicate/stall/sabotage the process. Disarmament was proposed seriously in 1899, 1907, 1918, 1932 and the 1960s, but never actually tried, because the military-industrial complex killed it off. Especially in the 1932 Geneva Disarmament Conference the military establishment and arms company agents stopped President Hoover's radical disarmament plan. Turkeys do not vote for Christmas. The military-industrial complex could try *every which way to stop disarmament at all stages of the process*. Disarmament will be a fight against them, not to kill and maim, but to make them proper servants of democratic government. They should co-operate. In "democratic" countries this should not be a big obstacle. Later we discuss military dictatorships. Armed forces need to be sure of continued civilian employment, pensions and economic security as they are closed down. Some states like North Korea may need some help.

Of course, many of the military know what is good and will support the process and it will take five years to reallocate them to their new jobs in public and private services. Having a new workforce of 28 million won from aggression and destruction is a major world success. Most soldiers know ending war is the greatest blessing of all and will work for it. They have expertise and skills which would shine in a variety of tasks.

E. Conspiracy Theories.

Because we have lived in a multinational armed world with conspiracies, secret services, James Bond and evil empires, it is easy for people to be worried about global conspiracies *after* disarmament. Someone will still attack us. What about the United Nations when they are the only ones with weapons after the rest of the world has disarmed? Surely someone at the UN could rule the world? Oh that is scary. We can't rely on James Bond. Some little Hitler might turn up disguised in a policeman's helmet, wanting to march somewhere. Or we could face aliens. It is all very worrying.

Actually, of course, it is not. When disarmament comes, defence is unnecessary. The purpose of attack becomes meaningless. Why attack? Even Hitler had to have a rationale for aggression. Attack on its own is an absurd, pointless idea. The Dutch folk of Breukelen have not thought of attacking Mijdrecht for a long time because they are at peace. It is militarism which breeds hitlers. Conspiracies have to make some sense.

The conspiracy industry needs examining. In ancient times conspiracies normally surrounded the throne or the emperor. In the modern era it has grown with the secret services, Ian Fleming, the Cold War, but mainly with a whole history of films which take people on journeys of suspense and cover up. Quite often the Goodies do the conspiracy to get out of prison, defeat the Nazis or prevent the world being blown up. Often, too, the Baddies need thwarting and some Good Guy comes along and gets them. The films major on fear and suspense to hold you. Now this film idiom has moved into the web and media news transmission and is exploited by the Secret Services to keep their show on the road. Two

Trump elections were surrounded, even dominated by, conspiracy theories racing through the media which were largely fictional. There are people creating conspiracies as a route to power. So, it is quite important not to believe conspiracies when they are not true. Aside propaganda we now have the kit to uncover any military build-up.

 The best antidote to this vast false consciousness is Jesus' words, "What is done in the secret places will be shouted from the housetops." As Jesus insisted, bringing this stuff into the light, having open information, requiring evidence, kills it. We might even envisage the Secret Service organisations around the world, the CIA, MI5, the Chinese MSS, the Russian FSB and many others could become the *exposers* of truths, the anti-secret service against all conspiracies instead of secret services. Of course, good news reporting and exposure already does much of this.

F. Eliminating Terrorism.

How can you disarm the world when a load of terrorists all over the place have dangerous weapons and are prepared to use them? It seems to challenge the whole possibility of world disarmament. But it does not. We need to understand three basic truths about terrorism. First, it is the normal response to colonial occupation. Al Qaida was formed because of the US occupation in the Middle East and most of groups exist around an actual or perceived military occupation whether Hamas in Palestine, the IRA in Northern Ireland or Islamic groups throughout the Middle East. We should reflect that Churchill planned moving over to a terrorist Britain if the Nazi invasion succeeded; it is an obvious reaction to military occupation. Now, with the relative military withdrawal of the US/UK from the Middle East, and the changes in the economics of oil, active terrorism has declined and will further. With world disarmament the main terrorist motive goes and people get on with peaceful living.

But there is another factor. We now know that the United States, and especially the CIA, has encouraged, trained and armed terrorists around the world, from Cuba and South America, to the Congo and other parts of Africa to Afghanistan, Iran and throughout the Middle East and over to Laos and other parts of the Far East. There have normally been several interventions a year around the world since 1945. In Afghanistan the CIA pumped in $6bn of arms and support, making many terrorists well off and deciding their career choice. In addition, terrorists have generally picked up US weapons left over from conflicts, as in Iraq, which have armed them for their work. Of course, the USSR had its mirror operations, but the United States led the field from 1945. For these two reasons the Big Boys have largely created the problem of terrorism about which they now complain. If the Big Boys stop this stuff terrorism would wither anyway.

Third, there needs to be a direct plan to close down existing terrorist groups. These are people with guns who have become professional lawless soldiers. This has two stages. First, in each area where there is a problem, a buy-back policy is in place for a number of months. Weapons can be bought back at a suitable price and then destroyed. If they are not handed over, then weapon owners become criminals and the UN and national police/armed forces move in to clear areas more systematically, fighting if necessary. They then confiscate without payment and terrorism is criminal. With no arms/ammunition production or rationale these groups wither and disappear. Certain areas like North Nigeria, DRC, Afghanistan, Pakistan and the Philippines might need special help, but this is not a great problem. Really, it is largely created by the vast excess of small arms manufactured year on year by companies who will sell to anyone who wants to pursue terrorism and old arms caches from the big boys. They especially need checking through tracing shipments and closing down the smaller arms traders. Eliminate that and terrorism will wither.

Fourth, we need to be aware that these people need jobs and retraining. They could be given motorbikes and the kit to do something better in life and they would change. Always you love your enemies.

G. Will States Oppose Disarmament?

Will States oppose Full World Disarmament? Let us look at a little parable. In 1945 two states, Japan and Germany, were completely disarmed, not allowed to manufacture weapons, and even had to pay quite a bit for their military occupation by the Allies. They were also among the worst damaged states in World War Two for obvious reasons. By about 1960 two world surprising "economic miracles" had occurred. Where? In Japan and Germany. They were both producing all kinds of useful things that were exported around the world and their economic growth was outstanding. Was it that the Japanese and Germans worked harder? Well perhaps they did, and the economics of this period were complex with Marshall Aid, reparations and control, but one obvious factor stands out. Military expenditure does not produce anything. The UK spent 6-7% of GDP on Defence throughout the fifties while Japan and Western Germany contributed perhaps 2% to the Western Allies for occupation. It was *not spending* 4-5% of GDP compound over a decade and a half which made the difference, the economic miracle. Even in a decade, that results in a real growth of more than 50% in the German and Japanese economies. The miracle was mainly *not* spending on defence. This is the bonus of disarmament - the peace bonus - bombers into hospitals, tanks into houses, missiles into schools, fighters into factories and drones into parks. Any leaders who ignored this bonus would have to be perverse.

Second, there is the truth. World leaders have said since 1945 that they are only for Defence, never for Attack. With no need for defence, do they mean it? Most medium sized states will agree on full abolition, as they already have in the UN Treaty on the Prohibition of Nuclear Weapons. It is likely that at least a hundred of them would sign up instantly to full world disarmament. If you are really only for defence, you sign. The big questions lie alongside two groups, the military dictators and then the Big Boys - the US and China, with India, Brazil, Russia, the UK, Iran, France and others as second level powers. If they have been telling the truth about Defence, they will sign. If they will not, the question is why?

Third, there is the world economy. Arming against recalcitrant states would cost and therefore we make them pay. Policing forces will only fall as any remaining threats go, and they therefore incur 30% extra import and export tariffs from everybody because of the costs of defending against a still armed state. Retain arms and be taxed heavily for the privilege. Aggression would be forcibly crushed by everybody. It would incur full damage reparations and face exclusion from the world economy. There is therefore no point in not disarming, because having arms is an act of *aggression* against other states, as it is domestically now.

Disarmament is not an option, but the requirement of international law. Simply, world peace requires swords into ploughshares. If you have six fully armed tanks in your garage, you are not a safe neighbour and should go to prison.

H. Ending Military Dictatorships.

As we have seen, there are a lot of military dictators around the globe, fifty or more. They have control over the State because the military supports the State and will put down any opposition. Sometimes Generals and Colonels are the Head of State. Notice it is usually the Army which is important – Generals Galtieri, Gowon, Musharaff, Lol Nol, Colonels Nasser, Gaddafi and many - more because the point about military dictatorships is keeping the populace placid on the ground, as we say. The military often have a well-paid relaxed life and so does the leader. In this sense introverted military dictatorships do not involve strong external threats, but there are many others that do threaten if they have big weapon bases. Most of Africa's seem introverted. North Korea is an external threat as are other states.

We might be surprised by how readily external threat dictators accept full world disarmament. Some actually do feel threatened by the West, and with good reasons. The bombing of North Korea in the Korean war left almost nothing standing and North Korea has been held in apoplectic fear. Pakistan is focussed around the tension with India. When the military confrontation with a far stronger power subsides, it might be readily welcomed. The internal dictatorships are more problematic. They tend to be in a band through central Africa and the Middle East into Asia, doing rather bad government and not being liked much. Yet, perhaps here it helps to see the problem of a military dictator. Once you start suppressing opposition views by force, views begin to cohere as opposition to dictatorship. They grow. Opposition by a new generation leaves the leader stranded, old, locked in his (always his?) military cabal and facing violent ejection. There is no way out of power. Perhaps the key to easy transitions here is to provide the leaders with an easy route into retirement. We could have a big retirement home for old military dictators. Of course, if a leader does disarm while in power, they are likely to get popular support for democratic government.

Otherwise, wide popular support for world disarmament undermines the base in which the militarised government puts its trust. It is cut off from arms and the kit that keeps populations docile. Other governments are going democratic. The relationships with multi-national corporations might become more transparent. In some states it will be tough. Egypt, for example, has a privileged military. Moving it over to democracy will involve steady determined reform. Not to change would involve inevitable defeat, weak dictators in a losers' club, isolated.

I. Democratic Reform.

We tend to forget that many so-called democratic countries will also need reform to get the military out of their privileged and dominant position. Militaries might try to line up with right wing groups in the old Fascist alliance against World Disarmament Reform. Many militaries, of course, are not anti-democratic. They may be more just and democratic than the rulers. Many, too, if their own peaceful career route through and after retirement is smooth, will not fight through self-preservation. The transition budget therefore needs careful design. The new purposes of the unarmed forces need articulation and planning. The links with arms companies need severing. Secret services need transparency. International military co-operation under the UN needs careful planning. The key to most of this is openness. If all of the issues are brought into the light and addressed, the full democratic transition to unarmed politics should not be difficult. Being unarmed is not a problem; it is the solution to a problem.

J. The Rule of Law.

Disarmament is not naïve, trusting that everyone will do what they have promised without accountability, but operates under the rule of law. Murder in war is the same as murder in Dagenham. Property damage in Homs or Aleppo is the same as property damage in Sydney or Grand Rapids. The underlying international law, to which policing holds us all to account, is that the possession and use of weapons is illegal, and killing people and damaging property is accountable to law and recompense, whether damage has been done by the United States or by the thug in the urban jungle is the requirement of the law. The dreadful double standard, whereby destruction in war is quasi legal, whereas destruction of property and person within a nation is punished, ends. The law of reparations is picked up and dusted down. Destruction will be paid for. It should need to be used rarely. Taking a bull on a lead into a china shop is culpable under the law.

Peaceful resolution rules through law and courts, settling disputes and trying crimes. The International Court system expands, acting more strongly, to address transnational issues of injustice and lawlessness. There can be early dispute resolution systems to precede issues which might cause problems later when one nation has ought to complain of against another nation. The big bonus is that most international disputes are easier to settle if arms, threats and superpowers are not around because the issues of justice are central. As well as disputes between nations, disputes involving multi-national companies also need addressing, as the recent history of tax evasion shows. Criminal punishment without fear or favour becomes easier when superpowers do not force their exemption with the gun.

K. Disarmament is policed by the United Nations.

The process of disarmament is to be administered by a policing body, acting under strict rules. This is not a vague process, but the required implementation of international law. Policing occurs in states and internationally. First, states are responsible for the arms and military they control and the destruction must be public, internationally verified and not reversible. In most states that process should lead to complete disarmament, but in some terrorists and criminals operate outside the law and with independent weapons, and these states ask for help internationally, so that multi-national armed groups clear areas of weapons and anarchy. They are backed by strong laws prosecuting weapons retention, terrorism and military intimidation. The beauty of this policing system is that as weapons are destroyed and repurposed, the size of the policing task diminishes year on year.

Our security about this process should be great. With contemporary surveillance equipment it should be possible to police this weapons' decommissioning rigorously and well. Obviously, several countries would be involved in the disarmament of any one country, insisting on information, access, detection equipment and so on. Weapon detection equipment might be a temporary growth industry. The mobile phone era allows effective whistleblowing against evasion. Any suspect facilities can be opened up to inspectors instantly. If you can be inspected at any time, it is extremely difficult to cheat or undertake clandestine munitions' operations of any significance. Criminal prosecution deters and it is not clear what purpose avoiding disarmament could possibly serve. In this way the steady disarmament of the world can be policed down to zero. Those who feel insecure without weapons can be given counselling and water pistols.

Some will try to argue that United Nations policing is the equivalent to the creation of a world-superstate. They should be assured by several things, First, the forces retained will be multi-national, as they are at present, preventing the creation of a single power bloc. Secondly, these forces will be run down as the need for them diminishes. Third, infringements by the United Nations forces would be subject to the same rule of law as everyone else. Fourth, the United Nations is not structured as a military force, but as a world democratic body. It is not committed to power over, but to living together in peace. It would be difficult to see it as a military threat; it would be a bit like midwives for infanticide. It is the stuff of poor conspiracy theories. The weaknesses of the League of

Nations in Ethiopia, Spain and Manchuria will not be repeated; there is a difference between law enforcement and militarism which we have all understood domestically for centuries..

L. Through to Disarmament.

So the World goes through to disarmament. This book is longwinded but millions soon understand the issue through seeing the suffering, thinking things through, observing the failure of war and they only need to carry peace through. Really, it is so easy to all disarm. The Big Boys will be far better for it. Military Dictators will depart their lonely lives. Slowly the war weariness of the nations over several generations will depart. The soldier becomes the friend. The threatening cross of fright is thrown in the canal. There will be no more bombed flats. No blood will gush from limbs through attacks. No refugees will wait. No war widows will weep. No armed self-righteousness will hog the airwaves. No nuclear disasters or wars will occur. There will be no pointless marching to follow orders. No one will plan to bomb power plants. No longer will the curse of war hang over any country. No pariah countries like North Korea will live outside. We live in the healing of the nations. No-one learns war any more. We have simply learned the truth that You shall not kill is required all the time. Instead of the god of destruction we have made for ourselves, the Lamb will preside.

Of course, we each have to do the work, a little bit of work, to grow full world disarmament. The first million voices are the most difficult. People understand this can happen, despite the success of the arms companies in making us fatalists. We, each in our way, can disarm the world simply by persuading ten people that it should be done. This is old fashioned democracy. We the people act in faith with understanding so that our governments make peace, really, by closing down the military system. "My peace I leave with you", said Jesus. We receive it, understand it, become it and pass it on.

You are a drop, a tear that must fall
From heavy clouds upon the churned earth,
Or ocean, wrapped around the world,
The billions, one to close the mighty show.
"We keep you safe by threatening we will war.
Our arms we sell for profit. We will smash
The world for freedom for we need control
Over the wrong, the right, to fight and kill."
Down on our knees we turn the right to wrong.
The world has goofed. The big boys messed it up.
And now we mourn the litany of war.
We rain our votes to bend all swords to earth
And grow the grain we need to let live live
And heal the nations, making his peace true.

23. WORLD PEACE.

A. The Rest from War.

Peace will come. The god of destruction that we have made evaporates to nothing. Perhaps we retain a few nuclear missiles to zap any incoming meteors in the next century or so, and we live peace. It is not some state of suspended animation, but a time when, on a global scale, we can do good for one another, know the richness of all tribes and nations and make what will last and be respected. Many of us live in local peace already. We go for a walk or holidays, live in a nice neighbourhood and do not fear death or destruction. Nothing will seem to change, but really our lives must be good for all. Now war touches everywhere. Then it will not happen. We give one another peace.

It is the deep biblical narrative of world history. It is Isaiah and Micah reflecting on doing it God's way.

> God will judge between many peoples
> and will settle disputes between strong nations far and wide.
> They will beat their swords into ploughshares
> and their spears into pruning hooks.
> Nation will not take up sword against nation
> Nor will they train for war any more.
> Everyone will sit under their own fruit trees
> and no-one will make them afraid,
> because we have listened to God.

It is not extraordinary, but ordinary, as the Germans talk with the French, the Japanese sup Scottish whisky and Russians and Ukrainians become friends. It is the healing of the nations, the end of Empires, the folding up of terror, and the gentle meeting of all nations.

We will finally nearly understand what Jesus of Nazareth was about, the ruler who wandered about doing good without controlling people, showing what healing might be like and giving the sword a bad name. Even when the Roman Empire, reluctantly, made an exhibition of its power over him, killing him on its cross, he had the last word and rather a big one. We have not known what we are doing, but we are forgiven. We have been given peace to share and it works. We love one another as we love ourselves and are at rest from war and the rumours of war.

B. The Healing of the Nations.

Then we will understand how long-term ill the world has been. We have devastated the Middle East leaving flattened cities, destitution in Afghanistan and elsewhere. Half the world cowers under military dictators. Militaries are trapped in their missions of destruction. Perhaps a billion are traumatized by war this generation and another billion further back. Where we now blame, we will see the sufferings of the past in the USSR, China, India and other western occupied nations. Both victims and assailants need healing. When we live in a ruling ideology which traumatizes, we are damaged. The West is full of arrogant selfish bastards, including me, hardened through winning and we will see we have been the problem. There are the open wounds of Somalia, Yemen, Syria, Sudan, Myanmar, Libya and now Russia-Ukraine. There were a hundred million refugees. Many Jews still suffer the Holocaust. Perhaps the world could have recovered from World War One in the 1940s, but something else happened. The world we have made needs several decades of peaceful healing, forgiveness and restoration; nothing else will do.

We fully disarm by 2030, try to address global warming and its calamities in the next two decades, and perhaps by the middle of the century there will be substantial healing from militarism as trees grow instead of bombs falling. It requires patience, insight and all of Christ's Beatitudes. Healing is like tree growth and it happens at about the same pace. Especially, the West needs poverty of spirit, the long wind down from being right and assertive. learning how we were wrong.

C. Humility and Undoing.

So often in life we need to undo things and the same is true in politics, but usually we do. We need new policies to address global warming. We need to do this and that and the other and activism is a large part of our response. Sometimes however we need to do less than nothing. We need to undo what we have done because it is haunts us and harms us. Now we have reached that time in relation to militarism. Here are some things we might face. We, the West, did not win WW2; the USSR mainly did, at vast cost. The Western Empires were mainly wrong and we all apologize. The West has harmed democracy. We have looting the planet of resources; now we steward. The US has run systems of control across much of the planet; they should own up and correct. Wealth needs to be spread. US military bases need full repurposing. We could think about population globally; where would immigration be good and why? Can refugee status be seen anew? We think through what is really good to buy, rather than stuff for our egos. We distrust the love of money and its ability to fuel evil.

We now see the true meaning of power in human life. We see that good power is constructive, like apples forming on trees, not destructive like bombs. We have seen through "power" as control over, the ability to manipulate people to my purposes and make them serve me. We have faced the fear of being killed. We have seen through the arrogant power of empire and why it has destroyed and demeaned so many, right through to Emperor Putin. We see through the competition to get to the top, the self-worship of the Big Boys in history. We see that might and the mighty have to off their thrones and all we little people are as important as them. We see that politics is about serving people for their good and justice, because you showed us this great lesson by washing feet and drying them with a towel. We see we live before God in blessing, growing like trees. We love and are loved despite our failings. We enjoy one another more than things. We know that service is the humility which makes life and democracy work. The lording people melt away. Thank You, Jesus. You have given us peace on earth, we have received it at last, have made peace, and are blessed to be children of God.

Appendix One. Wars since 1900

This gives an idea of the steady flow of wars and their damage. The costing is done mainly at today's prices through income loss calculated at a contemporary figure of $10,000 per person per war year if directly involved through invasion or action. This equalises across rich and poor. Obviously, it only roughly covers human loss, destruction, military costs in one assessment. There are some adjustments for other factors. Key: If possible, belligerent first. People in war area – P: Troops – T: Deaths (troops and civilians) -D: Wounded – W: Traumatized – Tr: Refugees R: Cost guessed in today's prices – C: Mainly constructed using SIPRI data after 1960 and Wikipedia.

1885-1908 BELGIAN CONGO under Leopold II. P: 30m. T: ? D: 10m. C: $6tn.
1899-1901 BOXER REBELLION (China/West) P: 30m, T: 500k, D: 100k W: 100K C: $120bn.
1899-1902 SECOND BRITISH/BOER WAR. P: 2.5m. T: 600k. D: 78k. I:98k. C: $50bn (215k in concentration camps)
1899-1902 U.S./PHILIPPINE WAR. P: 7m T: 215K D:200-400K C: $140bn (215k in concentration camps)
1900-1920 Britain, Italy/Somaliland. P:300k, T: 35k. D: 125k. C: $1bn. **(arial bombardment)**
1900 War of the Golden Stool (Gold Coast Governor, Hodgson, wanted Ashanti golden stool) P: 1m. T: 25k. D: 3K. C: $10m.
1900 France-Borno/Chad, Battle of Kousséri T:11K, D:1,200 W: 3k
1900-01 Kuwait-Rashidi War D:76k
1901-02Anglo-Arowar T:10k D:3k
1902-03 Ger/Fr/Brit – Venezuela (Naval War blockade)
1903 Britain-Tibet – Younghusband attacks weak Tibetan troops P: 1m T:10k D:3k C: $1bn
1903-7 Saudi-Rashidi War (Ottoman/Saudi War) P: small. T: 30k. D: 70k. C: $1m.
1904-08 German-Herero War (German take-over of S.W. Africa) P: 3m. T: 50k. D: 80k C: $50bn.
1904-5 RUSSO/JAPANESE WAR. P: 10m. T:2.5m. D:140k. I: 150k. C: $200bn
1905-7 Russian Revolution. P: 20m T: 50k?. D: 19k. I: 20k. C: $50-100bn
1905-7 Maji Maji Revolution (German/Tanzania) P: 2m. T: 100k. D: 150k? C: $5bn.
1906 British Bambatha Rebellion P: 2m. T: 20K. D:3K C: 1bn.
1907-11 Qing Dynasty Uprisings leading to 1911 P: 15m. T: 300k. D: 220k. C: $600bn.
1908 Young Turk Revolution. Ottoman Empire problems.

1908 Dutch-Bali. Colonial opium trade. T:1k. D: 200

1908 Dutch Venezuela. Naval blockade

1909 Quaddai War. France/Chad P:1m. T: 10K. D300K. C: $5bn

1910-20 Mexican revolution. (US and other western involvement) P: 15m. T: 545k. D: 2.7m C: $800bn

1911-12 Paraguayan Civil War D: 5k.

1911-12 French conquest of Morocco. P: 5m. T: 20k? D:120k. W: 15k. C: 20bn.

1911-12 Italian-Turkish War. P: 5m. T: 120k. D:23k. W: 4k. $5bn

1911-12 CHINESE XINHAI REVOLUTION. P: 500m. T: 300k. D: 220k. $5tn

1912-13 FIRST BALKAN WAR. P: 10m. T: 1.25m. D:500k. $200bn

1912-13 US occupation of Nicaragua. D: 1k.

1912 Negro Rebellion Cuba. D: 5k.

1913 Second Balkan War. T: 1.6m. D: 25k.

1913 Chinese rebellions.

1914-18 FIRST WORLD WAR P: 450m. T:80m. D:17m. I: 21m. Tr: 40m. C: $30tn. Plus 50-100m died through Spanish flu spread by the troops among those weakened by war and especially attacking the young)

1915-34 US occupation of Haiti. P: 1m T:10k. D: 2k. C: $10bn

1915-16 TURKISH/ARMENIAN GENOCIDE. 1m driven into desert to die.

1916 Easter Rising Britain-Ireland. P: 1m. T: 20k. D: 485. C: $2bn.

1916-24 US occupation of Dominican Republic. 1m. T: 2k. D: 1k C:5k.

1916-18 Arab Revolt.

1917 Kurdish uprisings.

1917-22 October Revolution, RUSSIAN CIVIL WAR, Ukraine War. P: 100m. T: 8m. D: 7-12m. R: 1-2m. C: $11tn.

1918 Finnish Civil War. P: 3m. T: 18k. D: 38k. C: 30bn.

1918-19 German Spartacist Uprising. P: 65m. T: ? D: ? C: $65bn.

1918-19 Hungarian-Romanian War. P:18m T:100k. D: 7k C: 180bn.

1919-23 Turkish War of Independence. P: 12-15m. T:5m. D:0.51m C: $600bn.

1919-21 Polish-Soviet War. (ignoring USSR Civil War impact) P: 24m. T: 2m. D:107k. $480bn.

1919-22 Irish War of Independence. P: 3m. T:70k. D: 1600. C: $6bn.

1920 Franco-Syrian War. P: 3m. T: 75k. D: 5k. C: $30bn.

1920 Iraq revolt against Britain. P: 5m. T: 65k. D: 12k. W: 8k+ C: $50bn.

1920 Turkish-Armenian War. P: 1m. T: 80k. D:200k. C: £1bn.

1920-50 CHINESE CIVIL WAR through to Communist takeover excluding WW2. P: 450m. T: 8m. D: 13m. C: $90tn.

1921-22 Soviet-Finnish conflict P: 3m.T: 13k. D: 1k. C: $3bn.

1923 Hitler's Beer Hall Putsch.

1923-32 Italian conquest of Libya. P: 225k. T: 2k? D: 50k. Concentration Camps 100k. C: incalculable.

1924-8 Afghan Civil War. P: 5m. T: 33k. D:15k. C: 20bn.

1925-7 Great Syrian Revolt - France. P: 3m. T: ? D: 4k C: $6bn
1929 Sino-Soviet Border War. P: 3m. T: 300k. D: 10k. C: 3bn.
1931-2 Japanese invasion of Manchuria. P: 10m. T: 200k. D:1k. $5bn.
1932 Salvadorian Uprising.
1932-5 Chaco War Paraguay-Bolivia. P: 3m in area. T: 360k. D: 180k. W: 40k. C:10bn.
1932-9 Soviet-Japanese border conflicts. P: 5m? T: ? D:50k. C: $10bn.
1933-6 Japan Mongolia Invasion. P: 2m. T: 110k. D: ? C: 5bn.
1934 Soviet invasion of Xinjiang. P: 5m. T:25k. D: ? C: 1bn.
1934 Saudi-Yemeni War. P: 4m. T: 67k. D: 2.1k. C: 1bn.
1935-6 ITALIAN INVASION OF ETHIOPIA. P:15m. T: 1.15m D: 500k. C: 150bn.
1936-9 Arab revolt in Palestine. P: 3m. T: 50k. D: 6k. C: 6bn.
1936-9 SPANISH CIVIL WAR. P: 25m. T:1.1m. D: 500k. C: 1.5tn
1936-9 British Waziristan campaign. P: 1m. T:100K D: 2K? C: $20bn
1937-45 Second Japan-China War subsumed into....
1939-45 SECOND WORLD WAR. P: 1.6bn T: 80m. D: 73m. I:27m. Traumatized: 500m. Cost $410tn.
1945-49 CHINESE CIVIL WAR/COMMUNIST REVOLUTION P: 500m. T: 2.5m. D:1.8m. W: .09m. Tr: 100m C: $20tn
1946-9 Greek Civil War. P: 7m T: 300k. D: 158k. R: 1m. C: $210bn.
1946-54 First Indochina War. France/Vietnam P: 10m (North) T: 8435k. D:900k. I: 120k+. C: $600bn.
1947 UK/PARTITION OF INDIA. P: 330m. T: 2m. D: 1-3m, say 2m. Refugees 14.5m + 6m later. C: $3.5tn.
1947-9 Kashmir. Pakistan/India War. P: 5m. T: 30k. D: 12k. W: 14k. C: 10bn.
1947-9 Israeli-Arab Palestine Civil War. P: 2m. T:185k. D: 23k. W: 25k. C: 2bn.
1948 onwards (60 plus years) MYANMAR DISTURBANCES. P: 20-50m. T: 800k. D: 200k. Displaced: 800k. C: ?100tn.
1948-60 Malayan Emergency. Low level insurrection. P: 5m T: and Police 451k plus 20K?. D: 11k. C: 50bn.
1950-8 Kuomintang Islamic Insurgency. P: 5m. T: 10k. D: 2k. $40bn.
1950-3 KOREAN WAR. P: 30m. T: 5.7m. D:2.5m C: $1tn
1952 Egyptian Revolution. Nasser takeover.
1952-60 Britain/Kenya. Mau Mau Rebellion. P: 5m. T: 55k. D: 50k-100k. 6 million bombs. 1m in Concentration Camps. 5k torture. C: 40bn.
1953-60. Cuban Revolution. P: 6m. T: 30k. D: 10k? Batista torture. $36bn.
1953 US Iranian coup d'etat. US overthrow of Mosaddegh D: 200. $1bn? Iranian loss of oil revenue to US $150bn?
1954-62 FRANCE/ALGERIAN WAR OF INDEPENDENCE. P: 10m. T:800k. D: 1.2m. W: 65k. R: 2m. C: $1tn.

1954-present Northeast India insurgency. P: 30m. T: 50-100K? D: 40k. C: $30mn.

1955-72 First Sudanese Civil War. P: 10m. T: 50k. D: 500k to 1m. C: 150bn.

1955-75 VIETNAM WAR P: 50m. T: 3m. D: 2.4m. W: 1.4m. T: 80m. C: $15tn.

1956 British-French Suez Invasion. P:2m. T: 0.55m. D: 4k. W:5k. C: $10bn.

1956 Hungarian Revolution. P:10m. T: 50k. D: 7k. W: 14k. C: $100bn

1959-75 US Vietnam-Laotian Civil War. P: 5m. T: 140k. D: 50K. C: $650bn.

1959-2011 Basque-Spain Independence conflict. P: 3m. D: 1k? W; 4k. Arrested 30k. C: $15bn

1960-65 CONGO CRISIS. P:15m. T: 30k. D: 100k. C: $750bn

1960-96 US/GUATAMALA CIVIL WAR P: 15m. T: 450k. D: 170k. $1.5tn.

1961-74 Angolan War of Independence. P: 5m. T:98k. D: 13k. $650bn.

1961 US Bay of Pigs invasion of Cuba. T:20k. D: 1k. C: $50m.

1961-90 US interference/NICARAGUAN CIVIL WAR. P: 5m T: ? D: 30k. $1.2tn.

1961-91 Eritrean War of Independence. P: 3m. T:230k. D:225k. C: $900bn.

1961-70 First Iraq-Kurdish War. P: 4m. T: 70k. D: 10k. Displaced 80K. C: $360bn.

1962-70 Egypt/Israel/West North Yemen Civil War. P: 10m? T: 300k. D: 150k. C: $8bn.

1962-90 Sarawak, Malaysia Communist insurgency. P: 1-2m. T: 15k. D:1k. low level C: $1bn.

1963-2000.Katanga Insurgency. P: 5m T: 30K+. D: thousands. R:600k. C: $200bn.

1963-66 Indonesia-Malaysia confrontation. Border K:1k

1963-76 Dhofar Rebellion. 1m. T: 20k. D: 20k. C: $1bn

1964-present COLOMBIAN FARC conflict. P: 20-30m. T:420k. D: 177k. abducted 27k. Displaced 5m. R: 340k. C: $1.2tn.

1964-79 Zimbabwe War of Independence. P: 5m. T: 40k. D: 20k. C: $375bn.

1964-74 Portugal/Mozambican War of Independence. P: 7.5m T:70k. D:60k. C: $200bn.

1964-82 Mexican Dirty War/US P: 40m. D: 3k. Tortured 7k. C : ?

1965-6 Dominican Civil War/US occupation P: 4m. T: 56k. D: 6k. $40bn.

1965 Indo-Pakistan War. Border P: 5m. T: 0.96m. D: 7k. big loss of kit C: $40bn

1966-1990 Namibian War. P: 10m. T: 200k. D: 17k. C : $800bn.

1967-1975 Cambodian Civil War. P: 7m. T:160k. D:290k. $560bn.

1967 Arab-Israeli Six Day War. P: 2m. T: 0.5m. D: 15k. C : $10bn

1967-1970 NIGERIAN CIVIL WAR -BIAFRA P: 13.5m. T: 360k. D: 75k. plus 2m in induced famine. 3m displaced and R: 500k. C: 450bn.

1968-2019 PHILIPPINO MORO CONFLICT. P: 40-60m. T: 150k. D: 120k. R: 100k. displaced 1m. C: $3tn?.

1968 USSR Czech invasion. P: 10m. T: 680k. D: 1k. R: 70-300k later.

1968-98 N. Ireland troubles.

1971 Ugandan Coup d'etat. Amin takeover. D: 5k plus 50k later. C: ?

1971-75 BANGLADESH INDEPENDENCE WAR. P: 63m. T: 775k. D: 1.5m W: 10k+. C: $250bn.

1973 Chilean Coup deposing Allende US help. Pinochet military dictatorship D: ?.

1973 Yom Kippur War. P: 5m. T: 1.27m. D: 14k. C: $50bn

1974-5 Iraq-Kurdish war. P: 5m. T: 190k. D: 12.5k. Displaced 600k. R: 280k. C: $10bn.

1974-5 Shatt al-Arab Iraq-Iran War. Prelude to the big one.

1974 Turkish invasion of Cyprus. P: 0.5m. T: 75k. D: 2k. W: 12k. Displaced: 250k.

1974-1991 ETHIOPIAN CIVIL WAR. P:32m. T:490k. D: 500k plus 1.2m from famine. C: $4.8tn.

1974-83 Argentinian Dirty War. 30k disappeared.

1975-2002 ANGOLAN CIVIL WAR. P: 7.5m. T: 540k. D: 600k. Displaced 4m. 70k mine amputees. $1.75tn.

1975 E. Timor invasion by Indonesia. P: 1m. T: 55k. D:185k. C: 1bn.

1975-1990 Lebanese Civil War. P: 2.5m. T: 40k?. D:120k. C: 37bn.

1975-1991 Western Sahara War. P: 0.5m. T:150k. D: 5k. C: 5bn.

1975-ongoing. Insurgency in Laos. P: 3-6m. D: 100k. Displaced 300k C: 16bn.

1976-82 Islamist uprising in Syria. Terrorism P: 5m. T: 20k D:10k C: $10bn.

1976-80 Turkey violence. D: 5k.

1977-92 MOZAMBIQUE CIVIL WAR. P: 10m. T: 100k. D: 1m (including from Famine) C: 100bn.

1978- present. Turkey- Kurdish War. P: 5m. T: 200k. D: 80k. 3k Kurdish villages destroyed. C: $200tn.

1978-9 Iranian Revolution. D: 3k.

1978-1989 CAMBODIAN GENOCIDE P: 5m. T: 200k. D: 2m. C: $500bn.

1979-92 Salvador Civil War. P: 4m. D: 75k. Disappeared 8k. Displaced : 0.55m. R: 0.5m. C: $40bn.

1979-89 SOVIET-AFGHANISTAN WAR. P: 14m. T: 400k. D: 1.25m. W: 3m. Displaced 2m. R:5m. C: $1.5tn.

1980-1988 IRAN-IRAQ WAR P: 54m. T: 1.9m. D: 500K C: $4.3tn. Major arms supplies from west to both sides.

1980-1986 Uganda Bush War. P: 5m. T: 50k. D: 300k. C: 30bn.

1982 Argentina Falklands Invasion. T: 20k plus two navies. D:1k. C: 10bn.

1982-5 Israeli-Lebanon War. P: 2.5m. T: 20k. D: 10k. R: 850k. C: 10bn.

1983-6 KURDISH REBELLIONS IN IRAQ. P: 5m. T: ? D: 110k. R: 1m. Halabja gas attacks.

1985-2000 Israel-South Lebanon conflict. Border long conflict D:2k. C: 2bn.

1986 US bombing of Libya. Punitive strike.

228

1987-89 Sri Lankan Civil War. P: 15m. T: 220k. D: 100k. W: 110k. Displaced 800k. Cost: $30bn.

1987-1991 Baltic States liberation.

1987 onwards. Uganda Lord's Resistance Army. P: 5m. T: 40K D: 100k. Displaced 400k.

1988-94 NAGORNO-KARABAKH WAR. P: 5m T: 80k. D: 25k. Displaced 1.1M.

1990-91 FIRST GULF WAR US/UN IRAQ. P: 17m. T: 1.6m. D: 35k. W: 75k. Captured 100k. Intense weapon war. Destroyed most of Saddam's weapons. C: $1.5tn

1990-4 RUANDA CIVIL WAR AND GENOCIDE. P: 6m. D: 700k mainly Tutsi.

1991 onwards SOMALI CIVIL WAR. P: 7m. T: ? D: 600k. Displaced 3m. C: $70bn.

1991-02 SIERRA LEONE CIVIL WAR P: 4m. T: 30K. D: 60k. Displaced and refugees 2.5m. C: $44bn.

1991-5 Croatia War of Independence. P: 4m. T: 200k. D: 22k. Dis. 300k. C: 16bn.

1991 Soviet Coup Attempt. End of USSR. Destruction of much USSR military.

1991-02 Algerian Civil War. P: 20m. T: 18k. D: 150k. C: $200bn.

1992-5 Bosnian War. P: 3m. T: 230k. D: 90k. C: $9bn.

1993-05 Burundi Civil War. P: 6m. T: 40k. D:300k. $70bn.

1993-4 Republic of Congo Civil War. D: 2k. Displaced 20k.

1994-6. First Chechen War. P: 1.2m T:76k. D: 107k. W: 52k. C: $2bn.

1996-2006 Nepal Civil War. P: 23m. T: 145k. D: 18k. C: $300bn.

1996-9 Zaire/Congo War. P:44m. T: 120k. D: 250k. R:200k. C: $100bn.

1998-9 Kosovo War. P: 1m. T: 100k. D: 14k. C: 2bn.

1998-9. Eritrea-Ethiopia War. P: 3m. T: 0.5m. D: 100k. C: $5tn.

1998 Guinea-Bissau War D:2k. Displaced 350k.

1998-2003 SECOND CONGO WAR. P: 48m. T: 110k? D: 350k violent, and 5.4m excess deaths. C: $200bn.

1999 East Timorese Crisis P: 1m. T: 12k. D: 2k. R: 220k. $2bn.

1999-2003 Second Liberian Civil War. P: 3m. T: 60k. D: 30k. 12bn.

1999-2009 Second Chechen War. P: 1.2m T: 100k. D:60k. C:$10bn

2001 Afghan Taliban Insurgency. P: 20K. T: 400k. D: 120k. C: $20bn.

2001-3. WAR IN DAFUR. P: 5m. T: 170k. D: 300k. Displaced 2.8m. C: $30bn Genocide

2003 WAR ON TERROR. Global War following 9/11. Different. Claim D: 90k. Displaced 37m. C: $5tn.

2003-21 IRAQ WAR. P: 40m. Total T: 2.3m D: 655? (Lancet) W: 117k. R: 3.7m. C: $20tn

2004-present. South Thailand War. P: 50m. T: 80k. D: 7k. W: 13k. C: $20bn.

2004 -present. Iran-Kurdistan War. P: 1m D: 1k. C: $10m.

2004-11. Niger Delta Conflict. P: 4m. T: 200k. D:3k C: $5bn (oil)

2004-present. DRC Kivu Province War. P: 3m. T: 60k. D: 12k or 100k+? R: 1.4m C: $160bn

2004-present. SAUDI-YEMEN WAR. P: 30m. T: 300k. D: 377k. R: 4m. C: $3tn. Heavy bombing

2005-10 Chad Civil War.

2006-present. MEXICAN DRUG WAR. P: 120m. T: (and police) 700K. D:450K? 60k missing. Drugs, inequality, violence, poverty. C: (possibly) $15tn to economy.

2006 Israeli-Lebanon War. P: 5m. T: 30k. D: 1k. W: 4K C: $100m.

2006-present SOMALIA WAR. P: 10m T: 30k. D: 17k. Displaced 1.9m C: $200bn.

2008 Russo-Georgian War. P: 10m. T: 100k. D:1k. Displaced 192k. C: $10bn.

2009-22 BOKO HARAM-NORTH NIGERIA. P: 30m. T:150k. D: 350k. Displaced 2.4m. C: $600bn.

2010 Kyrgyzstan Clashes D: 2k. R: 200k.

2011 NATO-LIBYAN CIVIL WAR. P: 7m. T: 250k. D: 10k. W: 50K. R: 200K. C: $600bn.

2011-present. SYRIAN CIVIL WAR P: 17m. T: 330k? D: 5.5m. 6.7m internally displaced. R: 6.6m. C: $18tn.

2013-20. SOUTH SUDAN CIVIL WAR. P:11m. D:383k. 2.1m internally displaced. R:2.1m. C: $1tn.

2012-3 Mali war. P: 21m. T: 27k. D: 4k. internally displaced 230k. R: 144k

2014-present. Second Libyan Civil War. P: 6m. T: 120k. D: 15-20K. R: 2m. C: $620bn.

2014 present. War Against Islamic State. P: 20m. T:100k. D:50k. Displaced: 7.6m. R: 3.3m. C: $100bn

2015-present. Turkish-Kurdish conflict. P: 5m? T: 70k. D: 6k. Displaced: 0.5m.

2021-present. Myanmar Crisis. P:30? m. T: 420k. D: 30k. Internally displaced 1m. R:40k. C: $0.5tn.

2022 RUSSIA-UKRAINE INVASION. P: 43m. T:2.7m. D: 200k? Displace persons 8m. R: 8m. $1.1tn.

2023 Sudan Civil War.

(World Cities badly bombed: Moscow, Leningrad, Smolensk, Kharkov, Kiev, Warsaw, Rotterdam, London, Plymouth, Birmingham, Sheffield, Liverpool, Manchester, Coventry, Bristol, Belfast, Cardiff, Hull, Mannheim, Lübeck, Helsinki, Budapest, Belgrade, Bucharest, Minsk, Sevastopol, Stuttgart, Hanover, Mannheim, Kiel, Bremen, Lübeck, Essen, Berlin, Dortmund, Dresden, Hamburg, Kassell, Pforzheim, Mainz, Bucharest, Milan, Turin, Genoa, Messina, Palermo, Genoa, Rimini, Treviso, Shanghai, Wuhan, Chongqing, Nanjing, Canton, Singapore, Tel Aviv, Bankok, Kanggye,

Ch'oean, Hoeryong, Kointong, Maup'olin, Nauisi, Sakchu, Sinuichn Uicho, Haiphong, Hanoi, Ha Long and many more...)

Footnotes.

1. At today's prices. From SIPRI and a range of other estimates. Much of the background scholarship for this book occurs in my *War or Peace? The Long Failure of Western Arms.* (Cambridge: Christian Studies Press, 2015), *Jesus and Politics* (Grand Rapids: Baker Academic), and *From War to Peace* (to be published soon) and the fuller references and evidence can be seen there.

[ii] Caroline Elkins *Britain's Gulag: The Brutal End of Empire in Kenya* (London: Pimlico, 2005)

[iii] Anthony Beevor *Stalingrad* (London: Penguin, 1999) 428

[iv] https://www.theguardian.com/world/2009/oct/13/benito-mussolini-recruited-mi5-italy

[v] Garrison Keillor *The Book for Guys* (London: Penguin, 1994)

[vi] E.g. in Nicholas Gilby *Deception in High Places: A History of Bribery in Britain's Arms Trade* (London: Pluto Press, 2014)

[vii] https://www.ft.com/content/cf26c3b6-650e-4711-8776-c70756cc49e9

[viii] Roy Jenkins *Gladstone* (London: Macmillan, 1995 610

[ix] Lord Grey of Falloden *Twenty Five Years* Vol 1 (NY: Frederick A. Stokes, 1925) 91-2 quoted in Noel-Baker PMOA 19.

[x] Philip Noel Baker The First Disarmament Conference 1932-33 and why it failed (Oxford: Pergamon Press 1979) 73

[xi] https://ranishtimilsina.blogspot.com/2012/08/the-1932-disarmament-conference-by.html

[xii] Philip Noel-Baker The First Disarmament Conference 1932-33 and why it failed (Oxford: Pergamon, 1979) 7-113

[xiii] Alan Storkey *War or Peace? The Long Failure of Western Arms* (Cambridge: Christian Studies Press, 1915) 246-253

[xiv] H.C.Englebrecht and F.C. Hanighen The Merchants of Death (NY:Dodd,Mead and Company, 1934) 228-234

[xv] https://www.presidency.ucsb.edu/documents/message-the-senate-the-manufacture-arms-and-munitions

[xvi] Edgar B. Nixon, ed., Franklin D. *Roosevelt and Foreign Affairs*, Vol. III: September 1935-January 1937 (Cambridge:Belknap Press, 1969) p 456 quoted in Anthony Sutton *Wall Street and the Rise of the Nazis* Introduction

[xvii]https://en.wikipedia.org/wiki/Munich_Agreement#German_invasion_of_rump_Czechoslovakia

[xviii] Historic Hansard 3/10/1938

[xix] Townsend Hoopes *The Devil and John Foster Dulles* (London: Deutsch, 1974) 47

[xx] Patricia Dawson Ward *The Threat of Peace; James F. Byrnes and the Council of Foreign Ministers* 1945-1946 (Ohio:Kent State University Press, 1979)

[xxi] Citation: "A Strategic Chart of Certain Russian and Manchurian Urban Areas [Project No. 2532]," (30 August 1945), *Correspondence ("Top Secret") of the Manhattan Engineer District, 1942-1946,* microfilm publication M1109 (Washington, D.C.: National Archives and Records Administration, 1980), Roll 1, Target 4, Folder 3, "Stockpile, Storage, and Military Characteristics."

[xxii] Henry Viner Brooks *Saving Europe* (Pravda Press, 2021)

[xxiii] Letter Churchill to Lord Robert Cecil 1/9/1944 (British Library Display)

[xxiv] https://www.bbc.co.uk/news/uk-57774012

[xxv] Basic reports https://en.wikipedia.org/wiki/Vietnam_War
https://en.wikipedia.org/wiki/Gulf_of_Tonkin_incident#First_attack

[xxvi] https://sites.tufts.edu/corruptarmsdeals/, Andrew Feinstein *The Shadow World: Inside the global Arms Trade* (London: Penguin, 2011), Nicholas Gilby *Deception in High Places: A History of Bribery in Britain's Arms Trade* (London: Pluto, 2014)

[xxvii] https://www.dailymail.co.uk/news/article-2852826/Tower-London-hosted-240-head-dinner-arms-dealers-moving-poppy-memorial-installation-taken-apart.html

[xxviii] Philip Noel-Baker *The Private Manufacture of Armaments* (London: Gollancz, 1936) 439-45, 449-510

[xxix] Nikita S. Khrushchev *Khrushchev Remembers* trans and edited by Strobe Talbott (Boston: Little-Brown, 1970) 518.

[xxx] "In Cheney's words: The Administration Case for Removing Saddam Hussein." New York Times 27th August, 2002

[xxxi] https://debtjustice.org.uk/press-release/argentina-still-owes-uk-dictator-debt-falklands-arms

[xxxii] Zachary Wagner et al. "Armed conflict and child mortality in Africa: A geospatial Analysis" Lancet 30/8/2018

[xxxiii] website of Global Security.org

[xxxiv] Claire Mills "Treaty on the Prohibition of Nuclear Weapons." (House of Commons Library 13/6/2022 No. 7986 p12

[xxxv] Wikipedia on WW1 and other background.

[xxxvi] Sunday People 2018.

[xxxvii] Elaine Storkey *Scars across Humanity* (London: SPCK, 2015) 133-151

[xxxviii] Siegfried Sasson Rhymed Ruminations (London: Faber and Faber, 1940) 39

[xxxix] Josephus Jewish Wars 232

[xl] Philip Noel-Baker *The First World Disarmament Conference 1932-33* (Oxford:Pergamon, 1979) 67

[xli] *Radio and Television Broadcast With Prime Minister Macmillan in London, 8/31/59*

Printed in Great Britain
by Amazon

22796204R00130